Treating Psychosomatic Patients

Treating Psychosomatic Patients: In Search of a Transdisciplinary Framework for the Integration of Bodywork in Psychotherapy offers a conceptual and therapeutic framework for all therapists who have to deal with the psychosomatic 'conflicted' body, as presented in anxiety and depression, stress and burn-out, medically unexplained symptoms and trauma.

The book introduces the transdisciplinary framework 'experiential bodywork' (EBW), drawing on theories and scientific findings from clinical psychology, philosophy, neuroscience, psychotherapy and myofascial therapy. EBW provides a roadmap for a better understanding of the processes that underpin body psychotherapy and body-mind therapies. On a practical level, EBW challenges the therapist to marry the power of psychotherapeutic techniques with the richness of hands-on bodywork and hands-off movement expression. With the 'armoured' body as an entry point, patients learn to feel their body from within and listen to what it tells them. In the sharpness of this awareness they discover a freer way of speaking, moving and being present in the world.

Through EBW, *Treating Psychosomatic Patients* offers a transdisciplinary, scientifically based framework for the integration of bodywork in psychotherapy, ranging from psychosomatics to trauma, and will be of great interest to psychologists, psychotherapists and counsellors in a variety of settings. EBW also helps somatic therapists, such as physical therapists or osteopaths, to better understand the richness and layeredness of deep bodywork from different psychological, developmental and 'embodied' perspectives.

Joeri Calsius (PhD) is a clinical psychologist, body-oriented, psychodynamic psychotherapist, physical therapist and osteopath DO. In his private practice, Joeri works with patients suffering from psychosomatic and trauma-related problems from a transdisciplinary perspective. He is an academic lecturer, teaches postgraduate courses in a number of settings and is author of several peer-reviewed articles and book contributions on bodywork in psychosomatics and trauma.

'An expression of an important evolution in the way man and body are approached, this book encourages the reader to become acquainted with the new developments that Calsius describes well, both in theory and in practice. In this book, Calsius introduces more body-focused work and more scientific underpinning for that work. The fact that the link between the psyche and soma always remains paramount in the experiential focus of Calsius' work is certainly gratifying. A versatile book, which I can highly recommend to professionals and others who are interested in the fascinating theme of "bodywork".'

Prof. Dr. Patrick Meurs, clinical psychologist and psychodynamic child and youth psychotherapist, Catholic University of Leuven, Belgium; Director at the Sigmund Freud Institute Frankfurt, Germany

'Anyone in clinical practice will enjoy this book, regardless of their own theoretical or therapeutic background. It makes you think, and that's what a good book should do. Hopefully it also encourages a better, embodied, understanding of our patients. Because that is still the basis of any successful form of care.'

Prof. Dr. Patrick Luyten, clinical psychologist and psychotherapist, Catholic University of Leuven, Belgium; Research Department of Clinical, Educational, and Health Psychology, University College London, UK

'In this special work, the author grants a clear and inspiring insight into the psychosomatic body, the physical ailments that arise from unconscious processes and conflicts, and what experiential bodywork is and is not capable of. He combines philosophical, psychoanalytic, physiotherapeutic and neuroscientific insights in an overarching transdisciplinary framework. For this, he draws on the work of the American philosopher Ken Wilber, among others. The book provides numerous new insights and connections. Recommended for every psychotherapist who has to deal with the effects of traumas or medically unexplained symptoms, but also for physiotherapists and body-focused therapists. A book that has everything it takes to become a classic.'

Dr. Nelleke Nicolai, author, psychiatrist and psychoanalyst, private practice, Amsterdam, the Netherlands

'This book presents an interesting, yet entirely fresh, framework of thought that straddles the interface between mind and body. An excellent piece of work, clearly written, this book provides food for thought for all those who work with psychosomatic problems.'

Prof. Dr. Stijn Vanheule, clinical psychologist and psychoanalyst, University of Ghent, Belgium

'The author of this book is one in a million, combining, as he does, both disciplines. This places him in a privileged position that allows him to create the much-needed bridge between body and mind. One of the great merits of the book is that it places psychosomatic complaints and care 'in the picture' and does not keep the discussion away from the reader. Another merit is that it both raises questions and provides a good and clearly substantiated view of the theories on which the framework used is based. The starting shot has now been given.'

Prof. Dr. Michel Probst, physiotherapist and psychomotor therapist, Catholic University of Leuven, Belgium

Treating Psychosomatic Patients

In Search of a Transdisciplinary Framework for the Integration of Bodywork in Psychotherapy

Joeri Calsius

LONDON AND NEW YORK

First published in English 2020
by Routledge
2 Park Square, Milton Park, Abingdon, Oxon OX14 4RN

and by Routledge
52 Vanderbilt Avenue, New York, NY 10017

Routledge is an imprint of the Taylor & Francis Group, an informa business

English edition © 2020 Joeri Calsius

The right of Joeri Calsius to be identified as the author has been asserted in accordance with sections 77 and 78 of the Copyright, Designs and Patents Act 1988.

All rights reserved. No part of this book may be reprinted or reproduced or utilised in any form or by any electronic, mechanical, or other means, now known or hereafter invented, including photocopying and recording, or in any information storage or retrieval system, without permission in writing from the publishers.

Trademark notice: Product or corporate names may be trademarks or registered trademarks, and are used only for identification and explanation without intent to infringe.

Original title: *Werken Met Een Lichaam Dat Moelijk Doet* © ACCO Leuven, 2017 (Second Edition 2019)

British Library Cataloguing-in-Publication Data
A catalogue record for this book is available from the British Library

Library of Congress Cataloging-in-Publication Data
A catalog record for this book has been requested

ISBN: 978-0-367-81946-0 (hbk)
ISBN: 978-0-367-34200-5 (pbk)
ISBN: 978-1-003-01095-1 (ebk)

Typeset in Times New Roman
by Apex CoVantage, LLC

It is with gratefulness, warmth and love that I dedicate this book to:

Liesbeth, Tristan and Adinda; my wife, son and daughter.
Laurette, Jos and Frederik; my mother, father and brother.
Philip; my mentor and friend ever since.
Raf; my best friend.

I shall be telling this with a sigh

Somewhere ages and ages hence:

Two roads diverged in a wood, and I—

I took the one less traveled by,

And that has made all the difference.

   'The Road Not Taken', by Robert Frost (1874–1963)

With thanks to Bunkerbouwers (Jan Foudraine, 1997)

Contents

List of figures   x
Foreword   xi
When reading this book   xv
Some opening reflections   xvii
Some testimonials   xxiii

Introduction: The psychosomatic body in a field of therapies   3
A divided landscape 3
A bit of history 5
What is body psychotherapy? 7
Body psychotherapy as a response to the psychosomatic body 8
Experiential bodywork as a roadmap for psychosomatic therapy 9

1. **An integrated look at the psychosomatic patient**   15
   Towards a transdisciplinary model 15
   The Four Quadrant Model 16
   The fulcrum *concept 22*
   Types of fulcra *and processes 23*
   The self-system 28
   Experiential bodywork as development-dynamic work 30

2. **The narrative patient**   37
   The request for help from an existential-phenomenological perspective 37
   The first words, the first look 40
   The unconscious appears in therapy 43
   The body appears in therapy 44
   Embodied self-awareness 45

    Embodiment and body awareness within experiential bodywork 48
    Working with levels of attention and awareness within experiential bodywork 50
    Experiential bodywork as a layered approach 51

3 The body in therapy: possible or not?   57
    A first sound 57
    Body and lived body 60
    Mentalisation as the capacity for reflective distance 61
    Focusing as the ability to listen to what the body says 62
    The body in therapy, a first possibility 64

4 The tense body   71
    The muscle armour, an echo from the past 71
    The muscle armour 2.0 75
    The myofascial middle layer in experiential bodywork 80
    An anatomical view of the myofascial middle layer 84
    The body as an entry point in therapy, a neurobiological analysis 88

5 The unconscious within experiential bodywork   99
    The unconscious as a matrix 99
    Types of unconscious 100
    The archaic unconscious 101
    The early body in detail: pleroma, uroboros and typhon 102

6 The psychosomatic body within the *fulcrum* model   111
    The unconscious in action 111
    A psychodynamic reading of the first fulcra *113*
    The psychosomatic body within the fulcrum *model 115*
    The psychosomatic conflict within the early fulcra *117*
    Anxiety within subject development 121

7 The practice of experiential bodywork   127
    The therapy room 127
    First encounter and anamnesis 128
    Four access routes to the body in experiential bodywork 134
    Working with a listening touch: a phenomenological analysis 138
    The development-dynamic treatment template 140

*Three, two, one . . . go! Getting started with the development-
    dynamic treatment template 143*
The uroboric armour and the myofascial middle layer 151
Experiential movement or bodywork in motion 152
The body in transference 157
Working with children in experiential bodywork 158
The pranic body in everyday life 160
*The psychosomatic body in therapy: a four-quadrant
    approach 160*

In retrospect	165
Bibliography	168
Index	193

Figures

0.1	The psychosomatic therapy landscape	4
0.2	Paradigms within the psychosomatic spectrum	10
1.1	The Four Quadrant Model	17
1.2	The Four Quadrant Model	17
1.3	The Four Quadrant Model and paradigms	18
1.4	The Four Quadrant Model	18
1.5	Russian dolls	22
1.6	Types of *fulcra*	24
1.7	The process of fusion/identification, differentiation and integration	27
1.8	The differentiation of subject and object	28
1.9	EBW within the quadrants	31
2.1	ESA and CSA	46
4.1	Some core structures of the MML	81
4.2	Three functional layers within the myofascial tissue	86
4.3	Interoception and the insula as core structure	91
5.1	The uroboros snake	102
5.2	The typhonic snake	104
5.3	Sub-stages within the early *fulcra*	105
7.1	The Four Quadrant Template for anamnesis	129
7.2	Therapeutic flowchart EBW	133
7.3	Phenomenological description of myofascial bodywork within EBW	139
7.4	Development-dynamic treatment template	141

Foreword

Body-oriented work in counselling, psychotherapy, physiotherapy and other therapeutic situations has traditionally not been self-evident within the very cognitive (clinical) psychology and behavioural sciences or the associated healthcare professions. Personally, I remember my quest, at the end of the 1980s, to write a Master's thesis on the body in psychotherapy. Although many researchers and potential supervisors said they thought it was an excellent topic, it was not recommended as a subject for my Master's thesis because it was too controversial, not sufficiently mainstream psychology or, for the time being, too little documented or empirically substantiated. Certain publications, such as Gendlin's (1978) on *Focusing* and Depestele's (1986) on *Lichamelijkheid in de cliëntgerichte psychotherapie* (*Physicality in client-centred psychotherapy*), were, therefore, welcome exceptions that filled a void in academia. Body-oriented work, or bodywork, was mainly found outside of this context, such as in *Mijn lichaam als kans* (*My body as opportunity*; Lambrechts, 1975), a book that also demonstrated the need for a body-focused approach in agogics, psychotherapy and other disciplines.

In my starting practice as a child psychologist in the paediatrics department of a general hospital, beginning in 1990, I very regularly met what Joeri Calsius refers to as 'clients with *a difficult body*'. I also started thinking about a creative and healthy psychosomatic interplay of body and mind, rather than interpreting the word 'psychosomatics' only in a pathological or symptomatic sense. These thoughts are also encapsulated in the title of Calsius' book about the difficult body: *Treating Psychosomatic Patients*. Two decades ago, I spoke about the affectively experienced body and befriending it (Meurs, 1998), mainly inspired by the tradition of phenomenological philosophy and experiential client-centred therapy. Today, Calsius discusses the kinetic and biomedical scientific backgrounds of the affectively experienced relational body, drawing on recent developments in behavioural sciences. The greater place that the neurosciences and the biofeedback now occupy in social care is probably no stranger to this. It is certainly gratifying that the experiential focus of Calsius' work always remains at the forefront in this connection between *psychè* and *soma*. In that sense, the publication of Calsius' book can also be seen as an expression of a significant evolution in the approach to man and body. This publication prompts us to familiarise ourselves with these new evolutions, which Calsius describes well, both theoretically and practically. The concept of *embodiment*, as a connection between the rather biophysical aspects of Calsius' book and the experiential perspectives, a connection also between the author being a body therapist and a psychotherapist, plays a central role.

In the first few chapters, Calsius considers the experience of the body, the experiential perspectives on physicality. This gives us a good idea of what the author means by 'the body that speaks' and 'the difficult body'. The body sends out signals, uses a language that is often not yet verbalised; the body speaks and acts up, while language does not seem to be able to get a handle on it for the time being. What the body transmits are signals of tension, pain and restlessness. The body behaves in such a way that clients seek help, often from doctors, but without there being sufficient medical grounds that explain tension, pain and symptoms. The symptom body, as Merleau-Ponty (1945) expressed it in phenomenology, is not yet a symbolic body, not yet a body that can express a person's connection with himself and the Other or the environment in a healthy way. To get to that body that communicates pain and tension and is still looking for words, or to make contact with the self that does not yet sufficiently inhabit and know the body, a purely verbal, cognitive approach is sometimes too ambitious. More body-focused work and more scientific substantiation of that work is exactly what Calsius offers in this book.

From a developmental psychology perspective, one could say that the body is for the first time energetically present between the baby and the parents, in the form of less or more intense feelings, affects, movements, dispositions, tension and relaxation, warmth, glances and caresses. Care providers offer words to welcome the physical baby (and its body language); they allow the baby to stir/move them. Emotions in that setting can flare up (pain, tension, pleasure, crying, etc.) and die down. The baby's body language is affective communication, directed at another person, the care givers. The first affects are situations that are well regulated at certain times, while at other times they are too weak (the baby that is not sufficiently attracted to the environment) or too strong (the baby that is too much affected and upset by experiences from the outside or from the inside). The first affects that the baby communicates physically are first of all forces, *les forces*. These powerful experiences of the baby in interaction with the environment are well regulated by the care giver, which helps the child to further express these affective forces and to make better use of this communication via signals, *les signes*. The care givers sometimes imitate something with hands and feet or facial expressions and thus add further meaning. They portray the child's message and make it clear that the baby signals can be recognised, shared and translated; the body and its signals are open to further representation and translation, *les images et les mots*. In this process, the signal-body becomes a symbolic body: the body can express itself and is focused on words and stories; the body wants to be understood and searches for a story to tell. The clients who are sometimes medically described as psychosomatic or somatoform clients became lost in this translation of affective power and signal (*les forces et les signes*) into imagination, story and language (*les images et les mots*) (Devisch & Brodeur, 1996). They may have been given the label *alexithymia*, the inability to read physically experienced dispositions and affects. The origin of the problem is not infrequently situated in the development of these people, in the fact that the people around them are unable to help them translate their emotions into words. As we now know, this relational aetiology is not the only possible way forward. Some people also struggle with aptitude, emotional inhibitions and personality factors, or a different sensory perception and sensory integration, which makes it difficult for them to maintain their relationship with their bodies. And where in the past it was often thought that offering words in therapy could offer a solution, Calsius works with the body to build the bridge and to include some very necessary intermediate steps in therapy. In this way, he prevents an overly verbal approach that is too ambitious for clients whose bodies act up. And perhaps books like Calsius's also make it possible for concepts like alexithymia to disappear into the background: clients with a difficult body can probably be better typified as people who still come to inhabit the body and take steps in it, expressing a different form of connection between *psychè* and *soma* than what we expect to be mainstream in our culture. With regard to this cultural mainstream, these clients start out with a deficit (they cannot read physical feelings and dispositions), but within their specific sensory nature, we can help them to further befriend and inhabit their bodies.

Calsius takes ways of being in your body as a starting point, the body with which a person reacts affectively to his environment, relations and culture, the body also at the interface of biopsychology and psychophysiology. Calsius manages to map out these recent interactions between psychology and medical science in an effective manner. Human physicality emerges from the first chapters of this book as a mode of being in which body and mind – *psychè* and *soma* – are one from the beginning and speak through, with and for each other. It is to be welcomed that in this *zeitgeist* of brain research and neuroscience, the biopsychological basis of body-focused affect-regulating work in therapy comes into focus. The notions that are less well known to care providers and that make the interface between *psychè* and *soma* conceivable (e.g. fulcrum, myofascial aspects, pleroma, uroboros, typhon, pranic body) are explained well, both theoretically and in terms of their practical relevance. They are linked to more familiar experiential, phenomenological and psychodynamic concepts, such as transference in body psychotherapy and experiential bodywork.

Once Calsius has introduced the history of the body-centred focus in therapy and situated the thinking about the *soma-psychè* unity, he adds a perspective to the tradition of the experiential psychotherapy in which body awareness and giving meaning to body language, up to a possible articulation of the felt body, are well addressed. In that part of the book, concepts such as embodiment and the body itself form the central theme. Focusing and mentalisation are discussed as topical and important techniques in which Calsius searches for an affective body-focused language that does not become too cognitive straight away.

Bodies also tell histories, in which people can be entangled (Schapp, 1980). The body as 'flow' and 'living life' then becomes blocked. In this context, Calsius speaks of the armour of pain and muscle tension. The use of these body signals and the search for their original meanings with which a client can move on in life are not only addressed but also scientifically substantiated in this book. Other challenging thoughts are 'the body as the unconscious', alongside 'the body as the biological basis of being'. In the final chapter, experiential bodywork is clarified, which makes this book eminently suitable for body-focused therapists with a listening psy-ear, for psychotherapists with a feel for the signalling and narrative body, for therapists who have an eye for pain and traumas that are encapsulated and hidden in the body that plays up.

This is a versatile book, therefore, that I can highly recommend to professionals and other parties interested in the fascinating theme of 'bodywork'.

Prof. Dr. Patrick Meurs

About

Prof. Dr. Patrick Meurs is a psychodynamic child and adolescent psychotherapist, a lecturer at the KU Leuven (clinical psychology), Odisee Hogeschoool Brussels (family sciences) and Universität Kassel (pedagogical sciences), as well as director at the Sigmund Freud Institut Frankfurt (psychoanalysis).

References

Depestele, F. (1986). Het lichaam in psychotherapie. In R. Van Balen, M. Leijssen, & G. Lietaer (red.), *Droom en werkelijkheid in cliënt-centered psychotherapie* (pp. 87–123). Leuven and Amersfoort: Acco.

Devisch, R., & Brodeur, C. (1996). *Forces et signes: Regards croisés d'un anthropologue et d'un psychanalyste sur les Yaka*. Paris: Archives Contemporaires.

Gendlin, E. (1978). *Focusing*. New York: Everest House.

Lambrechts, G. (1975). *Je lichaam als kans*. Averbode: Altiora.

Merleau-Ponty, M. (1945). *Phénoménologie de la perception*. Paris: Gallimard.

Meurs, P., & Cluckers, G. (1998). Het affectief ervaren lichaam (weer) te vriend: Psychodynamische therapie bij kinderen met psychosomatische symptomen. *Tijdschrift Klinische Psychologie, 28*, 167–185.

Schapp, W. (1980). *In Geschichten verstrickt*. Stuttgart: Klostermann Verlag.

van der Kolk, B. (2014). *The body keeps the score: Mind, brain and body in the transformation of trauma*. London: Penguin Books.

When reading this book

As the title suggests, this book seeks to offer a different perspective on the psychosomatic body in therapy. This 'different' view refers to an exploration from different angles and is referred to as 'transdisciplinary'. The central theme here is the psychosomatic body, which may seem tautological in a way, since both body and mind are always psycho-somatic. We will come back to this. From a clinical point of view, the psychosomatic body can be seen as 'a body that plays up' or a 'difficult body'. Throughout the book we will discuss why the body is playing up and for whom this is the case as well as what is meant by the term transdisciplinary. Firstly, let's take a look at the structure of the book.

We start with 'Some opening reflections' regarding the title and central theme of this book. In the introduction 'The psychosomatic body in a field of therapies', we outline the current therapy landscape, prevailing paradigms and tensions. In order to gain a better understanding, we briefly discuss the historical development of therapies relating to the psychosomatic body. This brings us to the domain of body psychotherapy from which we introduce the concept of 'experiential bodywork' (EBW). Throughout the book, we will gradually develop this into a conceptual and therapeutic framework for a more transdisciplinary approach to the psychosomatic or 'difficult' body. With Chapter 1, 'An integrated look at the psychosomatic patient', we start with a transdisciplinary analysis of the patient. To this end, we explore some concepts from the early work of the American philosopher and integrative thinker Ken Wilber on the development of the individual. We then attempt to apply these Wilberian concepts to the transdisciplinary structure of this book and the framework of EBW, in particular. Chapter 2, 'The narrative patient', represents an immediate dive into practice and a first attempt to look at the patient and his request for help from a number of angles. For this purpose, a number of psychodynamic and phenomenological concepts are defined that help to describe in detail the contact with the psychosomatic patient and to gain a better appreciation of it at the same time. We clarify, for example, how the body appears in the therapy room in a layered and unconscious way and the sensitivity this requires on the part of the therapist to listen to the psychosomatic body in a different way. At the same time, the question arises as to how the body can be approached in therapy in a 'conscious' manner. Whether or not we can get in touch with our body at all is central to Chapter 3, 'The body in therapy: possible or not?' In Chapter 4, 'The tense body', we come to one of the more central concepts from the practice of EBW, namely, the muscle armour.

Given its clinical importance, we dissect this intriguing phenomenon, drawing on psychological-psychotherapeutic and neurobiological theory and myofascial research. Chapter 5, 'The unconscious within experiential bodywork', and Chapter 6, 'The psychosomatic body within the *fulcrum* model', are closely related and deal with the early development of the individual, the role of body awareness and how this can lead to psychosomatic conflicts. Chapter 7, 'The practice of experiential bodywork', offers the reader extensive insight into many aspects of the concrete therapeutic work with a body that plays up.

Which phases does the treatment consist of? How is contact made through a listening touch? How are the working concepts from the previous chapters translated into the therapy? What is a four quadrants approach and how do you approach the body concretely? How about (counter)transference? How can you work with evocative movement and breathing, and with EBW in children? These and other interesting questions are covered at length and are backed by many practical examples and testimonies from patients. Although this book is not meant to be a therapy manual, after reading the last chapter, the reader will be more able to use EBW in their own practice. The development-dynamic treatment template provides a powerful guide in this respect. We end by making some final reflections with 'In retrospect'.

Finally, a word about language and terminology. A transdisciplinary undertaking requires a balanced relationship to jargon. A mere sum of the vocabulary of all the disciplines involved is not what we have in mind, even if this were feasible. Although this book is part of the broad domain of body psychotherapy, this does not mean that psychologists of all kinds should not make an effort. Chapter 4, for example, is written using strong somatic jargon, but deals with crucial themes for connecting with the tired body. We therefore invite colleagues to continue reading. Other chapters are often more in the comfort zone of psychologists, psychotherapists or psychiatrists – although somewhat dependent on their psychotherapeutic background. In turn, these require an effort on the part of body therapists. Again, we encourage to continue reading.

But even the attempt to integrate the various disciplines is hard work and has its pitfalls. Since one can never fully appreciate all the domains that are addressed, there is always the risk that this book falls short of expectations. An ongoing 'attempt' to strike an acceptable balance is called for. Readers with full expertise in some of the domains covered may expect more detail and nuance or may identify imperfections and lacking interpretations.

The transdisciplinary bridge then soon turns into a ramshackle construction. Where possible and necessary, the manuscript should then evolve further on the basis of their recommendations and corrections.

One final note. When we talk about the psychosomatic body – and we do so all the time – we refer not only to the psychosomatic complaint in the narrow sense but also to the psychosomatic body as it appears in various clinical representations, such as anxiety and depression, stress and burnout, as well as cases of trauma and functional somatic syndromes. Finally, when we talk about the therapist, the male and female therapist are meant, despite the use of 'he' or 'him'.

Some opening reflections

As a title, *Treating Psychosomatic Patients* can be translated into daily practice as '*a body that acts up*' or '*a body that is difficult*'. This can be understood in at least two ways. On the one hand, the body causes discomfort for the patient: it hurts, feels tense, is tired or just spent, which gets in the way of day-to-day living. This frustrates not only the owner of the body but often also the person to whom the request for help is made, namely, the therapist or doctor who has to work with the languishing body. This is the second connotation of acting up: the body that hardly cooperates in therapy, if at all. It does not respond in the way we want or expect it to. And yet, something has to shift, as the diktat in therapy goes. The question is, of course, *what* needs to happen or what can still be done. After all, in many cases, the patient has already taken many steps without the hoped-for result.

And then there is the book itself. One could question the need at all for a book about a difficult body. Or, rather, why *another* book because a quick look – or click – through the (digital) shelves tells us that there is no shortage of books that offer therapies, advice or answers, written by people with academic, clinical or personal insights. I have often wondered why I would like to add another book. Not only do most books end up in a second-hand bookshop, but also, and more importantly, many existing books already make a special contribution to the complex domain of the psychosomatic body. Perhaps everything has already been said in various specialist fields?

Yet, unwritten words kept knocking on my door, sometimes while I was reading professional literature,[1] sometimes after a lecture for my students, but often also after a long day in practice. Perhaps the latter was the main reason to get behind the laptop. It strikes me that as far as practice is concerned, scientific literature often only homes in on causes or diagnostics or treatment and not so much on the actual therapeutic process as a whole, that is, the practice. In the few cases that it does – more often in manuals than in articles – interventions are usually only considered from one specific angle or discipline. If a multidisciplinary approach is used, there is hardly any room for integration or the advice is limited to a sum total of therapies or interventions.

The latter is done, for example, in multidisciplinary centres such as pain clinics, where the patient can be conveniently slotted into a chain of consultations, therapies and exercise programmes. Whether this is particularly valuable for the patient, or useful for the healthcare institution, is an interesting question that falls outside the scope of this book. In any case, it can be observed from everyday practice that patients often return to their GPs and therapists after such a therapeutic process because their symptoms have been alleviated either insufficiently or only temporarily. Although there may be a number of reasons for this, I believe that one aspect of the problem lies in the overestimation of such multidisciplinary projects.

However well-intended these projects may be, there is a real risk that people will be treated much like an outpatient seeing a string of doctors and therapists who often know little about each other's areas of expertise and whose economic policy forces them to work alongside each other.

In a transdisciplinary approach, various areas of expertise are included and integrated so that it is possible to subsequently work within a new framework, thereby taking due account of the patient's frame of reference.

Perhaps this book's modest *raison d'être* is what is these days referred to as 'transdisciplinarity'. In their article 'Transdisciplinarity: context, contradiction and capacity', Russell et al. (2008, p. 462) first juxtapose transdisciplinarity with more obsolete concepts, such as multidisciplinarity and interdisciplinarity:

> In contrast to multidisciplinarity – in which disciplinary specialists work together maintaining their disciplinary approaches and perspectives – and interdisciplinarity – in which areas of overlap or intersection between disciplines are investigated by scholars from two or more areas – transdisciplinarity has been described as a practice that transgresses and transcends disciplinary boundaries. Of the various cross-disciplinary approaches, transdisciplinarity seems to have the most potential to respond to new demands and imperatives.

In this context, Groot and Klostermann (2009) use a continuum of mono- to transdisciplinarity, the latter being seen as a higher level of interdisciplinarity. They also point to a special feature of a transdisciplinary approach, namely, the cocreation of knowledge and action by integrating other actors of information and experience, such as non-scientific or societal sources. To sum up, the transdisciplinary approach allows the therapist to think, work and write while transcending different domains; several areas of knowledge are not only involved, but also understood. It is, therefore, not enough to consider different angles (multidisciplinary) or to think along with them (interdisciplinary); it is also necessary to learn to think from the new framework while including the patients' frames of reference (transdisciplinary).

Although still in its infancy, transdisciplinary thinking is gaining ground over reductionist paradigms (such as evidence-based medicine) around the difficult body. This is often due to the failure of a mono- or multidisciplinary approach (Satterfield et al., 2009) and we even witness the emergence of new disciplines with an original transdisciplinary way of collaboration, such as the domain of 'infant mental health' (Rexwinkel et al., 2011). Clinical conviction and scientific insight learn that complex phenomena, such as psychosomatic symptoms, chronic pain or medically unexplained physical symptoms, cannot be adequately understood and treated within a reductionist framework. We would even go so far as to claim that these symptoms are sustained by them. Certainly with regard to inexplicable ailments, there is still a great deal of uncertainty. Moreover, the diagnostic label appears to be highly dependent on the medical discipline consulted. This is how you will often end up with a diagnosis of irritable bowel syndrome when you visit the internist, chronic pelvic pain syndrome at the gynaecologist's, fibromyalgia at the rheumatologist's, hyperventilation at the pneumologist's, tension headache at the neurologist's, non-cardiac chest pain at the cardiologist's, chronic fatigue syndrome at the virologist's and temporomandibular joint dysfunction at the dentist's (Henningsen, 2016). As far as the proportion of unexplained conditions go, the numbers speak for themselves. In their book *Medically unexplained symptoms, somatisation and bodily distress: Developing better clinical services*, Creed et al. (2011) make an inventory of numerous available studies on various populations, settings, population groups and countries. They arrive at sobering numbers of more than one third in general practise and even more than half in specialized care. Since these authors worked with specific terminology such as 'somatoform disorders' (DSM IV) – 'somatic symptom disorder' in DSM V – or the more recently used 'bodily distress syndrome' (Ivbijaro & Goldberg, 2013; Fink & Schröder, 2010), we dare say that with labels such as 'stress-related disorders', which doctors and therapists bandy about intuitively, the figures could well be much higher still.

If we then look at the origins, the aetiological theories and findings relating to psychosomatic and chronic pain are almost too numerous to take in, certainly in the case of functional somatic syndromes. Although research points to significant correlations with pathological changes in brain structure and function, for example in musculoskeletal pain (Kregel et al., 2017), chronic lower back pain (Wand et al., 2010; Apkarian et al., 2004) or fibromyalgia (Kuchinad et al., 2007), and some authors even propose to consider chronic pain as a disease (Tracey & Bushnell, 2009), two leading review articles in *The Lancet* (Henningsen et al., 2007) and *Nature* (Denk et al., 2014) emphatically describe the influence of early affective learning experiences, personality traits and body perception – in addition to epigenetic, pain-processing and environmental factors – as risk factors in functional somatic syndromes and chronic pain. On the basis of recent research, the proverbial chicken-or-egg question does indeed tend to lean more in favour of early-childhood influences. For example, maltreatment and abuse in childhood appear to correlate with chronic back pain (Leisner et al., 2014), migraine (Tietjen et al., 2010) and, more generally, with a disturbed pain processing (Tesarz et al., 2016) or stress-related conditions (Van Houdenhove, 2007c).

But no matter how thorough these scientific sources may be, ultimately, they have to be translated into therapy, and that – by all accounts – is not always an easy task. In practical terms, few therapists will deny that psychosomatic patients often drag their share of negative life experiences with them, and scientists can prove this connection ever more strongly, but this does not mean that these insights can be used in a 'tangible' manner in the actual therapy room. And it is precisely here that this book wants to try to make a contribution, particularly in the transdisciplinary translation for the benefit of the therapist and his therapy. Throughout this book, we will see that the body does indeed occupy a special place in therapy and requires, by definition, a multi-faceted approach. The reason for this is that the body is not only intrinsically located in no man's land but also *is* no man's land. The body – just like the mind – is always psychosomatic, that is, both *soma* and *psyche*, so that 'psychosomatic' as a term is problematic and alternatives urgently need to be investigated (Vandenberghe & Luyten, 2010). In a metaphorical sense, working with a (difficult) body is always located between the body and mind, and requires several angles for the therapist to approach it from. We feel supported in this position by numerous authorities, such as Daniel Siegel (2010), Bessel Van der Kolk (2014), Alan Fogel (2009), Peter Levine (2014a, 2014b) or Pat Ogden (Ogden et al., 2006), who, over the past decades, have shed light on this complex area between body and mind in a clear and emphatic manner.

> *The body is not only intrinsically located in no man's land, it always is no man's land.*

This book seeks to adopt a transdisciplinary approach in at least two ways. First, in terms of content, we try to look at the difficult body in therapy from three broad angles, to arrive at conceptual alignment and – where possible – also to integration for clinical practice. To this end, we explore the body as an area in therapy between body and mind from a psychological, biological and philosophical perspective. More technically spoken, we approach the themes in this book from a psychotherapeutic and psychodynamic, neuroscientific and myofascial, and phenomenological perspective. Or put in a more imaginative way, we bring the psychotherapist, the body therapist and the philosopher together around the table for an open dialogue about the difficult body.

This book essentially seeks to transcend disciplines and hopes to reach a diverse readership, including clinical psychologists, psychotherapists, body therapists and doctors. The common denominator is always the body that speaks in the therapy. Therefore, this book aims to offer both a conceptual and a therapeutic framework to therapists – in a broader sense, providers of care – who work with the complex but also intriguing psychosomatic body as it appears in anxiety and depression, stress and burn-out, as well as trauma and medically unexplained physical symptoms. Since each therapist has his own expertise, this book wants to offer added value by inviting the practitioner to integrate other knowledge, insights or skills within their own practice. From a transdisciplinary point of view, however, this requires a certain degree of familiarity with the jargon of related domains and, a willingness to watch, reflect and, where desirable, also to act. As far as the latter is concerned, this book wants to leave enough room. For many readers, the added value could just lie in the theoretical and conceptual broadening of their views. Others may be hungry for more and actually want to work with their patients from this new perspective and integrate it in their work. This is also possible, provided that the right training is in place. Insofar as this book may be innovative, it certainly does not want to overturn the apple cart. While every therapist knows his comfort zone, we would like to reiterate that it is not a question of merely bringing together different disciplines and adding them up. The bridge to the neighbouring discipline must be actively crossed. For us, this is where the difference lies between eclecticism and integration. In addition, working within a transdisciplinary framework always involves taking a critical stance with regard to one's own discipline. In any case, transdisciplinarity goes hand in hand with an eagerness to learn.

Finally, this book mainly attempts to be practice based. In addition to being a passionate teacher and modest researcher, I am, above all, a curious therapist who perhaps prefers to look at his work as a craft and wants to write from the treatment room. That is why we will start from practice and try to gradually integrate theoretical concepts and new ways of thinking with a view to adopting a different approach to the psychosomatic body within the therapeutic process. Thanks to this integration, the book can evolve organically through these theoretical frameworks back into practice, without ever wanting to be prescriptive. When I compare therapeutic profession to that of a craftsman, what is essential is the thoroughness with which the métier and space for creativity are appraised. This is somewhat of a personal critique of the protocol manuals often used today, in which it is necessary to carry out and apply a series of techniques or interventions aimed at a specific symptom or problem. In my opinion, this not only (re)animates the illusion that the human being is makeable but also contributes to the idea that a specific technique exists (and is therefore necessary) for everything which should be selected methodically in order to lead to the best result. The fact that this usually lacks a broadly anchored background theory appears hardly relevant and is conveniently swept under the carpet of the expeditiousness of the many protocols. Not only is this lack of a theoretical framework an Achilles heel for fledgling therapists, but there is also no more room for what was once the basis of science: the wonder, the desire and the critical attitude to understand man and the world. By starting in the first chapter with a more philosophical stance, I will try to introduce this attitude of understanding or 'Verstehen' as the basis of a transdisciplinary approach to the psychosomatic body in therapy. Although the other chapters deal more explicitly with specific concepts or skills, this phenomenological-hermeneutical attitude of the therapist remains at least as important as the various strands of his therapy.

I would like to finish off by adding a relevant, personal note. No matter how crucial objective, scientific insights and knowledge are in addition to subjective experiences, what matters most is the therapist's personal growth. For me, this resonates with the revealing title *Van inhoud naar houding* (*From content to attitude*) with which philosopher Ilse Bulhof (1995) takes the reader through a process that shifts from content to mindset: 'From wanting to know exactly what

Socrates would once have said to what that means for you right now' (p. 82). Perhaps this is what distinguished psychiatrist Irvin Yalom (1980) meant when, with a metaphor from a cooking class, he referred to the cook whose dishes could not be imitated, because she 'threw in something' that could not be found in the recipes. He compares this with experienced therapists who, when nobody is looking, introduce something – 'the real thing' (p. 3) – into the therapy that cannot be captured in scientific research. So on the one hand, this shift from content to mindset is important – a process that many therapists will describe as 'growth' or 'experience' – but on the other hand, there is also the relationship between the two. Or as Bulhof (1995) puts it, of course, you have to know what Socrates said and meant before you can explore what it means for you as a person. As such, a transdisciplinary attitude goes hand in hand with study work, a serious but, above all, gratifying activity that has been relegated to the background at a time when refresher training or continued learning has to tick boxes and be quick fixes or simply represent experience and networking opportunities.

Note

1 Anyone who browses the professional literature is bound to question the value of many studies that are carried out and published, often without much background theory or clinical value for the therapist or patient. It would lead us too far to describe how one-sided, hyper-specialised and partly artificial the scientific world – with universities as standard-bearers – has become. Researchers – under the constant pressure to publish – have to create their research in such a way that a meaningful link with clinical reality is often lost. Or many professors stand in front of overcrowded auditoriums and hold forth on themes in which they have barely been able to gain personal clinical experience. Interesting books have been written on this very subject and editorials regularly appear in the media to which I am happy to refer.

Some testimonials

It is perhaps a good idea to start a book that attempts to offer a different view of the psychosomatic body in therapy with those who have experienced it. In the following excerpts, patients share their experiences, using their own words. Sometimes this happened during – usually after – a session but always following a vulnerable encounter with newly discovered and felt parts of themselves. Out of respect for the candidness of their words, we only refer to them by their initials.

> J. (39 years old):
> *Soon I felt better and better. A few weeks later (actually for the first time in my life) I had the feeling I could breathe freely. It felt like nothing I'd ever experienced before. I noticed a great clarity in my thinking and perception. It felt as if my body and mind 'functioned optimally', as if I suddenly had more options, as if everything went much more efficiently (automatically), (without emotional disturbance), 'without any interference on the line', with less tension. . . . I had gone from one extreme to the other, as it were.*
>
> *I realise that, of course, this isn't the case, because now that I have certain insights, I'm suddenly starting to feel better automatically, but if I manage to work on this consistently, if I finally dare to make decisions myself, break certain routines, automatisms and patterns, walk away from some people (and situations), 'work on myself' (becoming aware) . . . there is a good chance that I will be able to recognise certain triggers in myself more quickly and that I will not let myself be affected by certain situations, reactions. . . . That way, I will be able to distance myself consciously and feel better (in my skin).*

> T. (26 years old):
> *At the beginning of the session, I experienced some pain in the hip area, because of anxiety more than anything, because the pain woke me up this morning and I couldn't get back to sleep. Focusing on my belly made me realise that it held a lot of stress. I liked the quiet background music and the gentle stroking of my belly, as they were pleasant and relaxing. I did catch myself thinking a lot, but focused on how I could release the tension a bit. This went away when I started to focus more on breathing. Also, I felt more relaxed when I closed my eyes and had my belly stroked, but still the tension*

was really present over the rest of my body. In the meantime, I started to get a tingling feeling when I started to breathe more vigorously.

When you asked me to breathe in and out energetically, I was a little confused. The distinct tingling in my arms and face gave me a very strange feeling, as well as tears, which didn't really feel like tears. It was more like a feeling of letting go of control. Here, I had the feeling that it came from the bottom of my pelvis, and went up through my back. This relaxed me in those places, but I had the feeling that all the tension had shifted towards my arms and head. These were also the places where the tingling was at its strongest. I was shocked at how cramped my hands were when I looked at them. While this gave me an uncomfortable feeling, because it took a lot of effort to get out of it, I didn't mind, because my body told me to take it easy. Emotionally, this whole process was quite intense. I didn't expect this. The impact is quite big. I am still thinking about it a few hours later, but with a positive feeling.

M. (32 years old):
Difficulty breathing. . . . When the treatment focused more on my sternum, I noticed that my breathing stopped, that it was difficult to take my next breath. I recognised the pain of moments when I was overwhelmed by sadness. Then it feels like the floodgates open and pain gushes out. Physically, I get the feeling as if something is grabbing me by the throat/chest. I felt that pain again during the treatment. Immediately, I get a sense that I have to close those floodgates quickly, because it's of no use. It doesn't change the situation. It only makes me sad, while I live a reasonably happy life now.

Sense of sadness. . . . The reassurance helps me feel calmer, and I can breathe more easily. I feel a sense of sadness washing over me gently, but I felt okay about this, so I don't experience it as unpleasant. In the end, the tears roll down my cheeks, but this also feels good.

I realise that I always overthink things, try to anticipate things that I actually can't control myself. I've come to realise that I actually try to do this with everything in my life and that it's a shame, because it prevents me from enjoying the moment. Then I think back to what it was like 'before', before Daddy's passing, and I realise that I used to live much more in the moment.

Afterwards, I still feel calm and, above all, secure. It feels okay to allow this. Still, I notice that after that, I quickly switch back to my 'normal' self. However, the experience lingers, also because the day after I still experienced pain on my sternum. If I rub it, it hurts. I consider this as a sign my body is giving me, to show that there is sadness and that I need to do something with it.

When therapists in training are introduced to EBW for the first time this gives a lot of interesting testimonials, too. We illustrate this with two examples.

Rob:
A deep bodywork treatment is a journey from the everyday thinking to a deeper felt consciousness. A descent towards physical sensations that can express themselves in visual fragments or archaic images as a harbinger of felt dreaming. The therapist's handles invite you to have sensory experiences

away from language. Sensations dissipate compulsive thoughts and a different state of 'being' emerges. The body is felt and inner turmoil is channelled through subtle or abrupt movements. The body shakes off something in order to free itself.

Dream images and visual memories merge in a creative process under the rational surface. Physical stimuli and colours alternate with timeless moments of tranquil voids.

The body-mind unit does its own thing under the guiding hands of a silent therapist who directs the process. An old wound even starts to heal.

Sophie:
At first, I feel like I'm inhibited, kind of embarrassed to open myself up. It's a confrontation with myself and my neuroses, my thinking is still strongly present. As the intensity of the session progresses due to increased breathing, manual contact, movements of legs, pelvis . . . this feeling changes into a deeper intensity which I perceive as one of excitement, an internal driving force, making it easier for me to overcome my inhibitions and let go. It's as if I'm given the opportunity to let myself come out from within. When certain painful areas in my body are touched, I feel anger, and even a kind of aggression or belligerence, emerging. Later, when the session ends in a tranquil phase, I feel that my mind is more open and I get images from the past or spontaneous images that I have not really experienced, but that I feel come from within, my desires, my needs, my virtues. The next few days, I feel that I watch myself more carefully and that I notice things from my subconscious (e.g. in dreams) that would otherwise pass me by. The difference between my inward and outward personality then seems smaller and I feel more 'determination'.

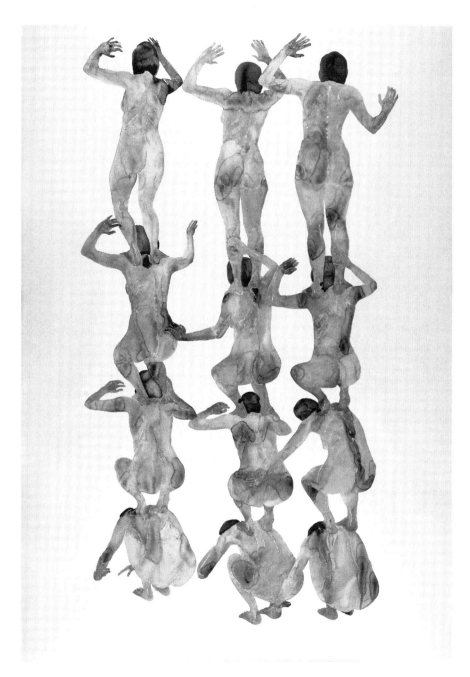

Bodybuilding, 2016, watercolour, 227.8 × 152 cm.

Introduction

The psychosomatic body in a field of therapies

Throughout the ages and cultures, the body has always played a crucial role in psychosomatic well-being. From yoga, as probably the oldest discipline that sees man as a psychosomatic unit (Feuerstein, 2001), right through to healing forms well into the Greco-Roman era, each time the approach was based on the reciprocal relationship between movement or touch, on the one hand, and psychological functioning, on the other. Hence the well-known adage *Mens sana in corpore sano*. Yet, this evolution has been unable to sustain itself into our postmodern era. Despite developments, such as psychosomatic medicine, psychomotor therapy, body psychotherapy or somatic psychology, a persistent dichotomy between body and mind gradually developed, which is still present to this day. A far-reaching consequence of this is the strict division of the therapy landscape between the poles *psyche* and *soma* at two extremes on a spectrum (Figure 0.1).

A divided landscape

In itself, this dichotomy does not necessarily have to be a problem and it is understandable that there is a need for therapies that explicitly focus on one or the other. These two sub-areas, therefore, correspond to pertinent disciplines, such as physiotherapy and psychotherapy, which, in turn, are underpinned by corresponding scientific domains, respectively the biomedical and rehabilitation sciences and the psychological sciences and psychiatry. Less obvious, however, is the central area of the spectrum. Here, one would expect psychosomatic therapies that work with both body and language. This middle ground has traditionally been quite a crowded space where many therapies and schools claim to adopt a holistic approach to the patient. The problem here is not the lack of therapies, but rather the scientific validity of their approaches, assumptions and treatment effects (see, for example, Courtois et al., 2015) or their problematic relationship with science (Mehling et al., 2005). The latter, however, only applies to a small proportion of these therapies and also occurs in the opposite direction, i.e. from mainstream science itself.

When we return to the central theme of the psychosomatic body and first look at the left-hand side of the spectrum, we come across the purely somatic therapies, such as physiotherapy, manual therapy or osteopathy, where intense, and often

4 *Introduction*

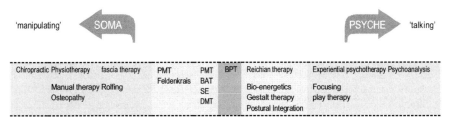

PMT: Psychomotor therapy; BAT: Body awareness therapy; SE: Somatic experiencing;
DMT: Dance and movement therapy; BPT: Body psychotherapy

Figure 0.1 The psychosomatic therapy landscape

Note: The location of the therapies in this figure is purely illustrative and is not an exhaustive list

successful, work is done on difficult bodies. For many patients, these therapies are often the first port of call on a long road of recovery. Physiotherapists occupy a privileged position here because of the numerous referrals they get from general practitioners. Manual therapy and osteopathy are seen as further, specialised stops and often follow the first phase of physiotherapy. However, since a considerable number of patients appear to derive insufficient benefit from somatic therapies alone, they end up in the psychotherapeutic system, but only in a second stage within our dichotomously organised healthcare system. 'If medication is not working, if the massage and exercises don't help, then maybe we should talk about it.'

On the right-hand side of the therapy spectrum, the self-evidence with which syndromes are treated is equally considerable. On the one hand, the positive effects of cognitive-behavioural strategies are often pointed out (Tang, 2017; Simons & Basch, 2016; Thoma et al., 2015; Monticone et al., 2015), although with conflicting results for disorders such as fibromyalgia (Minelli & Vaona, 2012). Sometimes these therapies are discouraged (Twisk & Maes, 2009). On the other hand, psychodynamic therapies, in general, are also proving valuable (Leichsenring et al., 2015; Driessen et al., 2011; Shedler, 2010), or more specific approaches, such as Dynamic Interpersonal Therapy (Luyten, 2014), in particular. However, within the psychological-psychotherapeutic setting, the body is not self-evident (Calsius, 2017a, 2017b). Meanwhile, the clear-cut division between body and mind persists: body therapy is not a conversation therapy and in mainstream psychotherapy, there is no place for touch or movement.

An exception on the somatic left-hand side of the spectrum is psychomotor therapy. This specialised form of physiotherapy has its roots in movement therapy and remedial gymnastics, developed as a holistic approach to psychiatric and psychopathological disorders and has a respectable, scientific basis (Larun et al., 2016; Vancampfort et al., 2012, 2013, 2014, 2016; Gyllensten et al., 2010). The problem with psychomotor therapy seems to be that it is rooted in the biomedical paradigm of physical therapy, as a result of which it finds itself in a bit of a stranglehold. On the one hand, clearly not a form of psychotherapy, psychomotor therapy uses a health paradigm that handles empirical parameters, such as physical fitness. On the other hand, psychomotor therapy works with elements such as body experience, self-esteem, internalising and externalising models, drama therapy and self-expression, which means it is much closer to psychological-psychotherapeutic models and does not fall under the hegemony of the randomised science method from the biomedical paradigm. The unwarranted price that psychomotor therapy pays for this is further exacerbated by its historical connection with second- or third-line residential psychiatry and consequently, its problematic inclusion in general practice. Nevertheless, psychomotor therapy can rightly be situated in the psychosomatic area of the spectrum, albeit to the left of the middle ground.

A bit of history

If we now leave the somatic part of the spectrum and move to the right, we end up in the psychotherapeutic section. Intriguing here is the history of a difficult, if not impossible, relationship to the body. For starters, if we look at psychoanalysis, touching was taboo. This is somewhat surprising, given that specific touches were originally even part of the catharsis method, as propounded by its founders Sigmund Freud and Jozeph Breuer (Heller, 2012; Totton, 1998). The body, therefore, continued to appear regularly and persistently in psychotherapy and eventually developed into a fully-fledged and autonomous movement, namely, body psychotherapy (BPT).[1] Historically, this movement is mainly associated with Wilhelm Reich (1897–1957), whose vision and approach we will discuss in more detail in Chapter 4. However, although Reich is generally regarded as the godfather of BPT, for Marlock (2015), the source of the very first systematic psychosomatic analysis in the West can be traced back to Franz Anton Mesmer (1734–1815) and one of his students, Comte de Puységur. Mesmer applied a theory of subtle, vitalising flows in the body and brain that could lead to psychosomatic disturbances in the event of a blockage. While he started therapeutically with magnetism that was in use at the time (to influence the aforementioned energy flows), Puységur used hypnosis to bring his patients to a 'lucid conversation' (idem). It was, however, French psychiatrist Pierre Janet (1859–1947) who, in his work at the Hôpital Salpêtrière, applied catharsis as a method on the basis of a 'psychological analysis' and investigated how neurotic structures and muscle tension were linked. He recommended touch and massage as therapy, which would later inspire Reich. However, the combination of catharsis, hypnosis and touch would, as already mentioned, form part of the early years of psychoanalysis, when Freud (1856–1939) applied forms of pressure and massage to create associations (Heller, 2012). Moreover, for Freud, the 'self' was first and foremost a 'physical self' (Freud, 1988 [1923]).

Although after Freud and before Reich, it was mainly Otto Fenichel (1897–1946) who proves to have been vital in the birth of BPT, we should certainly also mention Georg Groddeck (1866–1934) and Sandor Ferenczi (1873–1933). With his 'Active Technique', the latter made patients aware of their unconscious bodies in postures, movement or behaviour and is thus, in a certain sense, the forerunner of what is today called body awareness therapy. Where Fenichel focused on the muscular tissue and tonus in relation to mental processes, it is Groddeck who – for the first time – developed an integrated approach by applying deep massage techniques in the same analytical session with a view to influencing underlying emotions (Geuter, 2015b). Nevertheless, it is thanks to Fenichel that BPT will continue to develop through his contact with BPT's unsurpassed grandmother, Elsa Gindler, from Germany (1885–1961), who, as a reform gymnast and movement therapist, advocated a somato-educational approach without any psychotherapeutic ambitions.

Fenichel – married to a student of Gindler's – studied with her and inspired his student and later friend Wilhelm Reich with Gindler's approach (Weaver, 2015). From this cross-fertilisation of remedial gymnastics with his expertise as a psychoanalyst and his introduction to Elsa Lindenberg, dancer and pupil of the famous choreographer Rudolf Laban, Reich will create the basis for his character-analysis and vegetotherapy. He will develop these after his break with the International Psychoanalytical Association (Bassal, 2015). At this conference in Lucerne in 1934, Reich presented his paper on vegetative current, with which he introduced his theory of character and muscle armour (Büntig, 2015). From then on, Reich typically considered the body as a imprint for chronic tension, constriction and repression and the neurovegetative substrate to influence this (Reich, 1972; Totton, 1998).

After this important occasion in Berlin with Fenichel and Gindler, Reich was forced to move to Oslo, where he developed his theory and therapy, but no longer referred to it as psychotherapy. Although it falls outside the space available here, it is important to point to the historical cross-fertilisation that took place in Oslo with the tradition and knowledge within physiotherapy that were present there. The psychiatrist Trygve Braatoy (1904–1953), himself a student of Fenichel's, was first of all very influential for the physiotherapist Aadel Bülow-Hansen (1906–2001), who, in turn, integrated a psychoanalytical form of psychotherapy in her method of massage, posture exercise, breathing and relaxation (Bassal, 2015). In fact, this is the opposite of what Groddeck did before. Another child of the so-called Golden Age in Oslo was Gerda Boyesen (1922–2005), who would later develop Biodynamic Psychology, in which she does not only situate the concept of blocked and congested energy by suppressed affects in muscle tissue – as Reich did – but also in the connective tissue and abdominal organs. This is how Boyesen came to use deep abdominal massage for emotional release, which she referred to as psychoperistalsis (Geuter, 2015b). This second important period – after Berlin and Oslo – for the development of BPT is characterised by the reciprocal relationship with physiotherapy and leads to the establishment of the first Institute for Psychomotricity in Oslo.

Throughout all these developments and despite many criticisms of his approach and person – justified or otherwise – Reich remains forever associated with BPT through numerous concepts he introduced, such as character and muscle armour or grounding, which would influence generations of therapists inside and outside of psychotherapy. Partly because of the importance Reich attaches to breathing, posture and touch, these elements form the basis of various therapies within the Human Potential Movement of the 1960s and 1970s, such as Alexander Löwen's bioenergetics (1910–2008), Fritz Perls's Gestalt therapy (1893–1970) and Jack Painter's Postural Integration (1933–2010). But what does BPT involve today and what does it stand for?

What is body psychotherapy?

When Geuter (2015b) points out that BPT is historically based on three pillars, it is humanistic psychology that makes up the threesome alongside psychoanalysis and remedial gymnastics. This third pillar comes to fruition during the Human Potential Movement, which crystallised in the 1960s during Esalen Institute's heyday in California and was characterised by cross-fertilisation with Eastern philosophies and meditative traditions (Walsh, 1999). Fritz Perls (1893–1970), Eugene Gendlin (1926–2017) and Stanislav Grof (born 1931) are the main protagonists with their respective Gestalt therapy, focusing and holotropic breathwork (Heller, 2012). These psychotherapeutic approaches are body focused, holistic and embedded in a body phenomenology of the here-and-now. In the aftermath of this melting pot of eastern and western philosophies and psychotherapeutic currents, a multitude of body-mind therapies will emerge.

But given this rich history, what is meant by BPT? In their survey, Marlock and Weiss (2015a, 2015b) characterise BPT as an umbrella term for various methods, on the basis of an interesting grid with six axes: (1) treatment versus phenomenological learning, (2) energetic body versus the knowing body, (3) analytically insightful versus functionally development-oriented, (4) focus on non-verbal processes versus dialogue-based relation, (5) touch versus no touch and (6) regression versus working in the here-and-now. In this grid, the Reichian therapy can be situated at the extremes: treatment, energetic body, analytical, non-verbal, touch and regression. At the other extreme, Gendlian focusing can be typified as a developmental, phenomenological learning from the knowing body within a dialogue-based relationship in the here-and-now, where explicit touch is not used.

In addition to differentiations within BPT, the literature also points to the discrepancy between BPT and other psychotherapies (Geuter, 2015a, 2015b; Heller, 2012). What is characteristic about BPT is that both the physical and the psychological substrates are systematically integrated in the treatment, whereby the focus is continuously on both structural and process-like changes within the entire psychosomatic dimension (Geuter, 2015a). Furthermore, BPT distinguishes itself in particular by using a range of body-oriented interventions. These are explicitly aimed to promote a meaningful awareness process in which mental, emotional, behavioural and physical dimensions are connected holistically (Marlock & Weiss, 2015a). In addition, BPT also distinguishes itself in a fundamental way from psychomotor physiotherapy and other educational-therapeutic methods, such as the Feldenkrais method, the Alexander technique or eutony, where body experience is used without a clinical psychological-psychotherapeutic framework

(Geuter, 2015b; Heller, 2012). This characteristic, distinctive and, therefore, also unique identity of BPT was ratified in 1988 and 1996 by the establishment of the European Association of Body Psychotherapy[2] and the United States Association for Body Psychotherapy, respectively.

Body psychotherapy as a response to the psychosomatic body

So we have arrived at the domain of BPT, which is situated in the middle of the psychosomatic therapy spectrum. After all, trying to transcend the dichotomy between the body and mind is enshrined in BPT's very foundations. Working with evocative movement, hands-on bodywork and physical expression are the preferred points of entry to the patient's world of experience. The fact that the physical structures and processes are not the goal of the treatment, but 'a means' is one of the distinguishing features which sets BPT apart from various other forms of bodywork, such as physiotherapy or osteopathy. It goes without saying that influencing and, where possible, improving various aspects of physical functioning is also appreciated in BPT, but as mentioned earlier, it is not the intentional goal of the treatment. In concrete terms, for example, the relaxation and softening of muscle tissue (we will hereinafter refer to 'myofascial structures') in the chest area contributes to a better posture, deeper breathing or more freedom of movement in the back and shoulders. Nevertheless, the primary objective in BPT is primarily the experience and awareness that accompany these changes, such as being present in the world in a different way. For example, patients can, and dare to, straighten their shoulders, open up and establish contact and relationships in their environment from a more solid basis. Geuter (2015b) argues that the characteristic of BPT lies in the integration of body-focused and psychotherapeutic techniques, in which the simultaneous influence of both physical structures and psychological processes via awareness is central.

Does this not make BPT the ideal answer for the considerable group of people who fall by the wayside in other, more dichotomous approaches? In that case, the title of this book should refer exclusively to the domain of BPT. As a consequence, the *raison d'être* of this book could also be questioned, as there are plenty of specific and interesting reference works available on various forms of BPT. In addition, we even notice that therapies that were originally more dichotomous are now consciously and actively opening up for their complementary part within the therapeutic spectrum. There is a clear psychologisation noticeable within various body therapies, such as physiotherapy, manual therapy or osteopathy. Not only do they work from a biopsychosocial model, they also increasingly use behavioural therapeutic strategies, meditation techniques, such as mindfulness, or implement cognitive therapy around pain coping and perception. On the strictly psychotherapeutic side of the spectrum we see currents in which the body – or at least the physical experience – is granted a more obvious place and ethical dilemmas around touch are discussed (Ogden et al., 2006; Tune, 2005; Leijssen, 2001). Certainly experiential psychotherapies, such as Gendlin's focusing method (1969) or Perls's Gestalt therapy (van Praag, 1998) work consciously and actively with body awareness, physical presence and sometimes touch. Even within the psychoanalytical field, there are increasingly more people in favour of actively involving the body in therapy (Cornell, 2015) and who warn against the dangers of hyperpsychism (Orbach, 2006).

So also on the right-hand side of the spectrum, there seems to be a tendency to no longer only deal with the experiences of the body, but also with the actual integration of bodywork. The profile 'body-oriented psychologist', which was established by the Dutch Institute of Psychologists (NIP, 2011) describes the following competencies:

> The body-oriented psychologist NIP is able to apply a specific form of body-focused interventions in the field of posture, movement, touch, breathing patterns, voice expression, and focusing of attention, or a combination of these, with which the connection between body and psyche is made workable. He/she is also able to perceive the changing expression of the client (implicit knowing).
>
> (p. 10)

Experiential bodywork as a roadmap for psychosomatic therapy

The more we move to the middle of the spectrum in Figure 0.1, the more physical and verbal the therapies become, which translates into psychomotor therapy just to the left of the middle and the experiential psychotherapeutic approaches just to the right of it. At the same time, this middle line is not so much a schematic boundary, but an extensive area of BPT that is occupied by therapies that explicitly identify with a holistic framework and actually approach the patient in a more integrated way. This integration therefore does not simply presuppose the sum total of skills, techniques or strategies, but, above all, the inclusion of the paradigms that encapsulate both sides of the spectrum. Indeed, we must not lose sight of the fact that, although both sides of the continuum are distinguished by a difference in therapeutic methodology, they are also fundamentally poles apart by a totally different view of the world, in other words, by a different paradigm. Philosophically, this distinction originates, in part, in a hermeneutic 'Verstehen' versus a logical 'Erklären', which can then be understood as a phenomenological versus an empirical view of the world (Figure 0.2). The body therapeutic left-hand side appears to be biomedically grounded in an empirical 'measuring is knowing', whereas the psychotherapeutic right-hand side can largely be accommodated in a hermeneutical-phenomenological 'attempt to understand'.[3] Even coming from a scientific research background, this is a major difference, as this involves a quantitative Randomized Controlled Trial (RCT) method versus a qualitative 'n=1' approach, respectively. We will return to this briefly in Chapter 1, where we introduce a specific development-based model as a template for an integrated approach in practice.

So why does this book not deal with BPT as an alternative for straddling the body and mind? We have just left this question unanswered. The scope of BPT is

10 *Introduction*

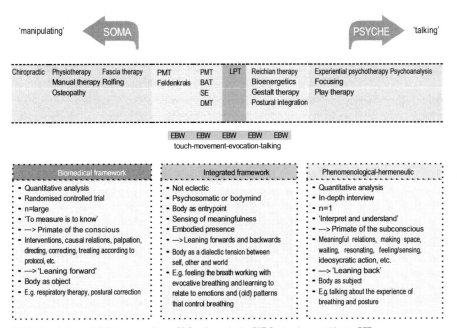

Figure 0.2 Paradigms within the psychosomatic spectrum

broad, but at the same time not always easy to demarcate for historical, conceptual and practical reasons. BPT has often found too little affinity with scientific research and has, for that reason, been unable to invest sufficiently in buttressing its specific foundations. Partly for this reason, it has not been able to juxtapose itself as a mainstream alternative next to psychodynamic, systemic, client-centred and cognitive-behavioural psychotherapy. This problematic relationship was not helped by the fact that some pioneers, such as Wilhelm Reich, Alexander Löwen or Jack Painter, chose to describe their therapies as a form of psychotherapy. At the same time, some more recent approaches, such as the Sensorimotor Approach (Ogden et al., 2006) or Somatic Experiencing (Levine, 2014a, 2014b) are not always clear in their psychotherapeutic identity either. On the other hand, the domain of BPT is clearly back in the picture, and explanatory mechanisms and treatment effects are gaining in validity based on scientific research (Röhricht, 2009). Especially in relation to psychosomatic disorders, trauma processing or difficult mentalisation and alexithymia, BPT's added value is increasingly emphasised (see, for example, Payne, 2015; Van der Kolk, 2014; Fogel, 2009; Ogden et al., 2006; Bloom, 2006; Totton, 2005; Schore, 2003).

At the same time, the effects of touch and body experience and their neurophysiological correlates are investigated more fundamentally (see, for example,

Schleip & Jäger, 2012; Craig, 2002, 2003, 2011; Herbert et al., 2011; Field, 2010; Tsakiris, 2010; Björensdotter et al., 2010; Schleip et al., 2005; Schleip, 2011). As a result, as mentioned earlier, the body appears remarkably more in the discourse of traditional psychotherapies, often because of their increasing neuroscientific relevance. Finally, within BPT itself, an evolution has been noticeable in recent decades in which, in addition to touch and hands-on bodywork focused on intrasubjective dynamics, more is being done through movement expression and behaviour from an interactive or intersubjective dimension (Cornell, 2015; Heller, 2012).

> *We want to establish a more innovative framework for an integrated way of working and thinking around the psychosomatic body in therapy. This will include the insights and guidelines of therapies within the psychosomatic middle ground and, at the same time, also compare them to the current scientific theories and research findings.*

Despite these positive evolutions within the domain of BPT and because of the sometimes-unclear conceptual context and problematic history, in this book we do not focus on BPT in the narrow sense of the word, but use an overarching coat hanger that we refer to as *experiential bodywork* or *EBW*. With this, we try to create sufficient, neutral space for a transdisciplinary approach that does not specifically belong to any current or school. However, we would like to spell out clearly that EBW itself is not a new form of BPT. Rather, in this book, we try to establish a more innovative framework for an integrated way of working and thinking around the psychosomatic body in therapy. We like to learn from the richness of many existing therapies within the psychosomatic middle ground by including their insights and guidelines, but also by comparing them with current scientific theories and research findings. With a transdisciplinary mindset, EBW tries to make a modest attempt to clarify part of the psychosomatic ground plan, to deepen some of its fundamental foundations and, above all, to build bridges. For when Heller (2012) states: 'Physiotherapists and osteopaths often notice that their work elicits intense and emotional reactions, but they do not have a frame of reference that allows them to deal adequately with such events' (p. 535), he actually refers to a half-truth to which EBW wants to formulate a response. In a somewhat concise way, body therapists have unique and interesting tools to penetrate the difficult body, but they are fundamentally lacking a suitable framework to be able to work with that which is released in the patient's experience. On the other side of the spectrum, clinical psychologists/psychotherapists have solid and effective frameworks to hold and guide patients through often turbulent, emotional waters, but lack the body-focused knowledge, expertise and tools. These are two half-truths that are more difficult to unite than expected. Since these half-truths relate to both the empirical-analytical and the phenomenological-hermeneutical paradigm, within EBW we use an integrated model in which these two approaches are contained. This model and the underlying integral view of the patient are central to the next chapter.

Notes

1 For a detailed genealogy, we refer the reader to Langfeld and Rellensmann 2015, and for a discussion of the philosophical precursors of body/mind approaches, we refer the reader to Heller 2012.
2 For a detailed description of the competences for 'Body Psychotherapy', as well as the associated ethical framework, see Body Psychotherapy Competencies (EABP, 2012).
3 Yet, not all therapies can be accommodated within this dimensional spectrum on the basis of their name or work domain. For example, behavioural therapy fits in better with the 'measuring is knowing' paradigm than would be assumed on the basis of its psychotherapeutic identity. At the same time, therapeutic currents may be too quick at times to assume a holistic label and to situate themselves in the middle of the spectrum.

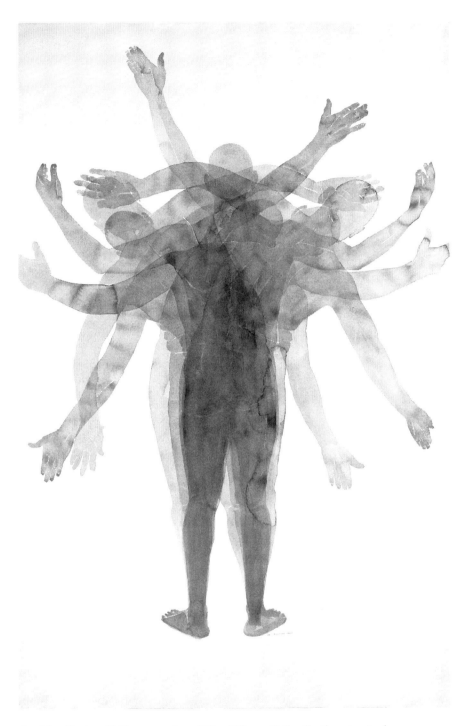

Big Man Waving, 2008, watercolour, 172 × 108 cm, Dell collection, Amsterdam.

1 An integrated look at the psychosomatic patient

In today's healthcare system, it is almost standard to map out the broad context in which the patient finds himself. Few people will question the importance of this. How this is best done and for what purpose it should be used in practice, is another question altogether. Academic studies prefer to work with a biopsychosocial model (Engel, 1980). Somatic therapists will therefore not only shed light on the somatic side, but will also consider the patient's psychological and social environment. In mental healthcare, it is the natural course of events that somatic data are added. Although biopsychosocial classification models, such as the ICF model,[1] offer an answer to earlier and one-sided bio-medical approaches, and even though they are now well established (Mahdi et al., 2017; Stucki et al., 2017; Gorostiaga et al., 2017; Linde, 2017; Muschalla et al., 2017), there are obvious weaknesses and shortcomings (Heerkens et al., 2017; Sabbe, 2010).[2] Within EBW, we opt for an alternative as a stepping stone.

Towards a transdisciplinary model

> *Within a transdisciplinary model for the psychosomatic body, there must also be room for development-oriented and process thinking, for the fundamental role of experience and meaning, and for the unconscious.*

In summary, the ICF model (WHO, 2002) departs from three perspectives, namely, the human being as an organism ('the body'), as an acting subject ('activities') and as a participating subject in an environment ('participation'). Here, characteristics, functions and disorders (body), activities and limitations (actions) are distinguished, alongside participation and participation issues. Finally, the ICF model also takes stock of possible influencing factors that are divided into two categories, namely, personal factors and external factors. The latter can consist of an extensive series of subcategories. The personal factors, on the other hand, are identified within the ICF model, but are not really fleshed out in any more detail. Despite the value and application outlined earlier, within EBW, we decide against using the ICF model, but opt for an alternative. Reasons for this include the fact that within the ICF model, there is hardly any room for development-oriented dynamics or process thinking, nor for the fundamental role of experience and meaning, and certainly not for the role of the unconscious as a phenomenon and factor in human functioning. This makes the ICF model too unrefined to use in an integrated approach such as EBW. It is also interesting to note that the ICF model does not deal with possible influencing factors, such as the individual's personality structure. It is also striking that the patient's experience is scarcely given any space, although it appears to play a crucial role as a risk factor in the development of functional, somatic syndromes (Henningsen et al., 2007).

The model that we use as an alternative within EBW is partly based on the work of American philosopher Ken Wilber (1949), in which a transdisciplinary vision of the individual's development is central. This author introduces a number of instruments and concepts, including the Four Quadrant Model and the developmental *fulcra*. Both are explained for the first time in this chapter. Whereas the ICF model hardly discusses the patient's world of experience, the family climate and the group dynamics in which he grew up, and certainly not the interactions between these factors, Wilber's concepts offer a special added value for a development-dynamic view of the individual. However, Wilber's oeuvre is not always equally undiscussed and has been subject to criticism, such as too little exposure to peer review and too many attempts to integrate fields of knowledge that are so far apart that it threatens to become a 'theory of everything'. These comments, mainly from academia, should rightly be taken to heart, but mostly relate to the later periods of his oeuvre. The concepts and vision mentioned earlier, which we try to translate within the scope of this book, originate from the early and mid-periods of Wilber's oeuvre, in which we agree with the academic-scientific attitude that he adopted at that time. In our opinion, this is not only his most productive period, but also his most innovative. Most critics of his work agree on this. The translation to therapy is made in Chapter 7. Here we consider the first concept: the Four Quadrant Model.

The Four Quadrant Model[3]

In essence, the Four Quadrant Model (4QM) has a simple basic form.[4] The individual is central to four quadrants, each representing a specific and unique aspect of human reality. The model is briefly explained step-by-step as follows. Wilber starts from the observation that each individual has a personal, private side that is his or her own, but is, at the same time, always part of different groups, such as a family, a family and a culture. In other words, we all have a private side and a collective side. So, with our patient in the centre, we first sketch a square with a private upper half and a collective lower half.

In addition, each individual also has an exterior that is visible and tangible and whose contents we can measure and even touch in one way or another.

This measurable exterior is opposite an interior that we can only experience and feel. The inside and outside are represented as a left and a right half of the square

An integrated look at the psychosomatic patient 17

in which we just placed the patient in the centre. The interesting thing about the 4QM is that Wilber overlays these four distinct sides or aspects of reality as planes in the model, so that four different combinations or quadrants arise (Figure 1.1). The model then consists of the central individual with his personal exterior on the top right, his personal interior on the top left, the interior of the groups to which he belongs on the bottom left, and the interior of these groups on the bottom right. In other words, the individual's measurable and visible aspects are in the upper-right quadrant, those of the groups to which he belongs in the lower-right quadrant. The aspects that the individual experiences are in the upper left quadrant, while phenomena that arise and are shared collectively belong in the lower left quadrant.

More concretely, the top right-hand corner is the quadrant of biological, physical properties and all aspects of behaviour (for these are quantifiable aspects). Top left is the quadrant of the personal world of experience of thoughts, feelings, emotions, intentions and self-image, while the bottom-left quadrant stands for values, norms and beliefs within family and culture, including psychological system dynamics and group processing. Finally, the lower right corner of the quadrant houses the socio-economic context, including characteristic features, rituals, regulations and environment. For clinical practice, we remember the following keywords: 'body and behaviour' (top right), 'inner-world of experiences and self-image' (top left), 'values, norms and prevailing climate within culture, group and family' (bottom left) and 'structures, codes of conduct and interactions within groups and the environment' (bottom right) (Figure 1.2).

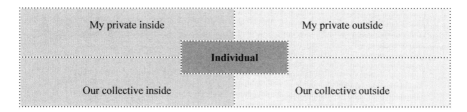

Figure 1.1 The Four Quadrant Model
Source: Based on Wilber, 1998b, 2000, 2001a, 2006, 2017

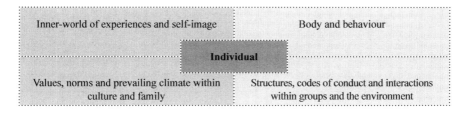

Figure 1.2 The Four Quadrant Model
Source: Based on Wilber, 1998b, 2000, 2001a, 2006, 2017

18 An integrated look at the psychosomatic patient

At the same time, Wilber points out that the 4QM can be seen as two halves that represent a specific scientific view of the world. The two quadrants on the right, can be approached with an empirical-analytical perspective and obey the 'measuring is knowing' rule, while the entire left can be accessed via a phenomenological-hermeneutical and dialectical approach in which interpretation and meaning are central (Figure 1.3). We recognise these two scientific perspectives as the characteristic paradigms of the spectrum of therapies that we outlined in the introduction. The 4QM, therefore, consists of a subjective left half and an objective right half.

A direct and clinical consequence of this for the therapist is the need to consider both sides if the patient is to be portrayed as fully as possible. In concrete terms, this means that the therapist does not merely zoom in on a child's problematic behaviour, for example, as is the case within the DSM culture, but that he tries to understand the meaning layer underlying this 'behaviour as a phenomenon'.[5] This is exactly why the ICF model misses the mark for the first time. After all, the ICF model is mainly concerned with the individual's external, measuring and visible factors and his or her participation in society. In the 4QM, this corresponds to the top-right quadrant and the bottom-right quadrant, respectively. In a certain sense, therefore, the ICF model focuses on only two of the four quadrants, i.e. one half of human reality, i.e. only the part that can be charted empirically. As said before, the 4QM tries to show human reality in a more inclusive way.

The 4QM, therefore, relates to several substrates that hide behind the *condition humaine*. Translated to professional healthcare, we can discover four of them (Figure 1.4). The biomedical substrate in the top right belongs to doctors,

Subjective side	*Objective side*
Interpreting and understanding →	Measuring and describing →
phenomenological-hermeneutic perspective	empirical-analytical perspective

Figure 1.3 The Four Quadrant Model and paradigms

Source: Based on Wilber, 1998b, 2000, 2001a, 2006, and 2017

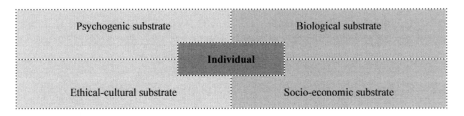

Figure 1.4 The Four Quadrant Model

Source: Based on Wilber, 1998b, 2000, 2001a, 2006, and 2017

physiotherapists, manual therapists and osteopaths. The psychological substrate of the top left quadrant belongs to the domain of clinical psychologists and psychotherapists, while the ethical, systemic and cultural-philosophical substrate in the bottom-left corner is more specifically the work domain of couples and system therapists, philosophical counsellors and ethical experts. Finally, the bottom-right quadrant is based on a socio-economic substrate where, in terms of professional healthcare, we can situate institutions such as public social welfare centres or employment agencies. Here, social workers are involved in debt mediation, support for problematic parenting situations or guidance in employment or training.

Although we must not lose sight of the fact that the 4QM as a didactic model is only intended as a coat hanger for inventory and differentiation, its strength also lies in its integration on the basis of the following basic principles:

- each individual can be situated within the 4QM
- and consists of at least 4 domains of expression, housed in four quadrants
- these are not reducible to each other
- each speak their own language
- each have their own entry point to reality
- are intrinsically intertwined
- and therefore, cannot be separated from each other's dynamics and influence.

Translated to patients, this means that we, as care providers, must ensure that the complex reality in which our patients find themselves is not reduced to less than four quadrants. In concrete terms, this happens when, for example, depression is reduced to a mere – usually hereditary – issue of a disrupted metabolism of serotonin and dopamine, without valuing experiences, thoughts and self-image as being at least as important and influential. In other words, depressive feelings and thoughts are not simply the result of a disturbed neurotransmission, but are a unique partial reality in themselves. In quadrant terms, the top left quadrant is not an epiphenomenon of the top-right quadrant, but equally a unique expression of the individual.[6] Subsequently, as a care provider, we must make sure that a balanced approach, such as 4QM, does not blind us to what is 'normal' in our patient's story. For example, when Horwitz and Wakefield (2007) suggest in their book, *The loss of sadness*, that we have all relegated normal sadness to an area referred to as clinical depression, they point to the DSM as the decisive factor. Distinguish at least four domains in which the reality of the patient expresses itself and be vigilant when labelling a patient as being 'abnormal' or 'pathological' too quickly. In addition to precise differentiation – for example, during the anamnesis – 4QM then also helps to select the right language or entry point to approach the patient.[7] What does the patient currently need most, what can he handle and what appears to be the most helpful? Around which possible entry points – talking, moving or touching for example – is there resistance or anxiety? What about self-reliance and can the patient rely on a stable support network if necessary, or is guidance needed at this level? We will return to this in more detail in the practice-oriented Chapter 7. Finally, the 4QM also offers the possibility to connect various elements in different quadrants. For example, there may be causal or maintaining relationships, a quadrant may weigh heavily on re-establishment processes within other quadrants, aspects of the request for help appear in only one or in all quadrants, or it is noticeable that certain themes in a quadrant are always linked to elements from other quadrants. We will explain this in a moment by means of a case excerpt.

> *The 4QM is enriching, because it helps to make an inventory of the patient's story, to differentiate, to relate to each other, to analyse and to select the most optimal therapeutic access route.*

Here, we can summarise that the 4QM is at least enriching, because it helps meticulously to identify, differentiate, relate and analyse the patient's story, as well as to select the most optimal therapeutic entry point. Precisely because the model explicitly leaves room for the entire world of experience and makes possible dynamic processes understandable in a nuanced way, the therapist can more easily achieve an integrated approach and at the same time more clearly define the boundaries of his own field of competence. The 4QM is therefore not a *carte blanche* for the therapist to do anything he wants.

Amir is a 28-year-old man of Moroccan descent; an IT professional, who signs on with pain all over his body, especially his back. He has been suffering for years, but over the past two months, the pain has been constant. When I examine him, I notice how cramped he is in his lower back and pelvis. Although he works out, he doesn't have much strength in his upper body, which also feels weak. X-rays and blood tests came back negative and medication doesn't seem to help, except for a Lorazepam tablet before going to bed. He still lives with his parents and is married for the second time. The first marriage went wrong after only a few months, Amir was just 20. His current marriage hasn't gone well either, especially now that his wife wants to start a family, and he doesn't like the idea at all. Amir himself attributes the difficulties to the cultural differences with his wife. His current wife – just like his ex, in fact – comes from Morocco, barely speaks Dutch and refuses to get a job. Amir was born in Flanders, speaks fluent Dutch and considers himself to be well integrated. He can't cope with his wife's conservative attitude and certainly doesn't want a child 'because that's how it should be'. When I ask him why he went looking for a partner in Morocco for the second time, he says that this was under pressure from his family. Both his parents agree that it is now time to start a family. 'If I were to say no, my father would never speak to me again'. Amir feels angry and powerless at the same time: 'I can't get another divorce now, can I? I'm so ashamed of myself, just the thought of it'.

If we place Amir's case in the 4QM, this would give the following picture: in the top-right quadrant ('*Body and behaviour*') we place the cramped lower back and pelvis, the weak upper body and associated loss of strength, but also the negative X-ray, blood tests and the medication he takes before going to bed. The fact that Amir is a 28-year-old man with Moroccan roots and a good command of the language is also part of this quadrant.

In the top-left quadrant ('*Inner-world of experiences and self-image*') we situate his feelings of shame, powerlessness and anger, as well as his opinion of himself as a well-integrated individual in society.

The bottom-right quadrant ('*Structures, codes of conduct and interactions within groups and the environment*') is the typical place for data such as the fact that Amir still lives at home, is married for the second time, so also once divorced, works as an IT professional and regularly works out. His wife, who comes from Morocco, does not speak the language and does not want to work outside the home, is also included in this quadrant.

The bottom-left quadrant ('*Values, norms and the prevailing climate within culture, group and family*') contains references to the atmosphere within the relationship and the family, such as the wife's traditional beliefs, the cultural difference with the family of origin, the pressure exerted by the parents, but also the potentially damaging attitude of the father if Amir does not want to have a child or has another divorce.

The interesting thing about the 4QM is the room that is left for interpretation and variation. For example, the wife's request for a child is situated in the bottom two quadrants: on the right because she's actually asking him, resulting in many arguments, but also on the left because, it is a very sensitive family issue, for example what the outside world will think and what they will say about the family. For Amir, this desire to start a family feels demanding, unreasonable and manipulative. We make a note of this in the top-left quadrant. The way in which his body reacts belongs in the top-right quadrant. This also gives us a first insight into the relationship between the quadrants and the way in which they influence each other. It is important to note that the patient's request for help is always noted in the middle, regardless of how it is formulated. So even though the request for help is 'back pain', we do not place it in the top-right quadrant (which would be the logical thing to do). The reason is that the 4QM wants to help analyse a request for help and to situate it in the broader context of the patient. So, for example, if the request for help is a 'headache', then this is placed in the middle of the quadrants (where the patient is located). If the patient then indicates that he regularly suffers from headache, this is indeed added to the top right as a physical aspect of the request for help. The headache in the middle of the quadrants as a request for help versus the headache in the top-right quadrant is therefore more than a semantic difference. Moreover, data from the anamnesis can sometimes be placed in several quadrants at the same time. For example, feeling tired is a physical-energetic issue (top right) and an experience (top left), but also a cultural *fin-de-siècle* phenomenon (bottom left) or as a diagnostic criterion within labour law or the insurance industry (bottom right).

The *fulcrum* concept[8]

No matter how much the 4QM contributes to a more integrated view, it does not shed sufficient light on our patient in an integrated way. Where the 4QM can be seen as a snapshot of the story that the patient brings and, in this sense, offers a kind of cross-section or horizontal analysis, a more vertical or development-sensitive analysis is lacking. In other words, an integrated approach to the patient also presupposes a process-dynamic view of the various developmental layers that make up the individual. Within Wilber's work, the concept of developmental stages, or *fulcra*, is put forward for this purpose. Wilber interprets a *fulcrum* as a milestone that occurs in the psychological development of the individual, such as developmental stages that follow one another.[9] Characteristic here is the typical order of the various *fulcra* as a succession of partial wholes or holarchies. We can compare this with a collection of Russian dolls (see Figure 1.5) that are ordered from small to large or from young to adult. Wilber argues that human reality should be considered as such a collection of part wholes, or holons, that transcend each other and are included in a continuous process of development and differentiation.

In contrast to a hierarchical structure in which the components are placed on top of each other and can function independently of each other, in a holarchical organisation, it is impossible to separate the components completely from each other. In a holarchy, every layer has the potential to actualise within the big picture. In other words, a previous layer of functioning within the development can, under certain conditions, step into the limelight under the influence of a particular context or trigger. Acting out in borderline patients can be an example of this, but also other, less mature forms of thinking, acting or feeling, which refers psychodynamically to the phenomenon of regression (de Wolf, 2011). Although this may take on pathological forms, these possible movements between layers or dolls should, in the first instance, be regarded as a healthy skill.[10] Here too, vigilance is required for an overly rapid diagnosis of the patient displaying 'pathological' behaviour. Within the psychodynamic domain, somewhat categorical

Figure 1.5 Russian dolls

An integrated look at the psychosomatic patient 23

classifications between psychotic, borderline and neurotic personalities, such as those propounded by Kernberg for example, are refuted by thinkers such as Klein and Bion, who point to a psychotic, borderline and neurotic zone of functioning in the individual (Vermote, 2011). Wilber (1999) continues on this functionally dynamic theme and sees development at its core as a process of 'transformations of consciousness'. The numerous dynamics and positions that characterise this process of transformation are meticulously described by Wilber in their healthy and pathological forms. We will return to some of them in further chapters, in order to better understand the psychosomatic request for help.

> When it is necessary to clarify development processes to the patient, I sometimes use the metaphor of a climbing wall enthusiast. While he is looking for a way up, using possible fulcra, the climber's feet and hands are always on a different level. His centre of gravity is always inside his torso, which is the most current and used level of development, or fulcrum, at that moment.
>
> Yet, this does not alter the fact that first of all, the feet (and therefore the preceding fulcra) play a crucial role in stabilising and 'providing a foundation' for the climbing process. On the other hand, the unique experience of climbing consists in the fact that the climber is always searching and scanning and, therefore, needs his hands. They also explore new heights and other support points to get up. These are the fulcra towards which the individual is working in their development. An additional aspect in the image of the climber are the hooks in the wall to which he secures himself, so that – if things go wrong – the fall is limited. Together with the person who secures and guides the climber from the ground (this could be the therapist), these points of attachment are part of the therapeutic process and framework. We will come back to this later.

In addition to a 'four quadrant' cross-section of our patient, we now also have a longitudinal, vertical '*fulcrum*' cross-section, which allows us to gain insight into his developmental layers and processes.

Types of *fulcra* and processes[11]

The use of developmental stages is, of course, not new in psychodynamic thinking. Freud got the ball rolling with his psychosexual stages and was followed by authors such as Erikson, with psychosocial stages, Piaget, with cognitive stages, and Kohlberg, with moral stages. Later on, these models were further developed on the basis of integrated views on development by authors, such as Graves (1970, 2004) and Kegan (1982, 1994). But also by Wilber, who refers to developmental stages as *fulcra*, based on his quest to use more theory-transcending jargon. This leads to ten *fulcra* according to basic structures of consciousness, spread across three major areas of development: the pre-personal, the personal and the trans-personal domain. Figure 1.6 lists the first six *fulcra* that, together, make up Wilber's pre-personal and personal development domains. Within the confines of this book, we first and

Fulcrum 0:	The fused or 'pleromatic' self[12]
Fulcrum 1:	The sensory physical self
Fulcrum 2:	The phantasmic-emotional or body self
Fulcrum 3:	The early conceptual or name self
Fulcrum 4:	The social or rule/role self
Fulcrum 5:	The formal-reflective or cognitive self
Fulcrum 6:	The existential self

Figure 1.6 Types of *fulcra*

Source: Based on Wilber, 1984a, 1984b, 1992, 1996, 1999, and 2017

foremost home in on the early, pre-personal *fulcra* up to and including *fulcrum* 3. Psychodynamically, these are the pre-Oedipal stages. It goes without saying that the personal *fulcra* up to and including 6 – related to the advancing ego development – are also of great importance in psychosomatic or trauma related bodywork. What Wilber refers to as transpersonal *fulcra* begins with the post-egoic or existential developmental stages 6 and 7, for which he relies, among other things, on various humanistic-existential movements, alongside thinkers such, as Viktor Frankl, Carl Gustav Jung and Roberto Assagioli. In order to portray the phenomenology, processes and structures of consciousness of the higher *fulcra*, Wilber mainly employs contemplative, gnostic and mystical traditions of both Eastern and Western origin. Although conceivably interesting for the central theme of this book, these developmental stages are not part of our further analysis.

> *Characteristic for* fulcra *is the holarchical structure as a series of Russian dolls that are all located in the largest doll. This largest version can be seen as the patient who presents himself in his most current or 'adult' form. But all other levels are equally present in it.*

The *fulcrum* concept is quite detailed, with Wilber using different processes that describe the developmental dynamics in both healthy-functional and pathological-dysfunctional directions (e.g. fixation and dissociation per *fulcrum*).[13] A basic axiom is that *fulcra* – like other authors' stages – can never be skipped during the development of the individual.

From now on, we will refer to the developing individual as 'subject' and speak of 'subject development'. In other words, how a person develops, whether or not through specific *fulcra*, can be very varied, but what is certain is that all individuals have to go through it one way or another. This refers to optional abilities that Wilber refers to as 'lines of development'. Another characteristic of *fulcra* is the holarchical structure described earlier as a series of Russian dolls, all of which are located in the largest doll. In practice, for the sake of convenience, the largest doll can be seen as the patient presenting himself in his most current or 'adult' form. However, within this large Russian doll, all other levels – from sufficiently to insufficiently or barely developed – are equally present. Let us explain this briefly by means of the phenomenon of pain.

The way in which a patient deals with pain does not always correspond to his most 'adult' level, but usually to previously developed parts. In other words, when people are in pain, smaller dolls come to the fore and can take over the direction of the more fully developed parts of the body. Crying, despair, clambering or getting angry and withdrawing are possible manifestations of a smaller doll in response to pain. In a certain sense, we can therefore interpret this as regressive coping.

So to put it simply, a therapist should, together with the adult doll who is reporting to the clinic, look at which dolls are still present in the treatment room. Incidentally, it is not always unhealthy or dysfunctional when smaller dolls of the individual appear on the scene, on the contrary. Since many patients are unable to make sufficient contact with their inner child – crying, for example, can be beneficial, especially in the case of pain and sorrow – they no longer have access to play, playfulness and the pleasure that goes with it. They find it difficult to give in to physical or sexual interaction and fusion, and struggle to renounce their rational, controlling and often over-critical way of life. Immersion in the moment, surrender to flow and giving in to enthusiasm or ecstasy require access to all dolls, from young to old. In a nutshell, a healthy fulcrum dynamic is vital for the healthy, individual functioning as a human being. As stated before, regression is also part of the normal being human and pain sometimes provokes regressive coping.

So according to Wilber (1999, 2000, 2001), development is the evolution of individual self-awareness – in short, the self. This evolution unfolds through the Russian-doll-shaped *fulcra* and through a succession of characteristic processes of fusion/identification, differentiation and integration. Wilber splits the developmental process for each *fulcrum* into a superficial and a depth structure. The depth structure then includes all potential elements that can be developed, while the superficial structure is a certain manifestation of a depth structure that is developed depending on the specific context. The unique, and thus context-dependent, variations by which a depth structure is expressed in a particular individual characterise the superficial structure. Wilber likens the depth structures with the floors of a building and the superficial structures with the layout per floor. Finally, Wilber (2000) opts for a specific process terminology: changes within the superficial structure are called 'translations', these within the depth structure 'transformations'. By means of this terminology, the diagnostic process in EBW is refined and the therapy can be better adapted to the patient's needs. For example, does a patient get stuck 'translating' on the same floor, is he looking for a staircase for the next floor or does he regularly return to a previous floor? If, for example, people in therapy come to the deep-sensitive learning or awareness of their being-in-the-world and can from then on consciously adapt to this as a source of information, then this is like the wall climber who clicks into a hook in the wall. From a developmental point of view, this ability remains sustainably acquired, just as you when you discover a new floor via a staircase – in other words, 'transformation' – you leave the previous floor behind. Another typical developmental-psychological achievement is the ability for mentalisation that will be discussed in Chapter 3. Under normal circumstances, the wall climber will always be able to rely on the ability to 'mentalise' as a wall hook offers him. Conversely, in stressful situations, people who have difficulty 'mentalising' will regularly fall back on hooks that were clicked onto the climbing wall before. These are called 'pre-mentalising strategies'. Let's briefly illustrate the normal *fulcrum* dynamics by means of an example.

A young toddler still functions in what is called magical thinking. This way of looking at the world is characteristic of the depth structure that Wilber will refer to as fulcrum 2 and 3. The possibilities of this level of consciousness are vast. For example, the child can play within an endless fantasy and the world can be discovered by means of magic powers and magical characters. Of course, there are also limitations, such as the fear that an animistic world full of living animals and things brings with it. Just think of the exciting, but also terrifying journey that Frodo and his companions have to make in The Lord of the Rings. Within the template of magical thinking (depth structure) there are many variations of applications and interpretations (surface structure) which the individual can try out (translations). At a certain point, however, the child will get stuck in magical thinking and discovers, with trial and error, that the world is somewhat different than The Lord of the Rings or, say, an average Disney cartoon would suggest. Magical wizards and talking trees are now giving way to mythical heroes, persistent training and quests, like Luke Skywalker's in the Star Wars epos who has to contend with his own father figure. Gradually, a next depth structure (fulcrum 4) unfolds where a whole new way of thinking and interpreting is discovered (transformation). The child will take some time exploring this new depth and will, full of hope, run back to the previous magical floor from time to time. But when the moment comes when the umpteenth shift of the furniture does not bring any solace, the child will also leave this new floor behind and start looking for promising prospects.

A final important element within the *fulcrum* concept is the developmental objects. In order to understand the role of these objects, we must first look at the typical process or template of development that is repeated per *fulcrum* and in which these objects 'emerge'. This is illustrated in Figure 1.7 as a threefold pattern of fusion/identification, differentiation and integration processes (Wilber, 1999, 2000) in which the subject first identifies with a certain level of development, then differentiates from it, only to integrate it eventually.

Since each level of development corresponds to one or more typical objects, this means that each time the subject has definitely rounded off a certain *fulcrum*

An integrated look at the psychosomatic patient 27

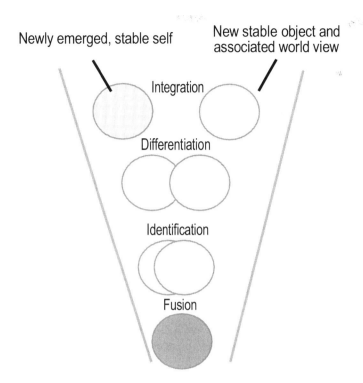

Figure 1.7 The process of fusion/identification, differentiation and integration
Source: Based on Wilber, 1999

as developmental landmark (integration), an associated object comes up (differentiation) with which the subject can work because it no longer coincides (fusion/identification). In Chapter 5, we will see that after *fulcrum* 1, the individual has the physical body at his disposal that has become a finalised, durable object, so that it can actually start using this physical body. The subject is at that moment a self that has acquired a physical body (object), where before, it used to coincide with it (fusion) and was therefore only a body. In this way, every *fulcrum* ends with a stabilised object, and in terms of developmental psychology, we mention the first three *fulcra* of physical, emotional and conceptual object constancy (Figure 1.8). Wilber (2017) paraphrases this in one sentence: '*The very key to your growth, development, and evolution is to make your present subject an object – that is, it is to look at your present subject instead of using it as something through which to view the world (and thus remain identified with it*' (p. 107).

Given the vital importance of the early *fulcra* in EBW, these are elaborated in detail in Chapters 5 and 6. Here, we remember that a *fulcrum*-sensitive analysis considers the developmental processes in which subject and object arise in relation to each other. So while the 4QM provides insight into the horizontal diversity

28 An integrated look at the psychosomatic patient

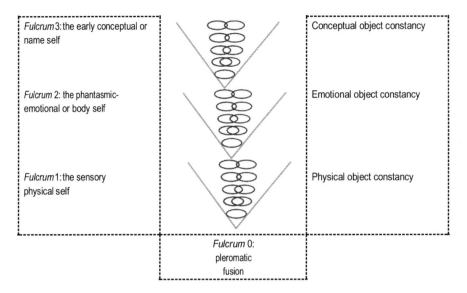

Figure 1.8 The differentiation of subject and object
Source: Based on Wilber, 1999

of the life story at that moment, the *fulcrum* analysis makes it easier to understand how the subject has been able to develop within this context and how this has, or has not, led to healthy and functional relationships with specific objects, such as his own body or emotions.

The self-system[14]

For an integral analysis of the individual, Wilber formulates, in addition to the 4QM and the *fulcra*, three other instruments, namely, lines of development, states of consciousness and typologies, which fall outside the scope of this book. Here, we will briefly consider a more overarching concept that various authors, from Jung to Sullivan, refer to as the self and that Wilber develops into the self-system. We have just underlined that, for Wilber, subject development is the evolution of individual self-consciousness, or the self. This self-system is characterised as the place where the following psychological functions (Wilbur, 1999, p. 92) take place:

- identification (locus of identification)
- coordination of mental processes (locus of organisation)
- processes around free will (locus of free choice)
- defence mechanisms (locus of defence mechanisms)
- integration of experiences (locus of metabolisation and integration)
- navigation to the next *fulcra* (locus of navigation).

An integrated look at the psychosomatic patient 29

In this sense, the self-system is the hotspot of deployable processes that the subject has at his disposal. This rather conceptual interpretation appears to be in line with the neurobiological view of the self as an organising medium that relies on various networks in the human brain (Gottwald, 2015).

The self-system is also continuously in motion as a psychodynamic phenomenon during its development and is certainly not an unchangeable or static given. Siegel (2001, in Forman, 2010, p. 25) speaks of a self as a state (self-state) that displays at least the following characteristics:

- a perception of the world
- an emotional tone or charge
- a memory trail
- a mental model of the self
- a set of behavioural patterns.

When we translate this into practice, it is strongly reminiscent of phenomenology, where the individual is seen as 'the perspectival origin of his experiences, behaviour and thoughts and seen as the centre of self-awareness, object-experience and meaning bestowing' (Stanghellini, 2009). Within EBW, we refer to this as the 'self-other-world'. During the anamnesis, the following questions can therefore help to explore how our patient relates to himself, the others in his environment and the world in which he lives:

- *How does the patient view the world of the other person?* (perception of the world)
- *What emotional experience does self-other-world give him?* (emotional tone or charge)
- *What role do memories and previous experiences play in relation to the self-changing world?* (memory trail)
- *What does he think about the self-other-world?* (mental model of the self)
- *How does he (re-)act in a self-other-world and how does he deal with it?* (set of behavioural patterns)

Sven works as a metal worker in a factory and sells second-hand sports cars on the side. Sven consulted me some three years ago and this time, he calls me in a convivial manner – as if we know each other well and only saw each other yesterday – to make an appointment the same day. His neck is completely stuck and he still has a lot of important work to finish. When I say that my diary doesn't allow me to see him that day, he reacts with incomprehension and says he will call another therapist who understands that he 'doesn't ring for no reason'. The next morning, a brand-new Porsche convertible pulls up and Sven gets out. Apparently, a mate of his had swapped appointments with him that morning. After he puts his car keys on my desk in an ostentatious manner, he says that although he understands yesterday's reaction, he's the one who's had to sort it out.

Sven is known to have a narcissistic personality. This excerpt is a classic example of a typical relationship to the self-other-world: the world must be at Sven's service and understand his problems without reservation (perception of the world). If the other person does not react the way he wants, Sven experiences this as an affront, reacts sarcastically and finds it self-evident that a mate gives up his place (emotional tone and pattern of behaviour).

In his memory, I am apparently labelled as a therapist who understands him and can help him (memory trail), so that is why he talks to me in an affable manner. He understands that I reacted incorrectly by not giving him an appointment immediately, but fortunately he has taken control of the situation and managed to save the day. This testifies to a self-image in which the other person fails (perception of the world); but fortunately, the person can still fix it all (mental model of himself).

Experiential bodywork as development-dynamic work

So far, we have learned to use the 4QM, the *fulcra* and the self-system to gain a more integrated view of our patient. It is also enlightening to situate EBW's own practice within these concepts; first of all within the 4QM.

In the following chapters, we will often refer to the tense body as a muscle armour that serves as a starting point for EBW. We will see that this muscle armour is made up of myofascial tissue structures and is therefore intrinsically connected to the top-right quadrant. Tensed muscles are, after all, tangible and even measurable (e.g. via EMG measurement). However, therapeutic processes within the domain of EBW are not primarily focused on parameters that belong in the top-right quadrant. We already described in the previous chapter that working in an experiential way implies working with awareness and experience processes and not – as in the case of physiotherapy or osteopathy, for example – only working with increased movement or strength. In other words, in EBW, we do not so much try to increase the movement of the shoulder girdle itself or the strength of the leg muscles as a measurable parameter. So, no training to increase strength or stretching for more movement, but the facilitation of experience and awareness. More freedom of movement in the shoulder girdle means that the patient can open up more to the world, breathe in more deeply and dare to stand up more in relation to others (self-other-world). More strength in the legs results in more felt stability, stronger connection with the ground and more flexible resilience in conflict situations.

> *Working from the myofascial armour or with evocative movement and breathing as an entry point results in continuous changes within the experience and awareness processes in which the patient finds himself.*

In short, what we are trying to set in motion via EBW does not so much belong in the top-right as in the top-left quadrant. Body experience and self-awareness are processes that have to do with experience (phenomenology) and the attribution of

An integrated look at the psychosomatic patient 31

meaning (hermeneutics and dialectics). In this way, we at EBW draw a distinction between the substrate with which our treatment starts and the substrate on which the treatment is focused. The treatment process at EBW, therefore, consists of the 'entry point' substrate in the top-right quadrant and the 'intentional' substrate in the top-left quadrant, respectively. Working from the myofascial armour or with evocative movement and breathing as an entry point results in continuous changes within the experience and awareness processes in which the patient finds himself.

At the same time, in Figure 1.9 we refer to the reciprocity between these two substrates: 'Chronic postural and movement tendencies serve to sustain certain beliefs and cognitive distortions, and the physical patterns, in turn, contribute to these same beliefs' (Ogden et al., 2006, p. 10). EBW is, therefore, not a linear process, but is always contained in a progressive, pulsating dynamic. This dynamic is, in fact, characteristic of all forms of BPT in which core processes that are related to procedurally established patterns of experience and behaviour 'that can express themselves cognitively, affectively, imaginatively, sensory, motorically or vegetatively during therapy' are central (Geuter, 2015b, p. 6, translation JC). The latter three forms (sensory, motor and vegetative) refer to the top-right quadrant, while the first three (cognitive, affective and imaginative) belong in the top-left quadrant.

In this way, EBW straddles quadrants in the literal sense, namely, on the border between the top-left and right quadrants: integrated work with the body (*Körper*) and the lived body (*Leib*).

Yet, it would be a capital mistake to think that BPT only deals with the top-two quadrants. In the next chapter, we will discuss in detail the importance of the

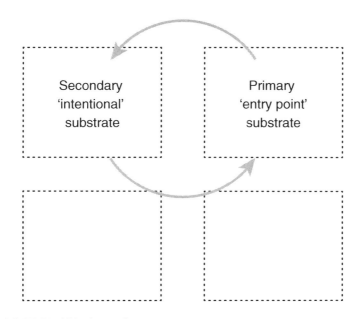

Figure 1.9 EBW within the quadrants

individual's narrative and capacity to attribute meaning, and in so doing, we will refer to the place given to the 'relational, dialectical' subquadrants. For 'being there' as an individual can never be separated from 'being with others' (Heidegger, 1999) or – as Alma (2005) puts it – 'being is always being-with, co-existence' (p. 33). So no matter how important the mutual phenomena and influences within the top quadrants are, working with people in BPT is always a question of all the quadrants that move:

> Although emotions and feelings are indeed grounded in bodily processes of excitement, and rooted in visceral, muscular, and vegetative systems, their primary significance does not lie in their homeostatic regulation of the body-mind through repressing or discharging them, but in their relatedness to 'others, imagined or real'.
>
> (Marlock, 2015, p. 158)

Then we can also situate EBW within the *fulcrum* concept. Working with psychosomatic conflicts often implies deep bodily tensions, anxiety or trauma, so that we have to work with procedural, pre-lingual and deeper brain networks that mainly tap into older layers of our development. We will come back to this in more detail. Put more simply, in EBW, we work with the smaller dolls in our patient as best we can. This assumes that as a therapist, we first learn to listen to the language, the words, the images and the behaviour that belong to these dolls in order to better understand the dynamics within the *fulcra* involved. The strength of EBW lies in the fact that during the treatment, we switch between these different layers or *fulcra* several times, in which we alternately hear/see smaller or more adult dolls speaking/moving. When we make contact with the body and then apply the bodywork more deeply, several deeper brain networks are activated that are barely under linguistic control, but have more to do with emotional memory centres, trauma or survival. Bar-Levav (1998) expresses the same vision in a plea for the integration of touch in psychotherapy:

> But how do we address and change such preverbal 'knowledge'? Surely not by talking from our cortex to the patient's. It is done by repeatedly establishing exquisite contact with the distrustful and scared infant within the adult patient. We persist until the fragile inner baby begins to feel safe in the therapeutic setting.
>
> (p. 53)

But no matter how much the process of awareness of old, deeply ingrained and often unpleasant experiences appeals to more basic *fulcra* and the physical memories of smaller dolls, the effect of the treatment very much depends on the linguistic or narrative integration of more recent dolls. Trauma work is never just a matter of letting the patient (re)experience a catharsis, but requires a sometimes-laborious process of integration within conscious and language-sensitive registers. EBW, therefore, always takes place within the entire individual, that is, in all *fulcra*.

An integrated look at the psychosomatic patient 33

Which brings us seamlessly to the last aspect within which we can situate EBW, namely, the self-system. As we will explain in Chapter 2, within EBW we always start from the narrative patient. When we listen closely, we hear in the patient's story the echo of the way in which he sees and experiences himself, the others and the world. In fact, we come across a blueprint of his self-system. The *fulcra* and the 4QM make it easier for us to take stock and analyse where and why the narrative gets stuck. Guiding the patient to detect, feel and, where possible, understand vulnerabilities and blind spots, is working with the self-system and should not be missing either.

Tools for therapy

- *We look at the patient's experienced, meaningful and measurable reality from two different angles.*
- *With the Wilberian Four Quadrant Model, we situate the patient as broadly as possible within the context of his body and behaviour, his inner-world of experiences and self-image, the prevailing climate within the groups to which he belongs and the related structural characteristics and social interactions.*
- *The Wilberian fulcrum model makes us aware of the various levels of development in the patient's narrative and the related layered presence of Russian dolls in therapy.*
- *By means of the 4QM, the fulcra and the self-system, we try to take stock, differentiate and analyse the patient's narrative in order to select the most optimal path in therapy.*
- *EBW is always development-dynamic work in which the self-system is contained in a pulsating process of fusion/identification, differentiation and integration.*
- *Making room for experiential work with deeply ingrained patterns and experiences always implies room for narrative integration.*

Notes

1 ICF stands for International Classification of Functioning, Disability and Health. The World Health Organisation launched the ICF model in 2001 after years of global dialogue and work in an attempt to offer an unambiguous frame of reference in a culture-independent language (WHO, 2002). Since then, the model has had far-reaching implications for care provision, education and policy-making.
2 Criticism of other, similarly inspired models, such as the diagnostic and statistical manual of mental disorders – in short, the DSM – is also growing (Van Os, 2014; Vanheule, 2014; Dehue, 2012; Vandenberghe, 2010; Smith et al., 2005).
3 See Wilber, 1998, 2000, 2001, 2006, 2017.
4 In *Integral Spirituality: A startling new role for religion in the modern and postmodern world*, Wilber (2006) refines the basic model by subdividing each of the four quadrants

again into an inner/outer perspective. This leads to eight perspectives that also correlate with either the number of methodologies for looking at the world: phenomenology and structuralism for the top-left quadrant, hermeneutics and ethnomethodology for the lower left quadrant, empiricism and autopoiesis for the top-right quadrant and finally, social autopoiesis and systems theory for the lower right quadrant.

5 Verhaeghe (2009) points to this in *Het einde van de psychotherapie* (*The end of psychotherapy*) and playfully introduces a new diagnostic DSM category: 'PEED'. This acronym stands for Pseudo Efficiency and Effectivity Disorder and refers to a serious problem in which the person concerned suffers from the delusion that everything has to be measurable, controllable and efficient, and displays the necessary dysfunctional behaviour to match (Verhaeghe, 2010, p. 170).

6 Although this kind of crude form of reductionism is gradually disappearing and people are nowadays starting from a multifactorial – *dixit* biopsychosocial – context, there is often still a subtle reduction in all directions within the 4QM in practice. Later, we return to a typical pitfall within some body therapies in which a muscle (e.g. the *M. iliopsoas*) is equated with an emotional process (e.g. anxiety or anger) and is treated as if it is also used to treat the emotion. In Chapter 4, we clarify scientific grounds for understanding such relationships between emotions and the myofascial substrate. Nevertheless, they remain two separate phenomena within two nonreducible quadrants. A muscle belongs to the biological substrate at the top right, while a feeling is an expression of the world of experience in the top left quadrant. Both should therefore not be confused with each other.

7 For example, a psychodynamic play therapist makes contact via a completely different route than a physiotherapist who teaches exercises, an osteopath who manipulates the spine, a behavioural therapist who asks to keep a diary, a systemic therapist who follows the whole family in therapy or the student counsellor. However, they can all be concerned with the same request for help and thus with the same patient.

8 See Wilber, 1984a, 1984b, 1992, 1996, 1998, 1999, 2017.

9 It is important to keep in mind that a fulcrum only marks the appearance of a developmental layer but not the total grasp of the new abilities to be developed. For example when the infant discovers the physical world and his own physical body at fulcrum 1, this is only the very beginning of a long road of developing and mastering the body which in anyway takes some decades to achieve. The same goes also for e.g. the emotional (F2), early cognitive-verbal (F3) and social (F4) realm of self-discovery. So a fulcrum always defines the appearance but never the result of a developmental stage.

10 Psychodynamically, a distinction is drawn between 'regression at the service of the ego' and 'regression of the ego', whereby the latter is considered pathological (de Wolf, 2011).

11 See Wilber, 1999, 2001a, 2001b, 2006.

12 The pleromatic or fused state is situated from conception to the early postnatal period. Afterwards the infant starts to differentiate itself from its physical surrounding and the sensory physical self starts to emerge. Although Wilber uses several descriptions such as pleroma for the total period up to the first fulcrum, in this book we choose to make a distinction between F0 as pleromatic and F1 as sensory physical self. Therapeutic implications will be discussed in Chapter 7.

13 For further explanation, see for example Wilber (1999). In his most recent work, Wilber (2017) uses the more imaginative terms 'addiction' and allergy for 'fixation' and 'dissociation' respectively.

14 See Wilber, 1999, 2000, 2001, 2017.

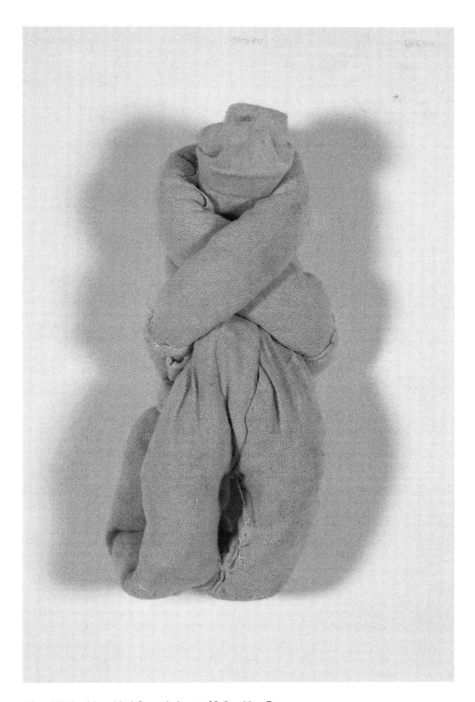

Blue, 2015, old padded flannel sheets, 22.5 × 11 × 7 cm.

2 The narrative patient

The transdisciplinary model that was the focus of the previous chapter lends itself well to the anamnestic phase of the therapeutic process involving the psychosomatic body. One would expect this second chapter to start with the anamnesis and how the psychosomatic request for help can be concretely mapped out according to the 4QM, the *fulcra* and the self-system. However, this would be impetuous and would overlook the important phase that precedes the anamnesis. We start this chapter the moment the patient registers, when a first interesting question arises, which does not always receive the necessary attention, namely: What actually happens when someone signs up for therapy? In other words, what motivates someone to go and see a therapist?

The request for help from an existential-phenomenological perspective

As outlined in the introduction, we attach great importance to understanding (Verstehen) the context in which the patient finds himself. We also want to get a feel for the processes and factors that bring the patient to the therapy room. That is why the therapist first of all questions the motivation for an individual to seek help: 'What is it that brings this person to me?' The element of 'movement' has a certain diagnostic value in the sense that the individual appears to be stuck and is no longer able to move sufficiently of his own accord. Within EBW, we do not only consider what has become stuck as a body that is physically stuck, as often appears in the request for help ('My whole body is stuck and hurts'), but as the patient's story that has become stuck. Drawing on narrative psychology we call this the 'narrative' (Bohlmeijer, 2012). This term refers to the story within which our lives take place and of which each person, as an author, partly writes the story lines. In a more psychoanalytical sense, we are speaking beings and we can only tell others and ourselves how the world makes sense to us and how we experience our existence as meaningful. A well-functioning narrative, therefore, forms a fundamental basis for arriving at meaning (idem). Siegel (2017) speaks of the 'tendency towards narrative as a system in which the "self" emerges' and which sets life in motion 'towards harmony by integrating in the process of making sense of my experience' (p. 121).

38 The narrative patient

Back to the question of what brings this person to the therapist. In fact, we have to insert an extra step and ask ourselves what happened *before* the moment of signing up. How should we take this? In a way, the process starts with the fact that something has happened in the individual's life, which has impinged on his narrative. Apparently, something has happened that the individual can no longer put into words. This refers to the existential dimension of the request for help. It can, therefore, no longer be included in the logic of one's own narrative, as a result of which the course of life at that moment becomes disrupted or is at least experienced as such. This is the phenomenological dimension of the request for help. The reason for this disturbance can be something big or small, a radical life event, but could just as easily be something seemingly trivial. Typical examples in practice include the loss of a significant other in the patient's life or unexpected changes in the relationship with significant others.

> *Ann-Marie, a primary school teacher, took early retirement at the age of 57. She is single and has never been in a steady relationship. Now that she has very little left to do in the day, she misses the children dreadfully. Over the past six weeks, she's been feeling listless and suffers from severe constipation and pain in her groin, something she hasn't experienced in years.*
>
> *Gregory's calling from his car for an urgent appointment. For the third day running, he and his girlfriend have had a massive row, but this time, she said she's had enough and slammed down the phone. He wants to talk to a professional as soon as possible and asks if I can fit him in today.*
>
> *Cindy returns after eight months. So far, her panic attacks have been well under control, but she's been at home since yesterday. The day after tomorrow, the trade union will come around to explain the restructuring at work.*

Patients are not always aware of possible underlying connections and often fail to establish a link with what may be at the bottom of the symptoms. People literally say that they don't get it, that they don't know any more or that they never saw it coming. It is therefore understandable for patients to turn to professionals to explain 'it' ('What's wrong with me, where does all of that come from?'). From a diagnostic point of view, it is interesting to put this same question back to the patients during the anamnesis in order to gauge their understanding of what is going on in their lives on the basis of their narratives: 'How would *you* explain what's happened to you' or 'How can you make sense of what is happening in your life right now? Straight away, it becomes obvious to what extent patients consider themselves to be part of the problem, or whether they put the blame outside themselves and engage in what is known as externalisation. In the early stages of the therapeutic process, these questions indicate the patients' ability to consider the broader psychological context of their condition ('I've had too much on my plate for far too long') or whether they are more likely to stick to a monocausal, physical or even 'mechanical' explanation ('It's my neck that is completely stuck and needs loosening'). In a way, we gain an insight into the way patients map out their own four quadrants and can then situate themselves within these.

> *As a practical tool, the therapist can ask himself, for example, where the patient is located on the spectrum between the extremes of 'internalising-externalising', 'mentalising-somatising' and 'contextualising-reducing'. Externalising refers here to the excessive recourse to 'external' causes, such as blaming others ('my ex makes my whole life impossible'), pointing out 'something' outside of myself as a source of all misfortune ('actually I should be living in Spain, because the weather here makes me ill every time'), but also considering my own body as an 'object' ('if I could just get rid of that fatigue and abdominal pain, I could start working again and be happy again'). Somatising stands for the mechanism whereby tension is only diverted through the somatic system.*
>
> *Familiar examples are the need to urinate more frequently at times of stress or abdominal cramps and stomach pains that arise during stressful events. But also chronic tension headaches in the case of continuous relationship problems or neck pain in the case of perfectionism can often be interpreted that way. Finally, 'reducing' refers to any form of narrowing the scope within which a situation can be understood, but in this case, refers more specifically to narrowing things down to only the quadrants on the right or – even more dramatically – to only the 'measurable' quadrant in the top-right corner. The extent to which the patient appears to be able to move towards the poles 'internalisation', 'mentalisation' and 'contextualisation' may, on the face of it, be seen as a positive thing, although there is the risk of taking this too far.*

In this way, we get a first impression of the way in which the individual behaves in the world and looks at this world.[1] In the previous chapter, we called this the self-system and referred to the *fulcra* within which a person functions at that moment. If the 'self-other-world' relationship is rather magically coloured, we can interpret this in a way that a therapist 'can take away the pain' – much like a wizard. In a mythical view of the world, the practitioner is seen as someone who 'knows it all' or has studies and books that contain the answer. People who adopt a predominantly rational view of the world, on the other hand, need scientific certainty or logic and feel comfortable with the words 'research has shown that . . .'. People, however, may be in a state of denial and reaction, or may gradually grow to accept their life situation at that moment. In general, patients who suffer medically unexplained physical symptoms often appear unmotivated for psychotherapy; they only want to reduce the symptoms and rationalise the problem in a compelling way. They show little interest in their own inner world or the part they play and moreover, often prove to be demanding (van der Moolen & Eisinga, 2004). Although the therapist is now only a few minutes away from the process of the first meeting, he is already able to pick up a lot of meaningful material and take it with him on the basis of the patient's stuck story. The narrative, embedded in an existential-phenomenological analysis of the request for help, is therefore an important working concept within EBW.

The first words, the first look

We are still going too fast, though, because between the event that causes stress and the explicit request for help from the therapist, there is a long road that is sometimes so long or so difficult that people simply cannot get the help they need.[2] On the other hand, we want to better understand the process that leads the individual to turn to a therapist. Here, we use the concept of objectal foundation as defined by Gilliéron (2005). Objectal foundation means that each subject organises his or her close and lasting affective relationships according to their personal economy, character, personality structure or psychopathology (p. 125).

Gilliéron (2005) adds that a stuck individual not only asks for healing of his symptom, but also seeks a certain relationship. The individual goes in search of another; he turns to the outside world and asks – at least implicitly – for help. In EBW, therefore, we draw a distinction between the explicit and implicit request for help. The explicit request for help refers to what the patient effectively expresses during the intake, usually what is bothering him and what he wants to get rid of. The implicit request for help relates to the objectal foundation and the relational tension hidden in it.

> *Evert suffers from continuous abdominal pains ('actually everything hurts') and has been feeling depressed for months. He would like to get rid of this pain as soon as possible (explicit request for help) because he is in the process of building a house for him and his wife, and everything is being put back anyway. During the first sessions, it turns out that the house is next door to his parents-in-law and that his father-in-law bothers him on a daily basis. Evert would rather just sell up, but knows that this would spell the end of his fresh marriage. On the other hand, he doesn't know if he would mind so much; he's at his wit's end and would like someone to explain all this to his wife, so that she would understand him better (implicit request for help).*

In order to understand this relational dimension – and thus partly the origin of the objectal foundation – the concept of the mirror stage (Vanheule, 2005) draws on the earliest dynamics or basic form between mother and child. The infant literally cries for help when it experiences hunger, pain or restlessness and in doing so, it sets the mother in motion to do 'something'. In developmental psychology, she is a central figure and plays a decisive role in influential processes, such as attachment and affect regulation. Psychodynamically, the mother is traditionally seen as the first object from which the child will learn to differentiate. This cry-for-help is stored deep and unconsciously in our brain like an evolutionary template and forms the basis for our earliest relational reaction patterns (Kinet, 2013, p. 105) and our attachment in particular. When the narrative is disrupted or simply is under tension, this template is triggered and activates the reflex to look for someone who can help. The individual suffers, understands insufficiently what is happening, if at all, and wants to be helped. He now turns to the other, and with this, his objectal foundation also comes to the fore more explicitly.

That is why Gilliéron points out that every request for help is also a question for a relationship.

Yet the objectal foundation is more than just an evolutionary pattern of seeking proximity. The objectal foundation also contains the early affective experiences the individual has had during the time of attachment. These experiences form the core and have a far-reaching impact on the development of the individual's identity. With a metaphor, we could represent the objectal foundation as the marinade in which we were raised as individuals and which still provides our deepest fibres with a certain palette of flavours today. The fact that we are marinated from the early, prenatal beginning is the part determined by evolution, but the ingredients that determine the marinade – and thus the flavour palette – are mainly formed by the interactions with significant others around us. Our earliest impressions, experiences and learning processes from the four quadrant environment in which we find ourselves appear to be able to weigh heavily on later health and behavioural problems and are already starting prenatally (Braeken et al., 2017, 2013; Van den Bergh, 2007). The marinade is, therefore, stored pre-lingually and physically and forms the earliest basis of our self-experience and identity. In this context, this pre-lingualism also refers to the importance of the literal precursors of language, such as sounds, vibrations, voice tone or timbre and phonetic rhythm: 'From the very beginning, language has meant a lot in an affective-existent sense, and it is not so much about what is said as that it is being said and how it is said' (Kinet, 2005, p. 118). Kinet (2013) continues Bazan's research (2010, 2007) into the relationship between semantics and affect:

> The dynamic past that affects our here and now (this could be interpreted as the marinade, JC) is, from a (neuro-)linguistic point of view, the result of an (early) child, affective conditioning of the sound fragments without connection with the semantics. Only later (after sufficient neocortical maturation) will the semantic register superimpose itself on it.
>
> (p. 47)

The fact that we are marinated from the early, prenatal beginning is the part determined by evolution, but the ingredients that determine the marinade – and thus the flavour palette – are mainly formed by the interactions with significant others around us.

In this context, Fogel (2009, 2011) also refers to research into the interactions of newborns and how these are accompanied by a range of involuntary sounds and movements involving the whole body, such as grumbles, hiccups, burps, sighs and coughs. As the marinade becomes more extensive and complex throughout our lives – we are talking about a learning history here – these unconscious forms of breathing, sound making, facial expressions and movement become more and

42 *The narrative patient*

more consolidated in the objectal foundation as an unconscious pattern of optimal or comfortable ways of relating to the self-other-world. We, therefore, see them come to the fore when people come under pressure, such as during times of tension, under stress, but often also in both acute pain and chronic suffering. George Downing (2015) speaks of 'a core repertoire of body organizing know-how (during approximately the first two years)' (p. 309) in which the young child learns various 'micropractices' (p. 310) and hereby introduces the term affect-motor schemata. These build up as a kind of physical narrative from the early effective interactions into a lifelong cluster of motor, cognitive and affective beliefs: 'Such affective-motor schemas can either activate, or deactivate, certain muscle groups, muscle tone and breathing patterns, and have a profound effect on the person's vegetative system and their body's metabolic processes' (Marlock, 2015, p. 157). Geuter (2015b), therefore, sees the affect-motor scheme as a core concept in BPT and points out that this deep priming of experiences can never be made fully explicit.

When Karin was younger, she was abused several times by her older brother for long periods of time and later also by the babysitter. It started when she was a toddler and lasted until she was 13 when her period started. In the session, she wants to talk about touch and why she still has such a hard time with this, even though she has been with a very sweet and gentle partner for years. When she describes a specific situation, she tells herself that she just has to brace herself. She closes her eyes, makes a scared/repulsed grimace and pushes her hands abruptly on her legs. This clustering of expression and movement is an example of an affect-motor scheme and takes place without Karen being aware of it.

For example, some people have experienced – and therefore learned – that a needy attitude works best in order to be able to live/survive or to ensure the presence, safety and attention of the other person. Others, on the other hand, have experienced that it is best to trust as few people as possible, as people usually didn't take care of them in the best possible way. They have had to deal with boundaries that were never respected, with others who got under their skin or who took pleasure in hurting them deeply. Their narrative endorses the advice to have as few interactions as possible and to rely on yourself as much as possible. Their objectal foundation is steeped in marinade, lingers for life and becomes more visible at times when pain, suffering or restlessness are a source of tension.

In other words, the individual who seeks therapy will always enter into an objectally founded relationship with the therapist. What's more, he will try to establish this relationship from the outset, precisely because it is missing outside the therapy room or has unexpectedly taken on a different form. With it has also disappeared the guarantee of safety, attention or satisfaction of other needs that were hidden in this relationship. For some, a care object has been lost, others are deprived of their sounding board, or they are asked to do things that they cannot offer. In concrete terms, this means for the therapeutic process that the therapist is on the alert for the objectal foundation from the very first moment of contact. The first signs and characteristics of this often appear at an early stage, such as when the therapist meets the individual in the waiting room or logs the individual by telephone and this in words, body language or behaviour. It is intriguing that the whole individual, including his objectal foundation, appears in the therapist's unconscious, such as his fantasy, intuitive emotional image or even dreams. The questions that the therapist asks himself in this respect may be 'How does this person make me feel?' or 'What image do I experience when I think of this patient?'

The unconscious appears in therapy

Back to the chronology of the therapeutic process. The individual feels ready to take the step to therapy. He now has the space[3] to sign up for a vulnerable and partly asymmetrical care relationship and thus becomes a patient[4]. Within this space, there is room for dialogue and expression, where the therapist tries to allow for as much free play as possible. Although the patient will partly consciously use, and fill, this speaking space to relay what is going on, the patient's unconscious also puts in an appearance. For this reason, EBW does not initially use a structured question-and-answer method, but works with an associative anamnesis in which patients can tell what they want, what they need or simply what comes to mind. In a later phase of the anamnestic process, a semi-structured template is used. We will come back to this in Chapter 7. A frequently used opening question in the associative part is 'Can you tell me what brought you here?'

Why is the patient's free speech so important? In the working concepts 'the narrative' and 'the objectal foundation', the unconscious processes in both patient and therapist become clear for the first time. Working with the body is already mentioned in the introduction as working in the margins and one of those margins is the boundary between conscious functioning and the unconscious, just as it concerns the boundary between the linguistic and the pre-language or non-language. Working from the unconscious, therefore, forms an important working method within EBW and will be discussed at length from Chapter 4 onwards. Here, we situate it in relation to the objectal foundation that emerges very early on, even before the first encounter. The patient already has a certain subconscious experience or fantasy with the therapist, even if he does not know him yet. Precisely because the patient has not yet met the actual therapist, will he have an imaginary experience of the as yet unknown therapist based on his unconscious experiences and memories with others from his objectal foundation? In other words, even before the patient has seen the therapist, he already appears in his thoughts, fantasies or dreams, at which point questions and sometimes even answers arise. Interestingly, the therapist appears in the place of a significant other and is, as such, already part of the patient's objectal foundation.

44 The narrative patient

> Will the therapist be someone who acknowledges ('validates') the request for help and the care and will he respond sensitively and appropriately? Or is the therapist someone who needs to be convinced with more theatrical behaviour? Maybe the therapist is someone who can leave suddenly or disappear abruptly, and the patient needs to be wary of this.

The care provider, therefore, already exists within the patient's subconscious in various ways. As a result, the therapist will be approached from the behaviour, emotions, thoughts and expectations that belong to the patient's objectal foundation. As already mentioned, the first encounter is, therefore, of value within the diagnostic process. Initial words, non-verbal impression, body language, general appearance and even the gaze are indicative of the objectal foundation and offer a first glimpse into the patient's narrative. Questions like 'Who or what brings you here?', 'Why *now*, do you think?' and 'What do you expect from the therapy?' are anchors within this early therapeutic process.

The body appears in therapy

We have just learned to appreciate how a disruptive event causes the narrative to stall, resulting in the objectal foundation to 'surface' or become explicit. As mentioned earlier, the therapist initially uses an associative anamnesis as a guiding principle during intake. Characteristic of this method of anamnesis is that its direction is determined by the patient's unconscious, whereby the therapist not only pays attention to the patient's words, but, above all, to the entire context of the encounter, including his own internal way of reacting (Gilliéron, 2005). Put in a more phenomenological way, the associative anamnesis is a relaxed listening tool that starts from seemingly naive, open and freely associating attention, rather than the therapist leaning forward in the conversation and concentrating on the search for what went wrong. Whereas the latter is typical of therapies on the somatic side of the spectrum, the associative anamnesis is the basis of a more psychodynamic or psychoanalytical questioning. Within EBW, we refine the associative anamnesis and listen to the body – leaning backwards and naively – or rather to what the body has to say. From Chapter 4, we will see that this happens to some extent when working with a so called 'feeling', listening' or haptic handle.

> *This speaking body is a kind of physical narrative that shares what it is like for the patient to be in the world like this. The individual's dialectic process between the body and the world settles down in the body and is also expressed through the body.*

This speaking body is a kind of physical narrative that shares what it is like for the patient to be in the world like this. In other words, the individual's dialectic process between the body and the world settles down in the body and is also expressed through the body. In the fourth chapter, we will specifically elaborate on this by means of one of the most central working methods in EBW, namely, the muscle armour. At the same time, this narrative body is reminiscent of the concept of 'embodiment' and its transdisciplinary embedding in many other domains.[5] For example, embodiment for Cooper (2008) refers to the existential fact that, as a human being, we not only have our own body, but that, as a body, we are inextricably linked to the world we inhabit. In this way, 'existing' can literally be understood as coming into physical being (derived from the Latin *existere*). People come into being in the world, which is what makes them vulnerable: they not only see, but also become visible (Merleau-Ponty, 2009; Carman, 2008). The existential-phenomenological question of the body is thus about the ontology of being a body and the way in which we first and foremost open up, enter, understand and join our world as a body. Heidegger (1999) goes one step further in his ontological vision of the body and states that we do not only experience this bodily being in the world from a certain disposition, but that it is our physicality that underpins this disposition. Cooper (2008) joins both Merleau-Ponty and Heidegger in summarising this as 'we apprehend our world in a direct and bodily way' (p. 21). Close to this, Röhricht (2015a, 2015b) joins Plassmann in paraphrasing embodiment as one of the very first 'introjects' that settle in the psychic apparatus on the basis of elementary, physical perceptions of 'being alive or embodied-being itself' (p. 240). In more recent literature on embodiment,[6] the body is conceptualised as a dynamic, organic place of meaningful experiences instead of a physical object that can be separated from the self or the mind (Mehling et al., 2011). A clinical repercussion that we later revisit is found in Wilde (1999, 2003), who points out that the chronically suffering patient changes not only in his physical body, but also in his embodiment, with all the consequences for bodily processes of giving meaning. Zeiler (2010) introduces the terms 'alienation' and 'spatial temporal contraction' to indicate how chronic pain drastically changes, and even disrupts, the patient's embodiment. As a result of the persistently negative stimuli that the body has to cushion, a serious disturbance and alienation of the embodied presence in the world arises, as a result of which the body is, as it were, cramped in one point in space and time, and is experienced as not of one's own or strange (alienation).

Very often, these people are totally absorbed by the now of pain and dysfunction, drastically narrow their living environment and range, and are preoccupied with pain-as-experience. At the same time, these phenomenological concepts are reminiscent of the central role of body experience as a risk factor in the difficult body (Henningsen et al., 2007), which once again underlines working with embodied self-consciousness as a quintessence in EBW.

Embodied self-awareness

Fogel (2009) continues on this phenomenological trail of embodiment and, based on neuroscientific findings, introduces two terms that are more closely related to the EBW therapeutic clinic, namely, 'embodied self-awareness' (ESA) and 'conceptual self-awareness' (CSA) (Figure 2.1). ESA is defined as the awareness of

> Embodied self-awareness (ESA)
> - Mediated through body and behaviour
> - Spontaneous, creative and open to change
> - Specifically, it's only lived in the 'now'
>
> Conceptual self-awareness (CSA)
> - Mediated by language and symbol
> - Rational, logical and explanatory
> - Abstract, transcends the 'now'

Figure 2.1 ESA and CSA

Source: Adapted from Fogel, 2009

movements, feelings and emotions and is conceived in the brain based on interception and body scheme. ESA happens spontaneously, is creative, concrete and only takes place in the present. At the other end of the spectrum, Fogel places CSA, which implies thought processes, is based on language and symbolism, works rationally and logically, and can go beyond the present. A therapeutically important aspect is that Fogel (2009, 2011) does not speak of embodiment, but of ESA at the moment we consciously experience our body. When we then name, shape and express this physical experience through language or symbols, the brain switches to other networks that lead to CSA. Although, therefore, ESA and embodiment differ from each other on the basis of whether or not they are conscious, the two concepts are also closely related, as is evident from the following quote: 'This means that thought patterns, emotions, forms of embodied self-awareness, muscle tension and relaxation act together as a dynamic system, each element of which influences and maintains the others to form characteristic postures of relating to the world' (Fogel, 2009, p. 196).

The ontological process of being-in-the-world that we remember from body phenomenology as an embodiment, thus, forms the unconscious physical basis of patterns that are expressed in typical postures and behaviours for the individual: 'Through our body, our movements and actions, we make the world our own' (de Haan, 2012, p. 215). The ability to become aware of this goes via ESA to CSA, after which this awareness is expressed in words, images and stories. On the other hand, these three distinguishable physical forms of experience – embodiment, ESA and CSA – are not entirely separate from each other and, together, form a fundamental pillar in the experiential work with a difficult body. In anticipation of the next paragraph, we can already situate embodiment, ESA and CSA within a spectrum that runs from subconscious, via preconscious, to conscious. Before we can integrate this in the therapeutic process of EBW in Chapter 7, we first have to explore how the subconscious relates to the body and body awareness. It is good to note that the concept of 'consciousness' is approached much more broadly today than it was a few decades ago, when it was often equated only with the higher brain structures, such as the cerebral cortex. Brain science now teaches that the whole body, with all its tissues and subsystems, is the substrate for consciousness and not just the neocortical structures:

> Not only the neocortex, but, in particular, some of the inner circuits among the brainstem, midbrain, basal nuclei, thalamus and the limbic system (probably with contributions from nerve cells of the intestine, the so-called 'gut-brain'), and also neurotransmitter substances that are found, not only in the brain, but throughout the body and in the blood, together determine the consciousness that is generated in the associative area, along with behaviour, perception, emotions, cognition and experience.
>
> (Gottwald, 2015, p. 128)

With the fundamental contribution of these deeper brain structures, a lot of attention is paid to other basal systems in the body, such as homeostatic control systems and the enteric nervous system. The latter is related to digestive systems and abdominal organs and sends, in absolute numbers, the neurons in the brain home. Damasio (2003, 2004) illustrated the fundamental role this homeostatic and enteric information plays in forming both body schemes and universal, basic emotions, such as anger, sadness and disgust ('primary emotions') and the preceding 'background emotions'. In view of the pronounced contribution of intestinal information (via the vagus nerve, which accounts for approximately 90 percent) to the creation of these basic forms of emotion, Damasio (2004) proposes to take the concept of gut-feeling literally. In his Somatic Marker Theory, he then substantiates how people make higher-order decisions based on rudimentarily stored patterns that are based on this physical – and therefore also visceral-homeostatic – flow of information. Conversely, these unconscious, physical signals or somatic markers provide an insight into the processes that take place when the individual finds himself in emotionally taxing situations or stress. At the same time, this is also in line with James-Lange's theory, who claims that an anxiety stimulus first leads to physical-physiological reactions, such as heart palpitations, sweating and organ reactions, only then to result in an emotion, such as anxiety. This is the result of an interpretation of the way in which the body reacts first and not from a mere top-down cognitive analysis of the situation.

The term 'gut-brain' challenges therapists and researchers to approach awareness-raising processes from a much broader and, therefore, also physical framework. On the other hand, this visceral homeostatic substrate (top-right quadrant) may also resonate with what we have come to know as the embodiment and ESA (top-left quadrant) and to which we will return at a later stage. Although it would lead us too far, it would be interesting to link research into the relationship between this 'brain-gut axis' and immunological defence systems (Van Oudenhove, 2007a, 2007b, 2010; Goehler et al., 2007; Mayer & Tillisch, 2011) with concepts such as embodiment and to examine how this relates to experiences such as 'being able to stand up for yourself in the world' or 'being able to come to terms with an event'. This brings us back to many of our patients: their anxieties, uncertainties and tension symptoms that often 'go right to the gut'. It is then somewhat strange that no single mainstream therapy is seriously concerned with the abdominal region in relation to emotional dysfunctions, let alone actually treats them.

Embodiment and body awareness within experiential bodywork

So far, we understand that ontologically, embodiment is both unconscious and existential, but also always deeply anchored. With Heidegger (1999; Van Sluis, 1998) we dare to label it as a disposition[7] (*Stimmung* in German) or an awareness: the individual is always in the world from a certain situation and participates in this world from a certain disposition. Since in normal circumstances, we cannot do without our body, we always face the world from our body and participate in our environment with our body. So the individual is a body in the world, but also discovers and unlocks it from his body (Carman, 2008). So, as a human being we are not just present in a 'corporalised' or 'embodied' form, but what we think, how we feel and what we do is embedded in our body, including all the processes that go with it. Even our language is imbued with physical references or metaphors (Lakoff & Johnson, 2003). Think for example of expressions such as 'fortunately that's behind us now', 'an albatross around his neck', 'I'm fed up to the back teeth with it', 'she has a lot on her mind' or 'I'm up to my ears in it'. The clinical anchoring of this fundamental corporalisation is what we encounter in EBW as the narrative or speaking body, and, as this was explained in this chapter, that is also what the body does from the word go.

We take with us that the speaking body grants an insight into the deep layer of our patient's embodiment.

In fact, the word choice *leiblich* versus *körperlich* is not coincidental and refers respectively to the phenomenological *Leib* (top-left quadrant) and the biological *Körper* (top-right quadrant). In other words, when we speak of the *Leib* or *Leiblichkeit*, we refer to the experiential dimension (lived body), while the term *Körper* refers to the biological substrate (body). Both are intrinsically connected to each other. We need a material-physical body to experience ourselves and others as a body. What's more, the physical dimension can be very decisive and restrictive with respect to the physical experience. Remember Wilde (2003), who pointed out that the chronically ailing patient not only changes in his body, but also in his embodiment. After all, as a human being, we have no choice but to experience our body. We cannot have our body outside our experiential dimension. So we always experience the body we have as the body we are. In concrete terms, this means that our patient who talks about his ailing body always does so as an experience of the body that he is.[8]

Although this sounds logical and plausible, it is noticeable that the patient usually brings his complaint from the idea that there is something wrong with his 'somatic' body (*Körper*) and not his 'lived' body (*Leib*). In the narrative, the body often appears as an object that one has, as a thing that is stalling or broken and only listens to physical or mechanical laws. In literature (see, for example, Fuchs & Schlimme, 2009; de Haan, 2012), this form of disturbed body experience

The narrative patient 49

is referred to as 'disembodiment', in which an individual is no longer connected to his body. There is also 'hyper-embodiment', which is when the person is fully immersed in the intense sensation of pain. In this state of hyperembodiment, psychological experiences are felt to be 'too real'. Such concrete thinking can ensure that psychological pain is felt as physical pain (Luyten & Fonagy, 2011). However, it should be emphasised that these two pronounced forms of embodiment to some extent fit in with normal functioning and cannot, therefore, be regarded as merely pathological. During bodily or sexual enjoyment, for example, but also when practising sports, the body, which is in a state of hyperembodiment, experiences these as pleasant and comfortable, while in the case of trauma, it is necessary for the body to be temporarily disconnected or disembodied.[9]

In order to stay close to the practice of EBW, it is especially important to remember that embodiment unconsciously takes place as a disposition in which the patient finds himself and to which he is also attuned. Clinically, we recognise this during EBW paradoxically when the patient becomes aware of his own embodiment and we, therefore, are technically beginning to speak of ESA.

Whereas initially, there was no awareness of one's own lived body and the way in which one is embodied in the world (embodiment), in therapy an early realisation of one's own lived body as a dynamic, organic place of meaningful experiences is now emerging instead of a body that is outside of it as a purely physical object (Mehling et al., 2011).

When S. shakes hands at the beginning of each session, I feel the frailty in her whole body, as if I could pull her over in one jerk. S. herself is not aware of this and compensates this absence of strength and grounding with an overinvestment in verbal speaking. Often, S. keeps rattling on and I have to ask her to be quiet. When S. is confronted with the weakness in her arms and the stiffness in her legs during the deep bodywork, she is initially shocked. Throughout the therapeutic process, she notices how she indeed 'hangs together like a rag doll'. Where she tries to be strong verbally, she invariably takes small steps backwards during upright contact with me. At the beginning of the next session, she tells me that she has noticed how she does this at work, at home, with her friends, etc. She finds out that she doesn't really like shaking hands at all, because she gets shaken up completely. It also feels like 'everyone is always pulling me'. During the evocative bodywork, we work with this and S. explores how else she can get in touch with herself. Pulling, pushing, looking each other in the eye and not shaking hands are all tried as an exercise, until she comes up with the idea that she might first have to work on standing firmly on her own two feet, with all of her lived body. This is followed by exercises that focus on the legs and grounding.

S. now understands more 'from within'[10] how she first enters the world with her body, unlocks it and walks up to others. She now learns to make contact with the existential phenomenological layer of her identity. This process of awareness of one's own embodiment is thus taking place across the ESA boundary. In concrete terms, this means that we can only become aware of the layer of the embodiment

50 *The narrative patient*

to the extent that it vibrates into the layer of embodied consciousness or ESA. Only then can we make contact with our experience of being in the world. The fact that this wording has a somewhat topographical feel is partly due to the layered networks in our brain that are considered responsible for the experiences we label as embodiment, ESA and CSA. Let's take a brief look at these networks and try to situate the three forms of body consciousness within therapy with the psychosomatic body.

Working with levels of attention and awareness within experiential bodywork

Within EBW, working from the aforementioned levels of consciousness occupies an important place. In addition to embodiment, ESA and CSA, we regularly refer to concepts such as *rêverie*, leaning back, explicit and implicit knowing, focusing and mentalising. Although there are clear, conceptual differences between these terms, for the sake of simplicity, we can divide them into two groups that are process-dynamic and even somewhat topographical in relation to each other. As far as the latter is concerned, distinguishable neural networks within the brain are described in the literature (see for example Vermote, 2015; Fogel, 2009).[11] From a process-dynamic angle, one level of awareness comprises forms of thoughtful, cognitive presence, such as conceptual self-awareness, explicit knowledge, along with analytical and hypothetical-deductive thinking. By means of language, symbols, analysis and concentration, the individual expresses himself through targeted speech and action. These processes relate to the upper layers of conscious reasoning and the associated cortical networks. In a certain sense, this is the highest level of linguistic, psychological or symbolic processing and represents a conscious, explicit naming in which the patient mainly thinks and speaks about himself. Hence the term conceptual self-awareness. This layer of consciousness is often prevalent in patients who are too much in their headspace, have become disconnected from their bodies or gut feeling and develop psychosomatic conditions.

> *Central is the mindful presence in the moment without judgment and this from a receptive and open posture characterised by leaning back, perceiving and receiving without the need for intervention or action. It is a state of simply being, as we know it in dreams, flow, meditation or peak experiences. It is about opening up and letting at the same time.*

The other level of awareness is therapeutically more central in body-focused psychotherapy and EBW and relates to terms, such as embodied self-awareness (Fogel), implicit knowing (Depestele), felt sense (Gendlin), *rêverie* (Bion) or mind-wandering (Vermote) and is partly in line with what Siegel (2009, 2010, 2017) conceptualises as mindsight and Csikszenmihalyi (2008) as flow. This is a very different level of consciousness. The focus here is on the felt contact with reality, in which the individual is present from a conscious experience of the here and now – also known as presence in the literature. It is the state of mindful presence in the moment without judgment or analysis. It is a receptive and open attitude in which leaning back, perceiving and receiving are central without the need for intervention or action. It is a state of simply being, as we know it in dreams, flow, meditation or peak experiences. It is about opening up and letting at the same time. Sports, music, art, meditation and therapy often provide the right context in which to tune into this state of mind. Within EBW, we work with these concepts when we refer to the general concept of body awareness or body experience, in which these characteristics are also explicitly described, as shown by the following definitions:

- 'Body Awareness is the subjective, phenomenological aspect of proprioception and interoception that enters conscious awareness and is modifiable by mental processes including attention, interpretation, appraisal, beliefs, memories, conditioning attitude and affect' (Mehling et al., 2011, p. 1).
- 'Embodied self-awareness is the ability to pay attention to ourselves, to feel our sensations, and movements online, along with the motivational and emotional feelings that accompany them, in the present moment, without the mediating influence of judgemental thoughts' (Fogel, 2009, pp. 1–2).

Experiential bodywork as a layered approach

Within the therapeutic process of EBW, the three positions of embodiment, ESA and CSA are always involved to varying degrees. In this way, we not only make contact with the lower layer of the unconscious body and embodiment, we also try to shift something 'upwards', towards consciousness (ESA) and, ultimately, linguistic expression (CSA). Crucial in working with three layers – embodiment, ESA, CSA or pre-implicit, implicit, explicit knowing (Depestele, 2004) – is therefore the layer in between, where the transformation processes occur, as a result of which space is progressively freed for spontaneous words, images, associations and experiences without these already being under the control of the conscious cognition. On the contrary, they bubble up from the pre-reflective and non-linguistic body of the lower layer to present themselves to our physical, and later linguistic, consciousness. The process thus arises in a certain sense in 'the depth' of the body, or to put it more accurately, of the being-there-as-a-body. This depth is the pre-implicit level that precedes the implicit level of *rêverie*, mind-wandering, dreaming, creativity or experiencing flow and felt sense in the focus process. 'This deeper knowing is also physical; it is a deeper version of what will become implicit, bodily-sensed meanings or felt sense; it is that from which they will form; so it can only be physical' (Depestele, 2004, p. 114).

In Hebbrecht (2016), we recognise an 'imagino-poetic capacity' here, as the ability to create images and words intuitively and organically. Indeed, when we invite our patient to feel their body 'from within', we use the whole body as an entry point and facilitate this imagino-poetic capacity in the patient. Contact with one's own body, the sensing of embodied meaning (felt sense) and the courage to let go of mental-cognitive control always herald a burgeoning or advancing awareness and facilitate an evocative process in language, movement or catharsis.

52 The narrative patient

I sometimes liken this process with the image of opening a bottle of lemonade for the first time. The uniqueness of soft drinks lies in the refreshing combination of taste, smell and effervescence. But untouched, no fizz is visible yet, as it is still 'stored' in the drink itself. The gas bubbles that will form when the cap is loosened – this could happen in the therapeutic process – are still in a silent, even invisible state of pure potential (pre-implicit knowing or embodiment). However, when the process is stimulated, the bubbles 'arise' and make their way up through the liquid and bottle – the urge to actualise – to finally burst open and release their aromas. The true spectacle of the bubble is then the in between layer of transformation processes (implicit knowing or ESA), reaching the outside world, with a specific result in smell and taste, as it stands for the upper layer of explicit knowing or CSA, where words are spoken and stories acquire meaning.

Interestingly, Vermote (2015) points out that brain research shows that these conscious, linguistic networks of reasoning and cognition located in the top layer cannot be simultaneously active with the deeper, slow systems of mind-wandering, flow, dreams and intuitive expression. In concrete terms, this means that during the treatment, our patient cannot simultaneously stay in the in between space of body experience (ESA) and talk about football, the weather or politics (CSA). On the other hand, the therapist must be able to work from this space if he really wants to make contact and be able to feel and sense.

When I lean back as a therapist and let my mind wander, I am open to images, words and insights that the patient's body whispers to me that would never have come to me otherwise. At the same time, I invite my patient to let go of cognitive thinking for a while, to have the courage to feel, to explore and also to invite images, words and insights that his own body impart. He too would never have thought of these otherwise.

All these processes will be discussed further and will be elaborated within the practice of EBW in Chapter 7. Here, we remember that EBW can essentially be understood as layered work across various levels of awareness.

Tools for therapy

- *We are sensitive to the existential and phenomenological layer within the story or narrative of the patient. How does this layeredness make its presence felt in body and language when the patient has got stuck in his narrative?*
- *The narrative brings us into contact with his marinade of objectal foundation and early learning processes about the relationship with himself, the other and the world.*

- *The anamnesis is initially associative in nature and then gradually evolves into a more specific questioning of themes that emerge using the four quadrants and fulcra from the previous chapter.*
- *EBW is always layered work in which we want to give maximum room to the discourse of the unconscious, the creative and the pre-reflective. Various levels of awareness and processes of perception, such as ESA and CSA, alternate during EBW, but are always anchored in the embodied presence-in-the-world or embodiment.*
- *The therapist works from a backward leaning, embodied and open presence that makes him sensitive to what is happening above and below the conscious radar, both for the patient and for himself.*

Notes

1 These different ways of looking at the world were already conceived by Claire Graves (1970, 2004) as a system of memes and later developed into a spiral-dynamic model of human evolution as clusters of values, norms and beliefs (Beck & Cowan, 2004). This is similar to Wilber's bottom-left quadrant where these memes are situated.
2 This is what Depestele et al. (2003) call the therapeutic space zero or 'pathological space' in which the client does not yet have room to make contact with his situation and experience, as a result of which it is not yet possible to speak.
3 Depestele et al. (2003) speak here of an initial space within the therapeutic process, which they call 'the relationship space'.
4 In various therapeutic currents, there is also talk of client, while at the same time emphasising the symmetrical position. Within EBW, we point out the importance of an asymmetrical relationship and speak, for the time being, of a patient.
5 In Merleau-Ponty's phenomenology, physical interaction with the world occupies a central place. He draws an essential distinction between 'le corps-objet' and 'le corps-sujet'. The body as an object is the body that we have, the purely physical body that is scientifically accessible. The body as subject is the body that we are, our body as a signifier (Bullington, 2009; Wilde, 2003). Fuchs and Schlimme (2009) also refer to the terms *Körper* and *Leib*, the former referring to the biological body and the latter to the (lived) body. In our normal everyday actions, we are not focused on our body, but on the world and on what we are doing. Usually, our body functions implicitly in the background. Only in specific situations does the body become noticeably present as a biological entity; for example in case of hunger, thirst, lust or fatigue (Denys & Meynen, 2012). Our body also comes to the fore in case of pain (Wilde, 2003). This shift from the body as an object to the body as a subject is a natural given. But in chronically ailing patients, this biphasic movement stagnates, which fundamentally disrupts their participation in the world (idem).
6 Embodiment is reminiscent of other concepts, such as body image, body scheme and body awareness (Roxendal, 1985). Nevertheless, there are fundamental differences. Body image is the perceived form of our body, the mental image of our own body, in terms of size, shape and characteristics (Blaskeslee & Blaskeslee, 2007). Body scheme, on the other hand, is predominantly somatosensory and is involved in tracking and adjusting the constantly changing position in space during movements (Blaskeslee & Blaskeslee, 2007; Fogel, 2009). This includes exteroception – processing input from outside the body, such as touch, smell, vision, hearing – and proprioception, which

includes the perception of joint positions, muscle tension, movement, posture and balance. Body awareness is defined by Mehling et al. (2011) as the subjective, phenomenological aspect of proprioception and interception – or the perception of sensations from your own body – that enters consciousness and is adaptable through mental processes.

7   Prins (2008) points out that the individual is always 'attuned' and always understands his world from a certain disposition: 'The disposition is the "medium" in which our existence takes place, it is the condition of the possibility of every self-experience and of every experience of the world' (p. 162). We may be inclined to perceive disposition as a feeling, since we, as humans, always have a certain feeling when we experience ourselves. For example, we can feel happy, cheerful or depressed and sad; in short, we can experience a certain affect each time we think about ourselves. This is the perspective that Damasio takes with regard to disposition, which he distinguishes from his concept of background emotions. However, this is not what Heidegger means when he talks about disposition, because any physiological, psychological or anthropological interpretation of the phenomenon of disposition falls short (idem, p. 161). In addition, the origin of disposition is undecided, while feelings are always naturally object-bound.

8   Qualitative research provides enlightening insight into how illness and suffering can have a major impact on the (lived) body. Overcoming boundaries can, therefore, lead to fundamental, positive changes in these dimensions of experience and existence (see, for example, Calsius et al., 2015).

9   Zeiler (2010) points out that during most of our day-to-day activities, our body is in the background and oscillates within a spectrum of hyper- and disembodiment, without getting stuck in both extremes. She describes this background position as disappearance, in contrast to dys-appearance, which is less functional and can be compared to disembodiment.

10 In experiential psychotherapy, the term 'felt sense' is used for this purpose.

11 Vermote (2015, pp. 7–8) refers to classifications according to Lieberman (and Kahnemans). C-system: Neocortical structures such as the lateral prefrontal cortex, posterior parietal cortex, hippocampus and surrounding medial, temporal lobe structures. These are responsible for explicit memory, reasoning and controlled social cognition, are influenced by language and purpose and have a controlling effect. X-system: Connected to deeper brain structures, such as the amygdala, ventromedial prefrontal cortex, basal ganglia, lateral temporal cortex. Operates procedurally, without words, automatically and without explicit memory. Is strongly emotion-driven, works on intuition and sees affective connections without being aware of them. It is active in processes of creativity and gives rise to the formation of diagrams that ensure that one intuitively knows what to do in complex situations where reasoning fails.

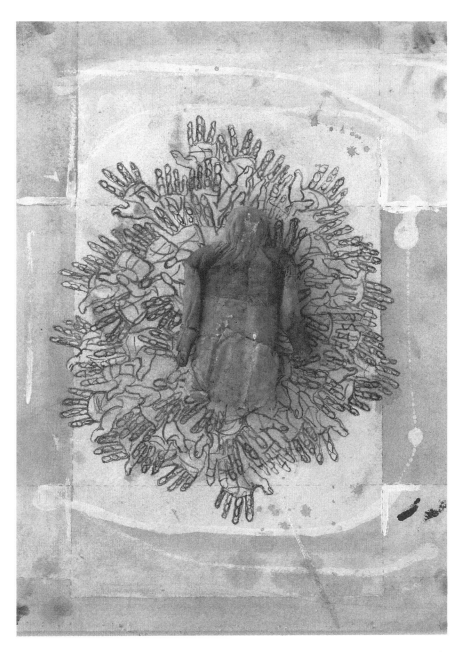

Light Weight, 2015, collage with conté, watercolour, acrylic, old sheets and starch, 42.5 × 32 × 4.5 cm, private collection, Enschede.

3 The body in therapy
Possible or not?

Making contact with one's own body is a recurring theme in various therapeutic schools and is often referred to as 'experiential'. The body that is negatively charged in situations of pain, suffering and anxiety, is explored for as a more positive experience in the present moment by means of numerous techniques. Each time, the importance of body awareness in the now is emphasised, with the final goal being what Fogel (2009) sees as 'coming home to our selves, in line with the true Self'. Cooper (2008) summarises the rationale as follows: 'Hence, the more that therapy can help clients to reconnect with their physical being . . . the more that clients can experience the fullness of an embodied life' (p. 269). Even within EBW, the experiential, experienced contact with one's own physicality is a crucial pre-condition. However, on a more critical note, it is important not to simply skim over the presupposition behind this statement, which is based on a predominantly humanistic view of mankind. In concrete terms, awareness of one's own physicality is always assumed to be attainable. In other words, the individual is able to get in touch with his body. But is this assumption justified? In other words, is the individual really able to fully experience and get in touch with his own body? What's more, can we come home in our lived body?

A first sound

It is worth considering this question from a psychoanalytical angle, inspired by a transdisciplinary approach, all the more so because this may clear the path for a different, and perhaps more nuanced, point of view. From a Freudo-Lacanian point of view, the fundamental importance of the body is already emphasised in relation to the development of identity. In Chapter 2, a brief reference was made to the mirror stage. It is during this dynamic that the body image is created, because the mother helps the child incorporate the fragmented body experience into a 'healed' experience (Vanheule, 2005). This leads to a first total experience, this is 'me' (Verhaeghe, 2003). The interconnectedness of physicality and early affective interactions is even more keenly focused on the importance of the skin as a place to touch and be touched (Anzieu, 2006; Cluckers & Meurs, 2005; McCarthy, 1998). Ogden et al. (2006), therefore, point to the specific importance of touch in this very first phase of life: 'The primary sensations at the very beginning of life are physiological and tactile, and the primary form of communication immediately after birth between parent and newborn is through touch' (p. 42).

Another interesting concept is that of 'second skin', which Esther Bick (1968, 1986) coins as a metaphor for the coping that a baby has to show when there is insufficient safe contact and containment or when there is just too little delineation and, as a result, a deluge of intrusive stimuli. What is even more interesting is that Bick links this second skin to the tangible skin contact via the 'actual skin' and, at the same time, describes how this coping externalises itself via the body, such as rigid musculature, extreme tension, holding breath or inane staring at an object (Bloom, 2006). However, when there is sufficient safe and nurturing contact through the actual skin, the baby increasingly experiences a sense of identity and containment. During this process of mirroring between mother and child, we gain our first physical experience through the other: 'The most intimate part of ourselves, "our" body, is provided by the Other' (Verhaeghe, 2003, p. 186). In other words, the individual or subject receives his or her own body image through the Other as a first layer of identity. This has far-reaching consequences, since it would mean that the basic layer of our self-identity – in short, our ego – is not just physical, but is primarily provided and founded through the other person. Verhaeghe (idem) clearly states 'The first Other is that of the body' (p. 295). This Other (we have already seen that this is often the mother), therefore, plays a critical role when it comes to their healing capacity, encouraging the baby to experience his/her body as a whole. In addition, in this phase, the other person 'does' something that is perhaps even more important, especially in relation to the later development of symptoms. The other helps to protect against the anxiety that goes with discovering one's own body. This anxiety appears to be partly incorporated via the other person. But how should we make sense of this?

From a psychoanalytical point of view, the original, pure or own body is thought of as massive, traumatic and, thus, overwhelming for the infant. Lacan (2004) speaks of the 'real' body and refers to this overwhelming experience as *jouissance* (Harari, 2001). The pure, somatic body, from the unconscious layer of embodiment, is rough and raw and continuously bombards the infant with sensory stimuli. At the same time, these impressions, coming from the body, are not editable with language, words or imagination, simply because these skills have not yet been developed. Bion (Vermote, 2005) calls these rough and raw stimuli '*beta* elements' and points to the mother who filters these stimuli, so that they become manageable for the baby (see Chapter 5). The first Other thus helps to channel the traumatic anxiety that goes with being in the body. In addition, we learnt that the subject's first body image is presented to him for the first time via the other person in the mirror stage. It is the mother who, through touch, play, feeding or caring, helps to discover where and then what the body is. In the lap of these early interactions, the small child gradually acquires a healed body awareness, literally, it becomes more and more whole. This healed body is, therefore, the first 'something' with which the child will identify, as a first form of self-awareness. In Chapter 5, we will explore this further with Wilber as the 'physical self'. Mooij

(2002) also points out that the primacy of our self-experience lies with the other person: 'Initially, a child cannot identify with himself because this "self" is first and foremost an empty place, but he identifies with an image that is offered to him from the outside' (p. 111). The presented body image is thus the first layer of our later self-identity. For Freud (1988 [1923]), the ego was, therefore, first and foremost a body-self or, more specifically, a body shell to which psychological content was added later (Verhaeghe, 2003). The clinical relevance of this should not be underestimated: to the patient, the body is both familiar and unknown at the same time, which often makes it anxiety-provoking.

But what does this mean for the question of the possibility of the body in therapy? The psychoanalytical discourse sees the body as impossible in a way: on the one hand, the body that I am is outside my scope of experience, because it is too massive, overwhelming and frightening, on the other hand the body that I have is originally handed by the other so that it is not really mine, but just an identification.

So we lose the real, pure biological body that we are, from the word go. Verhaeghe (2009) captures this succinctly:

> Our body is part of what is Real, which straightway means that we have lost our real body from the moment we have acquired symbolic thinking. We may 'have' it, but the mere 'being' is hardly an option. According to our use of language, we have a body, while, in reality, we are a body that has a language of its own.
>
> (p. 87)

But this loss also has an important advantage, since we can work on our language-symbolic body and thus control it to a certain extent. The impossibility of one's own body consists in the fact that we can no longer coincide with it – we can no longer be it completely. And in those cases where this coinciding does occur, the individual is overwhelmed by the anxiety of disappearing as a subject. We see this, for example, in a psychosis, in which the individual is overwhelmed by what is happening with, or in, his body. We also see this in the case of the panic-stricken patient who becomes completely distraught in a vicious circle of physical stimuli that are not amenable to a reasonable assessment. This is also reminiscent of what Glas (2002) writes about the impossibility of relating to anxiety:

> Coming closer to anxiety then means: imminent structural loss, an exposure to the forces of formlessness, dissolution of the 'I'-self relationship. In the extreme, it means that it is impossible to relate to anxiety: the 'I'-self relationship dissolves into anxiety.
>
> (p. 56)

It seems that coming closer to one's own pure and original 'real' body is tantamount to exposing oneself to the forces of the formless. Simply put, it seems impossible to coincide with one's own body, to be familiar with it or, as we often hear in therapy, to come home to your own body.

Body and lived body

In the analysis from the previous section, we wanted to set things straight. There is, after all, a risk that within various experiential and body-focused approaches, it is too easy to start from the seemingly obvious assumption that the body is simply accessible by means of therapeutic interventions that are aimed at body awareness. It is recommended that frequently used treatment strategies, such as 'becoming aware of your body' or 'becoming one with it and coming home to it' be tested to see if this is feasible. On the other hand, it is also true that this is, to a certain extent, a conceptual-philosophical debate in which one either agrees or disagrees with a certain vision. Supporters and opponents will point out the shortcomings of a certain paradigm, such as the psychoanalytical framework, or will simply not identify with it. Thus, the Freudo-Lacanian framework at its core remains a discourse based on a lack or rupture in reality and a deficit in the subject. A concrete consequence of this is that we, as humans, are driven throughout our lives by a desire to eliminate this shortcoming. The body of some patients indeed speaks strongly from the desire to coincide, or merge, in the physical experience, for example during therapy. On the other hand, the subject is a speaking being, precisely because it has been cut off from its own pure body by language. In short, the psychoanalytical framework states that as speaking beings, we miss 'being a body' and have to make do with 'having a body'.

Although this view is, to some extent, adopted by various thinkers within the existential paradigm, existential-humanist authors often rely more on 'being human' as a possibility, and not as a shortcoming. Even though we have been thrown into existence, we are not so much determined by being cut off as we find ourselves in a position to grow, to actualise ourselves to acquire more authenticity, individuation (Jung, 1995a, 1995b, 1999) or authenticity (Heidegger, 1999). A transdisciplinary exploration of these sometimes divergent positions is, in fact, enriching for the therapist, who can better grasp certain aspects of the therapeutic process. Gendlin (1969, 1993), for example, in his therapeutic approach of 'focusing', takes a completely different view of the body compared to the psychoanalytical model. Where focusing is aimed at learning to listen and opening oneself up to what the body offers as a deep sense of knowing, the physical presence in oneself can only be an illusion for Lacan. The body, therefore, installs a deep philosophical – more specifically ontological – gap between these two thinkers, in which a deep embodied knowing contrasts for Gendlin with the illusion of knowing one's own body in Lacan's case (Soenen & Van Balen, 2004). This also fits in seamlessly with the historical struggle within the philosophical body/lived body debate and focuses on the field of tension between the mentioned 'having' and 'being' of the body. Do we, as humans, mainly have a body or are we a body? Slatman (2008) offers a more inclusive vision in which having a body cannot be opposed to being one: 'Physical identity ultimately means nothing more than that "I am the body that I have". I am this strange body' (p. 213). Intuitively, this fits in well with the therapeutic practice of working with a body that acts up. Indeed, in the narrative, we often hear how the patient relates to his body as a strange 'something', a thing that no longer works the way they would like to, and is therefore acting up. So, it remains important to give this disturbed relationship with the body the necessary attention in therapy. We will therefore briefly consider two therapeutic interventions that are known within mainstream psychotherapy, namely, 'mentalisation' and 'focusing'. The fact that both are, in a way, two sides of the same coin but also fundamentally different, makes it very interesting from a transdisciplinary point of view for the therapist, who has to work with the psychosomatic request for help.

Mentalisation as the capacity for reflective distance

Mentalisation is seen by founders Allen et al. (2008) as the most fundamental common denominator in psychotherapy and is described as a cognitive, intellectual activity in which the mental and insightful development of one's own emotional experiences is central.[1]

> It is the ability to recognise intentions and feelings in others and oneself, to understand interpersonal behaviour in terms of mental states and to situate all this within a psychic reality that is connected to the external reality but can still be distinguished from it.
>
> (Kinet & Vermote, 2005, p. 7)

If this process is more focused on the body, then Spaans and colleagues (2009) refer to 'body mentalisation' as 'the ability to perceive own and other people's body signals, to be receptive to them and to experience connection with underlying mental states. . . . a subtle sensing of physical signals and the related mental states' (p. 241). Body mentalisation is, therefore, about the ability to transform physical experiences into words and images, so that the patient has more control over what happens to his body. In this way, the panic-stricken patient learns to distance himself from the sensations that overwhelm him by means of words and language. By naming what is happening and what is being experienced, a distance is created from the immediacy of the experience. The patient acquires a form of control over the inconceivable way in which the panic appears in the body. We can, in fact, take this literally, as the clinical concept of actual pathology teaches us, in which something of the body presents itself, but cannot be identified or communicated. As a result, the body reacts without any symptoms that mean anything (Verhaeghe, 2003, 2015). Body mentalisation in this sense is rather focused on promoting a learning of how to operate or control the body and does not correspond to what sums up mindfulness, for example. Allen et al. (2008) prefer to use 'a psyche-oriented mindfulness'. An important difference, however, is that mindfulness is pre-reflective, perceptual and not evaluative, while mentalisation is more deliberate, cognitive and focused on mental states. This means that mentalisation is not so much aimed at the physical knowing, or the pre-reflective aspect of our self-experience. Nevertheless, Luyten et al. (2010) refer to mentalisation as a multi-dimensional concept in which they also distinguish an implicit and automatic form of mentalisation. The latter is not conscious, non-verbal and non-reflective

62 The body in therapy

and is characterised by a parallel, and much faster, processing in the brain than its explicitly controlled counterpart (p. 161). This implicit form of mentalisation already appears at the beginning of the baby's second year of life (idem). In the next chapter, however, we will see that underlying capacities and networks of body experience are operational even earlier in the development. Moreover, Luyten et al. (idem) extend their multi-dimensional analysis of mentalisation with 'external' and 'affective' mentalisation, which are also closely related to the body. They refer to specific brain networks, such as the fronto-parietal and mirror neuron systems, which are highly body-based. At the same time, one might wonder whether these dimensional extensions do not overlap with what is meant by focusing.

Focusing as the ability to listen to what the body says

Paying attention to one's own physicality and practising conscious embodied presence are central skills within existential-phenomenological therapies. The importance of (re)learning the contact of being there as a body is a pillar within Gendlin's focusing (1969, 1993, 2008; Gendlin & Olsen, 1970). Leijssen (2009, 2010) outlines focusing in nine phases as a natural process of inner listening and indicates that this presupposes a 'becoming silent' in which attention is brought inwardly, to subtle physical sensations that invite welcoming recognition.

When she goes on to point out that you can try to express this inner experience in words or images, then it is here, among other things, that the ability to body-mentalise and focus can come together. Let's briefly illustrate this with a case excerpt of patient R. who has been for an oncological check-up with his wife.

> *'After the X-ray, we had to wait in the room that had become familiar. My wife was sitting next to me and that felt good, different than before. I saw her face from the corner of my eye, although I really wanted to surreptitiously see whether she was tired or worried, I was surprised by what I noticed, what I really saw. Never before had I seen the pain she had suffered for years, not even in a look or in the serene peace with which she had silently carried her anxiety and fight around the cancer. I realised that I was responsible for most of this pain in her face and that my egocentricity had made me cold and insensitive to the little cries of despair that she must have had often without ever imposing herself, without ever putting anything in my way. Suddenly I felt very bad.'*
>
> R. said that he would never forget that moment there in that waiting room, because just then, in that waiting silence, there was a song on the radio that he knew from way back, but had never taken in the lyrics. It was a song by Spandau Ballet – he couldn't remember the title – but in it, the vocalist sings with deep gratitude to his mother: *'and when she smiles she shows the lines of sacrifice'*. R. continues: *'I had the greatest trouble holding back my tears. I felt an almost unreal convergence of anger, pain, guilt and powerlessness in my body, but at the same time, I knew deep down that it was good that I was experiencing this now and that I was probably not ready to experience it before. I then grabbed her hand and I still don't know why, but she winked and gave me a little smile'.*

R.'s experience initially straddles a position somewhere between body mentalisation and focusing. R. mentalises his own physicality and tries to name what he is experiencing at that moment. However, when the track touches him deeply, he suddenly struggles to find his words and the authenticity of the physical experience slaps him in the face. He now feels and knows deep down – in one single moment – that he has never really known his wife, let alone allowed her in. Only now does he realise what he has done, while a seemingly banal song plays in the background. Realising this is what is experientially called a felt sense, in which an inner knowing, that transcends words and are anchored in the physical presence, clearly comes to the fore. Plasmans and Van Asten (2016) work here with the beautiful, layered metaphor of 'empathetic bodies' as a kind of physical alternative to what precedes when the body already knows, but the mind is yet to catch up. Such a specific moment, when words fail, is interpreted by Depestele et al. (2003) as a focus space:

> Further on, at certain moments of expressing this reflectively, he [the patient, JC] notices that he is stuck. He is in touch with an experience, but there is no more text. As soon as he focuses his attention on this wordless experience, the patient creates a platform whose supports are formed by his focus on the one hand and the indistinct point on the other: the focus space.
> (p. 183)

This is, in fact, what R. does when he allows the feeling, transforms it into an action (grabs his wife's hand) and then tries to find words. Focusing is about a deeply bodily felt process of change in which the conscious self is naturally involved, but is at the same time something deeper than this conscious self:

> [The change step, JC] occurs and happens to the knowing self; this self is included in it and taken to new 'insights', new self-knowledge. The change step comes from a process by which both the conscious and the unconscious are supported: that process was jammed, now it is moving.
> (Depestele, 2004, p. 119)

From this quote, we understand that R.'s experience does indeed go beyond what is meant by mentalisation. This distinction becomes even clearer when Depestele (2004) describes the process of change in terms of explicit and implicit knowing:

> An implicit knowing, a felt sense, is a not-knowing knowing. It is at the same time a knowing, a knowing that there is something; and at the same time a not knowing, a not knowing what it is, a not yet explicit knowing.
> (p. 110)

We could therefore paraphrase the focusing process as a process in which the self-considering self consciously learns to make room to listen to frequencies of knowledge to which one's own radio had not yet been tuned. Explicitly expressing what is being felt is not the most important objective, but rather the inner movement of what was already known on a deeper, implicit level. Leijssen (2004) talks about the importance of 'the right distance' with regard to the inner world of emotions, feelings and thoughts as an optimal inner relationship.

The body in therapy, a first possibility

If we revisit the working concept of 'embodied self-awareness' (ESA) from the previous chapter, we can already see that Fogel (2009) indicates that this form of body awareness can be approached from several ways or 'entry points' (p. 69). One of the central entry points in EBW is the integration of experiential myofascial tissue work with a 'listening touch' from ESA. In Chapters 4 and 7, we will discuss in more detail this listening touch and the muscular body armour that gradually installs itself as a protective structure over time in response to threats, anxiety or trauma. It is important to note here that these tissue tensions relate meaningfully to who we are and how we participate in the world as individuals. They have a meaningful relationship with our narrative and are an imprint of our relationship with ourselves, the other and the world. In this context, Mooij (2006) speaks of 'a hermeneutics of the body' in which non-intentional actions, sexuality, breathing and digestion express 'something'. Working on the tissue involved often leads to a liberating sensation in which suddenly clarity in experience, feeling or memory ensue. Fogel (2009) refers to this as the 'participatory memory':

> Participatory memories are lived re-enactments of personally significant experiences that have not yet become organized into verbal or conceptual narrative. . . . When experiencing a participatory memory, one is not thinking about the past. One is directly involved in a past experience as if it were occurring in the present.
>
> (p. 260)

Tissue tension is meaningfully related to who we are and how we participate in the world as individuals. They have a meaningful relationship with our narrative and are an imprint of our relationship to ourselves, the other and the world.

We also recognise in this description the (temporary) inability to translate the physical experience into words, while during the tissue work within EBW, a deep embodied knowing already manifests itself from the state of ESA. In experiential psychotherapy, this is reminiscent of the 'focus space' in which the patient is in contact with the experience, but there is no longer any text:

> If the patient can take the time to stay in touch with such an indistinct element and he tries to capture the essence – while questioning and waiting – first as a

specific physically felt quality and then with a quality-descriptive word, then a word or a few words can appear which – after letting them resonate a few times – continue to encapsulate the element.

(Depestele et al. 2003, p. 182)

We can further situate R.'s therapy against this background. The profound work on those body tissues that were an expression of his suffering – his muscle armour – was accompanied by both pain and relief. The alternation of a sometimes-relentless manual pressure on specific tissue points with soft and listening touch triggered a catharsis as a participatory memory several times. The supportive guidance of his experience with the help of words or images was several times at the basis of a bodily felt memory in the here-and-now. For example, there was that session in which working the muscle armour around the sternum, neck and jaw proved the catalyst for the next experience.

> Th.: 'Can you feel what I'm doing, R.?' [The pressure is slowly increasing]
> R.: 'This is almost unbearable, that's how sharp it feels'.
> Th.: 'Try to stay with this feeling'.
> R.: [Tears start to roll over his face] 'I thought I would have felt the worst pain in my bed, alone. Oh man, man, . . . I can't bear this anymore'. [The tears turn into crying and a fight against the pain.]
> Th.: [The pressure is no more than 6 on a scale of 10, but still R.'s reaction is disproportionate] 'What do you feel now R.? What kind of pain is this? Is this like the pain in your body over the past few weeks?'
> R.: 'No, damn it, this is just unbearable . . . you just cut through me . . . Man, man, ma . . . Ma . . . Ma . . .' [R. gets really angry, jolts up and hits the table. He cries incessantly now and asks, weeping, why this is necessary, why I do this to him.]
> Th.: [After a while] 'Is it possible to capture your emotion and pain in words or images now?'
> R.: [Gently recovering] 'I'm cold and feel sick . . . alone, alone at home, no one is there with me. [Silence, eyes still closed] It feels like someone is beating me with a heavy bar on the inside of my throat and chest. . . . I'm home alone and they're just not coming home, I've really been waiting a long time . . .' [Bodywork is being phased out and R. opens his eyes].

> Next, the images and words that presented themselves were given space. This is how R. tells us that he was back home in his parental home. I tell him that his angry and painful cries no longer sounded like 'man, man, man' but like 'ma-ma (mother)' at some point. R. hesitated, but indicated that he indeed felt that he was crying like a little boy and that it also felt as if it was that little boy had actually been on the treatment table.

After these EBW sessions, a lot of images and memories came up related to the experience of little R. That's how he was alone in the flat, for the umpteenth

66 *The body in therapy*

evening, and saw how he was thrown back and forth as a plaything of his emotions, his life, his suffering.

> *That evening, an image emerged that was ultimately different from the many representations and insights that he had often shared after a therapy session. The image was initially created by looking at the webcam on top of his laptop, but would gradually evolve from 'camera' to 'night vision device'. During the last phase of his therapy, R. often tried to explain to me what was so different since he had seen this night vision device as a metaphor. Although he felt deep down that this image encapsulated what he actually couldn't put into words, it was difficult to explain for him. He emphasised that he had never been so sure in his life that things were good the way they were. He now saw what it should have been like, without understanding why it had gone the other way. He experienced it as something that had ruined him and had impacted on his life, causing something in him to snap. The 'snapping' – however frightening it had been for a long time – had now made room for a deep sense of peace and confidence.*

This process is very much in line with the 'space for self-symbolisation' that Depestele describes (2000). The feature of this phase is shown in the following quote and at the same time describes what happened to R.:

> After the session, new ideas and associations sometimes appear unexpectedly out of nowhere. The patient must be open to this and receive it; otherwise it will be lost. These new ideas happen to the patient without him doing anything. It is the deeper process itself that has led to an unquestionably forward-looking symbolisation: we can refer to this as self-symbolisation. This inner space of experience is formed by the deep experience that opens itself up spontaneously and by the receptive patient.
>
> (Depestele et al., 2003, p. 183)

Although what is described here as a self-symbolisation actually happened to R., it is difficult to pinpoint specifically when this started. The process of ESA during EBW cannot simply be charted in hierarchical or linear chronology. It is rather a searching, shifting and pulsating movement that tries to anchor itself in many forms of consciousness. The dynamic, moving and even organic nature of this awareness process is explained well by Leijssen (2009) when she describes focusing as a broadening of consciousness:

> The process which takes place during focusing, implies a subtle balance between going somewhere and allowing something to come to you, deliberately striving and letting go, working and receiving, controlling and being touched, committing and surrendering. The moment of change happens to the person as something that gives itself, that surprises, that also evokes gratitude.
>
> (p. 112)

Tools for therapy

- *In EBW, we encounter different bodies, such as the developmental psychological body that was touched, nourished and cared for, the psychodynamic body that learned to organise and maintain itself within the early affective learning history, but also the overwhelming, 'impossible' body of psychoanalysis that is seemingly difficult to unite with the idea of the body as a possibility for self-actualisation and 'coming home' within the humanist-existential traditions.*
- *Mentalisation and focusing are well-known concepts and techniques within mainstream psychotherapy, both of which can be incorporated in an integrated model to treat the difficult body. In this respect, mentalisation is more situated near CSA on one end of the spectrum, whereas focusing is similar to the pre-reflective nature of ESA. Working with the felt sense also resonates strongly with what happens during deep experiential bodywork.*
- *The experiential dimensions of pre-implicit, implicit and explicit knowing relate to the layering of embodiment, CSA and ESA within EBW.*

Note

1 Fonagy (Fonagy et al., 2015; Allison & Fonagy, 2016) corrects this vision and mentions in his more recent works 'epistemic trust' as the most fundamental factor in psychopathological images.

Blanket, 2014, collage on paper, 30 × 16 × 4.2 cm, private collection, Rotterdam.

4 The tense body

A difficult body is often tense in several ways. First of all, it feels tense for the patient; the body feels awkward, is too constricting or just too limp and fails to cooperate. In addition, it also maintains a tense relationship with the world. A cramped posture, whether or not it is conspicuously constricted, can translate into inhibited or hesitant movements, as well as reckless or impulsive actions. The tension, however, is also in the body itself, more specifically in the myofascial tissue. This was formerly referred to as the muscular tissue, or the muscles. In the introduction, we already mentioned Wilhelm Reich, who introduced the idea of a muscle armour in the first half of the last century. The term 'myofascial' refers to more current views in which the close, functional relationship between the muscles (*myo*) and the associated connective tissues (*fascia*) is emphasised (Huijing & Langevin, 2009; Schleip et al., 2012). Myofascial refers to all these structures that shape and influence each other. In this respect, the myofascial tissue organises itself not only as local tension, but rather as a pattern of tension lines that are functional and necessary to a certain extent. In this fourth chapter, we will discuss in detail this clinical phenomenon of the myofascial tense body as armour, the way in which it comes about and what it means for EBW. To this end, we predominantly use the top-right quadrant, in which current research shows that the concept of muscle armour needs to be further differentiated into different functional somatic layers and systems. This degree of anatomical and neurophysiological knowledge is essential for at least two questions in psychosomatic practice namely 'Where should I start on the muscle armour' and 'How can I best carry out my manual approach'. This 'where' and 'how' are fundamental, if you want to be able to work with the body as an entry point in an expert and sophisticated way. Just as a psychotherapist does not just chat with his patient, it would be a sad misconception to think that the body therapist just feels and massages his way round in a random manner.

The muscle armour, an echo from the past

The idea of a body organising itself on a muscular level in tension lines to form a certain pattern of posture and movement is not new, certainly not in myofascial body therapies such as Rolfing, osteopathy or more recent methods

(Chaitow, 2016). One of the pioneers of body psychotherapy (BPT), Wilhelm Reich (1897–1957), already spoke in the last century of a muscle armour that was part of a more global character armour. In doing so, Reich went much further than psychoanalysis at the time, establishing a link between typical patterns of tension and blockages in the body, on the one hand, and the character structure of the individual, on the other hand. As a Freudian-trained psychoanalyst, he initially situated these armours within a paradigm of drives, blocked *libido* and censored aggression. However, Reich's pioneering work was ultimately his therapeutic approach, in which he actually started to work with the body. As a basic principle, however, he did insist on the importance of catharsis,[1] in which blocked energetic processes that have jammed the somatic structures are released.

Although we will clarify later that contemporary BPT certainly no longer works exclusively with emotional discharge or only seeks out catharsis, Reich has caused a fundamental shift. In *Function of the Orgasm* (Reich, 1973) he himself spoke of 'the breakthrough into the vegetative realm' with which he gave his therapy its own unique interpretation. In order to understand this, we must first take a step back to the origin of the muscle armour.

For Reich (idem), muscle tissue is the structure that stores and retains energy. He regards this energy as a kind of biopsychic energy which he calls 'bio-electricity' (p. 272). Conversely, he observes that every time he releases tense muscle tissue, there is a discharge of one of the three basic excitations that he believes the body knows, namely, anxiety, anger/hate or sexual energy/libido. So chronically tense muscles block and store biopsychic energy associated with basic drives and emotions. On the other hand, the latter are released when the tension is removed from the muscular tissue (idem). In psychoanalytic jargon, one speaks of *Besetzung* or cathexis. Within the Reichian bodywork, this reciprocal relationship between tissue and emotion forms a therapeutic foundation and is based on an intrinsically present, healing and self-regulating capacity of the body. Put more simply, Reich assumed that if the armour could be shattered, the rest would follow. When we stylise this, the therapist turns out to be a kind of intermediary, a facilitator who, as an expert, presses the right buttons so that the body is unblocked and the innate repair mechanism can be mobilised. In terms of strictly somatic therapies, 'manipulation' of the tissue must lead to a correct 'release'. With Reich, the patient must arrive at the correct 'catharsis', which often meant crying, shouting or hitting.

Although we have to guard against an overly caricatural representation here (because crying, for example, does indeed often have a healing effect), it is true that today, on the basis of research, we are urged to indulge in some fine-tuning. For example, Cornell (2015) points out that Reich did not see that his 'breakthrough into the vegetative realm' was usually a 'breakthrough into the infantile realm' (p. 94). Furthermore, Reich had little eye for the interpersonal field of interaction, holding or (counter-)transference and saw himself rather as an objective observer who, like a natural scientist, can stand outside the process (idem). Reich also saw the armour as something to be broken or even attacked, 'attacking the muscular armour' (Raknes, 2004, p. 22). This fitted in with a rather harsh therapeutic approach, often resulting in violent abreactions (Totton, 1998). This method is also approached differently in the light of current psychotherapeutic views. In this chapter, we will discuss in more detail the relationship between bodywork and subcortical processes concerning regulation, emotion and memory. While BPT is a powerful entry point to the infantile domain of experience and memory, it also requires the right framework and expertise for working with this vulnerable, fragile and often unstable part of the patient. On balance, every therapy – including EBW – hinges on the way it is able to guide the patient towards integration of all the elements that have been set in motion during the therapeutic process.

The echo of lasting change and integration can also be heard in the reworded narrative.

We revisit the muscle armour. Reich (1972) defines this as 'the experience-dependent development of a protective shell of muscle tension grown over time in response to a history of threat, anxiety and trauma' (in Fogel, 2009, p. 196). He describes 'the spasm of the musculature' as 'the somatic side of the process of repression and the basis of its continued preservation' and notes: 'It is never an individual muscle but rather muscle groups which belong to a functional unit' (Reich, 1973). These definitions were excellent at the time and are still very enlightening for clinical practice to this day. First of all, we are talking about a muscular protective layer that has been created on the basis of experiences over a longer period of time and in response to threats, anxiety or trauma. This tense tissue structure is, in fact, the somatic expression of a process of suppression that organises itself into functional muscular patterns, rather than into isolated local tissues. Finally, this pattern formation also contributes to the survival of the muscle armour. The ego is thus partly formed and influenced by these physical tensions (Totton, 1998). If we then look at the characteristics that Reich attributed to the muscle armour, the clinical reality becomes even more recognisable, especially for body therapists who work specifically with the myofascial body or psychosomatic disorders (translated from Heller, 2012):

1   the muscle armour makes coordination between different parts of the body unyielding and stiff
2   the muscle armour reduces freedom of posture and movement
3   the muscle armour obstructs breathing
4   the muscle armour reduces the perception of what is happening in the body
5   the muscle armour suppresses vitality (libido) and absorbs the anxiety that arises from this suppression.

From this description, it is clear that Reich (1994) was no longer a Freudian psychoanalyst, but focused on the body as a biological substrate and entry point in therapy. The latter is also evident from the central importance he attached to breathing and grounding of the body during therapeutic work. Totton (1998) points out that Reich equated breathing as a technique with the importance Freud gave to free association. In practice, what appeals most to the imagination is that Reich saw the muscle armour as a structured symptom in which both the unconscious impulses and the forces that had to control these impulses were contained. It was, therefore, only a small step for him to then analyse character structures on the basis of these typical armour patterns. In BPT, this analysis is called 'body reading'. So, in addition to a listening touch, the ability to read the body plays a decisive role in EBW. When we described earlier that for Freud, the ego is first and foremost a body-self, then he meant that the ego must try to control the biopsychic energy that holds sway in the unbound self. Although Reich and Freud are largely on the same page with regard to the ego, a remarkable difference lies in the importance that Reich attaches to the musculature as a substrate for this binding of energy:

> The muscular armour is first formed through its participation in the repression of specific affects and their repression. However, gradually, these tensions also influence other muscles and cause general compensating postural disturbances. It thus creates a structure of tensions that follow bodily causal chains built parallel to mental defenses and then influence the way the mind inhabits the body and what surrounds it.
>
> (Heller, 2012, p. 450)

For Reich, the reciprocal relationship between body and *psyche* literally consolidates in the muscle tissue that gradually becomes like a concrete armour, which means it will be maintained.

A patient, for example, suppresses anger that under no circumstances may be expressed. The muscles that are involved in this process of blocking off and keeping inside are charged with the energy of anger. Gradually, these muscles become more and more dysfunctional: they get more rigid, resulting in reduced mobility, sensitive hardened areas, congestion and stasis in the tissue and a decreased body awareness. Jaw, chewing and respiratory muscles, but also voice, facial expressions and eye muscles are affected. The affect anger is thus partly lifted and shifted to the armour, where the energy is bound and locked into the somatic structures of the body. The jaw, chewing, respiratory and mimic muscles are, therefore, the somatic expression of this anger (expression-substrate), but at the same time they are also responsible for not letting it come out (suppression-substrate). Deep myofascial work in this region of the body is, therefore, in a certain sense 'double' work, or perhaps more accurately 'de-duplicating' work. The paradoxical task of the armour – both expression and suppression – is eliminated or, at least, exposed.

As Reich has just pointed out, these charged tissues reinforce the disturbed pattern of suppression, but they also often appear to stimulate the underlying emotion, so that the vicious circle continues. Accordingly, Ritz et al. (2013) describe how respiratory muscles in anxiety patients start to function as triggers for anxiety. Because, for example, the tense muscles between the ribs (intercostal muscles) or deep in the neck (*mm. scaleni*) obstruct the adequate expansion of the chest, the panic-prone patient becomes anxious again with sudden and deep breathing. This happens, for example, during more intense breathing while practising sports, climbing stairs or just feeling sudden emotions.

The muscle armour 2.0

Since the muscle armour, as a working concept, occupies a fundamental place within EBW, we have to ask ourselves how this concept can be translated into current scientific frameworks and theories. In what way can this well-considered, clinical concept, which arose solely on the basis of empirical observation, be underpinned by scientific findings? In the introduction, we stated that this body is often tense in several ways. Tension should be understood here as excess (hypertonia/hypertension) or insufficient (hypotonia/hypotension) charge.

Oddly enough, the patient does not have to be aware of this; he often does not know that his body is tense. That is to say, sometimes he does know from a reflective position, such as CSA and is a kind of reporter about his own body. But he has no contact with his body from ESA and, in that sense, does not really know what he is talking about. The initial phase of 'body reading' and 'listening touch' is important during EBW to visualise the tense body for the first time. Allow me to clarify this by means of the following case:

> S. is a 37-year-old man who suffers from irritable bowel syndrome and tension headaches. Since his adolescence, he has suffered panic attacks, albeit sporadically. With his sagging, sway-back posture, S. makes an unfit impression, which is reinforced by excessive sweating on his forehead and very pale complexion. On his diaphragm, there is a tight band with his rib sides folded inwards. Although he is not an obese type at all, his lower abdomen is remarkably convex and slack. S.'s legs seem frail and literally subordinate to his torso, and are turned inwards with his feet pushed away. His arms seem to be stockier, which is due to an imbalance in the fitness training. They lack functional strength and look more like the shoulder pads rugby players wear.
>
> When I touch his neck, I notice how rock-solid the myofascial tissue is here. The skin feels clammy and cold and gives the impression of being adhesive. Underneath, the muscle tissue is tense with hardened areas here and there that react very sensitively. With gentle movement, the stiffness is even more noticeable and it appears that articulated movement of the neck is difficult; it moves as one block. The muscles on both sides of the neck (sternocleidomastoid muscles) are taut and this tension extends to the floor of mouth and face. When we listen to the hyoid region at the front of the neck, it appears to function in a very 'retracted' manner, which makes swallowing difficult. Inside the mouth (intrabucally), we find very sensitive tender points at the jaw joint and it is difficult to open his mouth wide. This tension continues via the sternum (sterno-mediastinal region) to the abdomen, which is inflated and tight, reacts hyperactively to touch and shows no movement when breathing. This appears to be a combination of a tickly, painful defence system.

The idea of the myofascial substrate as an imprint of – or at least significant in relation to – psycho-emotional processes and disruptions can be found in older (Sainsbury & Gibson, 1954), but also in recent literature under various headings. For example, reference is made to the relationship between breathing, posture and chronic pelvic floor complaints (Lee et al., 2008), but also between breathing and lower back pain (Smith et al., 2006), posture, movement patterns, body experience and chronic pain (Haugstad et al., 2006), jaw complaints and neural abnormalities in the limbic system (Younger et al., 2010; Gameiro et al., 2006), trauma and chronic pelvic floor complaints (Fenton, 2007; Fenton et al., 2012), respiratory musculature, anxiety and hyperventilation (Ritz et al., 2013) and trauma and skin disorders (Gupta & Gupta, 2012; Gupta et al., 2005).

But how are we supposed to understand the origin of this myofascial tension? In other words, what causes the muscle armour? Reich (1973) himself thought of this in terms of a biopsychic energy that moved as 'vegetative currents' that he saw coursing throughout the body (p. 268). These currents do not follow an exclusive anatomical structure (e.g. blood vessels or nerves), but rather spread in a diffuse manner 'like dye in clear water and are reminiscent of the concept of "Chi" from Chinese medicine' (Heller, 2012, p. 469).[2] In therapy, they are stimulated by deep bodywork, powerful breathing or grounding. Clinically, the patient perceives them as a tingling sensation, hot or cold chills, itching, pins and needles, muscle spasms or physical sensations of fullness, emptiness or tension, for example. When this vegetative current of energy becomes blocked, an affect blockade ensues, causing problems of tissue flow on a somatic level and defensive rigidity on a psychological level (Totton, 1998). The suppression of libidinous energy, which is central to psychoanalysis, thus acquires a concrete somatic topicality from Reich: it takes place *in* the muscle armour. Character structures are then understood as character armour that represent a whole range of affect blockades.[3] In other words, for Reich, the armour is a defensive muscular organisation to suppress forbidden, undesirable or impossible impulses. In this way, he literally builds a psychosomatic bridge and pays explicit attention to both sides of the bridge. On the somatic side, one even zooms in on the level of histological and physiological processes in muscle tissue and tries to understand how the armour is created:

> In becoming rigid, the muscle tissues acquire a particular metabolic quality that afterwards will influence the vegetative dynamics and the functioning of the sensorimotor system. It then becomes possible to conceptualize that the defense system which structures the ego is in connection with these systems that structure and inhibit the behavioural repertoire.
>
> (in Heller, 2012, p. 425)

In therapy, currents are generated by deep bodywork, powerful breathing or grounding. The patient perceives them as tingling, hot or cold chills, itching, needle pricks, muscle shocks or physical sensations of fullness, emptiness or tension. When this vegetative flow of energy is blocked, an affect blockade is formed, causing problems of tissue flow on a somatic level and defensive rigidity on a psychological level.

Interestingly, myofascial research confirms similar physiological processes. Simons and Mense (1998) conclude in their review 'Understanding and measurement of muscle tone as related to clinical muscle pain' that muscle tension is partly determined by the viscoelastic and physiological state of the myofascial tissue and this independently of conscious muscle activity. On the other hand, certain fascial layers that surround the muscle (in particular the *perimysium*) appear to have contractile properties with which they determine the degree of passive muscle stiffness, especially in the case of tonic or postural muscles (Schleip et al., 2005, 2006, 2019). This is not, therefore, about muscle tissue itself that stretches, but about the fascial packaging around the muscle. Later, we will see that both the muscle part (*myo-*) and the packaging part (*fascia*) are sensitive to stress and can tense up independently of each other. This is indirectly strongly determined by unconscious influences such as mood or stress level in which personality traits, such as alexithymia or negative affect, play a role. The degree of tension of the armour is therefore a myofascial phenomenon. Clinically, we already recognize this when we want to gain an impression of the patient's depth tension. Often, the tissue feels hard and taut, without any obvious reason. Typical examples are neck and neck muscles[4] (such as the sternocleidomastoid muscle and the scaleni muscles) or the suboccipital muscles under the skull that contract when the patient lies on his back and, therefore, do not actually require any activity from these structures. Instead of a soft, tender quality, we find stiff, taut musculature that forms a sleeve from neck to skull. But equally, therapists will recognise this 'unnecessary' depth tension at, for example, the deep adductors, soles of the feet, diaphragm and iliopsoas or jaw musculature. Many patients also unconsciously tighten their legs, as if to brace themselves, or their arms, literally making fists without realising it.

Another indication of unconscious effects on myofascial tension can be found in Abbott et al. (2013) and Hinz et al. (2012), among others, who point to the role of myofibroblasts in determining the basal tonus of connective tissue. These connective tissue cells can contract and are known, for example, for their role in wound healing. Myofibroblasts appear to be present in places where this was not expected, such as in the fascial tissue.[5] Schleip (2003a, 2003b) and Schleip and Jäger (2012) put forward the hypothesis of a phenomenon called fascial pre-tension that is caused by these myofibroblasts. Under the influence of stress and independent of muscular activity – remember the muscle part – this fascial pre-tension could then lead to increased tension of the fascial tissue – remember the packaging part – and thus 'lock' the body in that particular location. This could partly explain the development of the myofascial armour, On the other hand, we already mentioned that the defensive armour arises as a reaction to early childhood experiences of anxiety, trauma and threat. This path is also supported by scientific findings. For example, there is extensive research that confirms the relationship between childhood abuse and chronic back pain (Leisner et al., 2014), childhood abuse and migraine (Tietjen et al., 2010) and abuse and disturbed pain processing (Tesarz et al., 2015, 2016). A model that can help to understand how traumatic experiences can lead to far-reaching changes within the myofascial body and the development of an armour, can be found, for example, in Porges (2009).

In his 'Poly- vagal Theory', he situates trauma within a spectrum of normally elevated sympathetic activity to a state of extremely elevated sympathetic and parasympathetic activity. This extreme condition is called 'tonic immobility' and is characterised by a paradoxical activation of both the parasympathetic 'rest-and-digest' and the sympathetic 'fight-flight' (Levine, 1977, 2005, 2007, 2014a, 2014b). For this seemingly contradictory situation, Porges refers to the oldest, dorsal branch of the *vagus* nerve that controls the most basic survival system of 'death feigning'. When fighting or fleeing no longer seem an option, a switch is made to a total shut-down that is often accompanied by a decrease, or loss, of consciousness and manifests itself in tonic immobility. This is seen in (severely) traumatised patients who often tend to dissociate and experience deep somatic disorder, but also in people with medically unexplained symptoms or chronic pain where the body then appears cold, silent or even 'dead'. Within Porges' dimensional model, severe trauma, chronic neglect and abuse are dominated by the system of tonic immobility and being closed down, while more acute or one-off trauma activates the evolutionary less fundamental fighting/flight system (Levine, 2005). Patients with unexplained symptoms do indeed seem to be stuck in this first dimension more often. Central to many more recent forms of BPT, such as the sensorimotor approach (Ogden et al., 2006), Somatic Experiencing (Levine, 2014a, 2014b) or Van der Kolk's trauma therapy (2014), is therefore the guidance of the patient towards an optimal arousal zone or 'window of tolerance' (Siegel, 1999) between the more extreme positions of hyper-arousal (fight-flight) and hypo-arousal (tonic immobility). For a more detailed analysis of the concept of tonic immobility and other trauma models, please refer to the website of this book.

Levine (2005, 2014a, 2014b) situates trauma – or rather, the traumatic effect – in the stagnation of these response systems, as a result of which incomplete physiological reactions continue to harass the body and further compromise recovery. Payne et al. (2015) point to the consequences of this failing situation for the completion or 'complementing' of the systems set in motion and define trauma as 'biological incompletion, frozen in time'. If the intended or programmed actions for survival, such as movements and postures, cannot be accomplished, then the discharge system fails for the extreme amount of energy that has been released. Because of this inability to discharge, the energy cannot be evacuated from the body and becomes lodged in the tissue, particularly in specific neuromuscular patterns.

In a sense, this is nothing new, since trauma was for Freud 'an increase in tension that could not be adequately removed by the neuronal system' (Verhaeghe, 2006, p. 15) and was harmful 'as long as it was frozen, fixed, unresponsive and therefore not reduced' (idem, p. 18). Schore (2001, p. 68) also describes how early affective object relations are encoded in the neuromuscular system: 'The neuromuscular and autonomic nervous systems encode patterns of early object relations, so that there may be a long-term autobiographical memory of a pathological internal object relation, that becomes the unconscious working model'. Even this – the far-reaching influence of early affective experiences, attachment and environment – is in itself anything but new in psychodynamic thinking and reminds us of a number of previously introduced concepts. There is the marinade metaphor from Chapter 2, for example, which can be freely translated as the objectal foundation that is defined from the outset in the myofascial system and the autonomous nervous system, thus helping to shape the way in which the individual is present in the world (embodiment) and tries to understand himself, the other and the world (narrative). We will see that the non-verbal brain, in particular, is responsible for process-related and emotional memory storage, together with various basal control systems at brainstem level. The neuromuscular and neurovegetative basis of the objectal foundation thus contributes to the unconscious working model of early, internalised object relationships. Bloom (2006) summarises these Reichian elements in the interest of the body as affect-regulator: 'Because the body plays a key role in affect regulation (through the inhibition of breathing or tightening of musculature, for example), its significance would seem central in the study of primitive psychic states'.

This affect-regulating dynamic of the body is also evident in Tronick's Still-Face experiment (Mesman et al., 2009; Weinberg et al., 2008; Weinberg & Tronick, 1994) (available via YouTube). If one looks closely at the reaction of the children during this test, it is striking how the body indeed functions as a regulator of tension, stress and emotions. As the mother tunes out and stares into space, the physical stress increases in the small child that starts to become tense and frantic. The whole body is involved, from facial expressions to fists and trunk. In an attempt to evacuate this charge, the whole muscle armour starts to move, combined with screaming and finally crying. This is, in fact, reminiscent of Bick's second skin, which we described in the previous chapter, where the coping of absent containment also took place via rigid muscle tension and blocking the breathing. A similar pattern of affect-regulating dynamics through the body is also observed in a totally different and, this time non-threatening, situation, like in the Marshmallow test (available via YouTube). Here, too, there is a form of stress, since in this test, the children are asked to postpone eating a piece of marshmallow that is in front of them. Depending on their age – and therefore the possibilities for parking this pleasure ('delay of gratification') – we see that, especially the young children, bring out a whole battery of physical coping strategies, ranging from wobbling to grimacing or even knocking on one's own head, in an attempt to evacuate the excess energy through the body and the myofascial tissue. This makes it clear that the concept of muscle armour also requires a more development-dynamic perspective.

Let's take a young child who grows up in a family climate where there is hardly any room for emotional exploration. Mother cannot adequately mirror the emotional inner world and father can only tolerate the drives of the little child by blocking them off massively with grumpiness, shouts or aggressive behaviour. In this way, the child learns that anything that comes from his or her own confused inner world is undesirable and threatening or simply 'not allowed'. Normal tantrums or crying, for example, are not allowed, because they are not tolerated by the environment and lead to threats. Mother barely

> *picks up the signals and she can't give them back according to the child's needs and father's reactions are very frightening. As a result, the child has to do something to keep the situation livable. The latter, however, is not about a conscious, intentional action by the child, nor is it preceded by analysis and planning. On the contrary, the one-year-old child does not have any tools at his disposal with which he could deal with something consciously. There is no shared (symbolic) language yet, operational thinking is far from present and speaking is not an option. At least, if we interpret speaking in a narrow sense, because the child does, of course, use a language, also speaks and has early mental processes that focus on the body, the physical. So the only thing it can do is react with its body, largely unconsciously. Throwing a tantrum or being absent and not interacting, vomiting and spitting, not making bowel movements, avoiding eye contact and freezing when a loud voice is used or just keep on trying to catch someone's eye until they react.*

From this vignette, we understand that the muscle armour can be easily updated to contemporary visions and findings, taking into account the complex influence between biological structures and processes, on the one hand, and psychological experiences and learning history, on the other hand. In terms of structure, for example, a distinction can be drawn between the fascial tissue and the underlying muscle tissue, both of which can react with tightening (contraction) in case of stress or trauma. Clinically, this means that the muscle armour is myofascial and not – as previously thought – only a matter of muscles. At process level, central neuromuscular and neurovegetative control systems contribute to the development of the myofascial armour. Various models, such as the polyvagal theory, window of tolerance, tonic immobility or biological incompletion, clarify each aspect of these complex interactions that make us see why the body reacts the way it does. At the same time, models such as the Core Responses Network (Payne et al., 2015) and the Preparatory Set (Payne & Crane-Godreau, 2015) underline that the impact of trauma always requires a multimodal approach, of which the myofascial system is only one part. In addition to these enlightening neurobiological insights, the psychological perspective teaches us that the armouring of the body should primarily be understood as a form of affect-regulation. As far as myofascial armour is concerned, we remember that continued exposure to negative context and experiences through numerous processes actually impacts on the tissue and the body changes both on a structural and on a process level in the hope of being able to provide some answer or simply survive. And this brings us back to the definition of Reich, which is where we started. After this brief clarification of the how and why of the muscle armour, let's take a look at the what and where.

The myofascial middle layer in experiential bodywork

In the first part of this chapter, the muscle armour was described as a layered structure within the tense body of the patient. This multi-layered structure will be discussed in the next chapter where we will map out the developmental psychological growth of body awareness based on Wilber's *fulcrum* concept. In the

The tense body 81

second part of this chapter, we look at the muscle armour from a biological, top-right quadrant perspective and start with a lesson in anatomy. Although the anatomical reality also requires sufficient nuance, for the sake of simplicity, we could also speak of successive bodies, namely, as three concentric layers: an outer one, a middle one and a deep one. The outer layer can then roughly be seen as the larger movement muscles, while the deep layer represents the (myo-)fascial tissues just around the spine. The middle layer consists of myofascial structures of functional systems, such as chewing, swallowing, breathing, digestion or sexuality. Anatomically, this layer is therefore situated in the face and neck region, chest, abdomen and small pelvis, plus some deep structures in lower and upper limb measures. It has a complex, but intriguing, structure. In EBW, we speak of the myofascial middle layer (MML) (see Figure 4.1), which we consider to be an important treatment

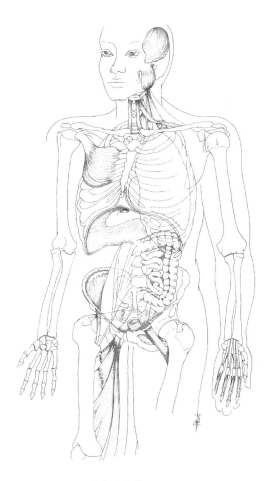

Figure 4.1 Some core structures of the MML

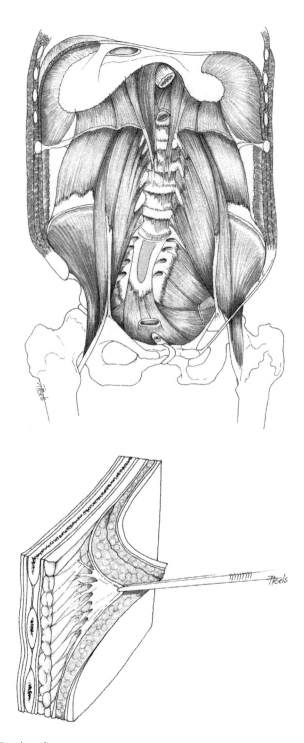

Figure 4.1 (Continued)

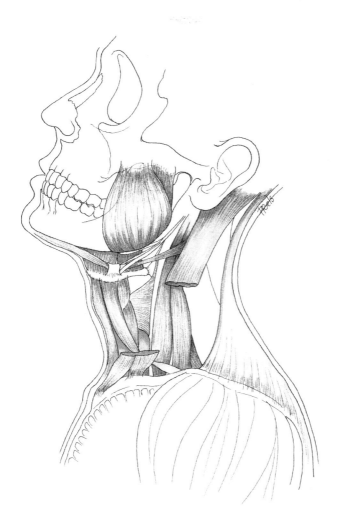

Figure 4.1 (Continued)

substrate when it comes to the psychosomatic body. In Chapter 5, we will discuss in detail the early body development of sucking, chewing, breathing, swallowing, digesting and excreting with which this MML is closely interwoven. This early body will be known there as the uroboric-pranic body. Here, we will first consider the myofascial structures that shape this body in the top-right quadrant.

A first observation is indeed that this MML consists of the myofascial layer that is one of the first to be stimulated in subject development. Functions such as sucking, drinking and swallowing, but also breathing, screaming, crying, digesting and excreting are not only our most basic functions, they are also our first attempts

84 *The tense body*

at processing the outside world. It is interesting to note that many psychosomatic and unexplainable complaints are related to these basic systems of functioning and regulation – and thus with the uroboric-pranic body and the MML. Just think of hyperventilation in case of panic, digestive complaints or irritable intestines, teeth grinding in case of stress and difficulties in the sexual arena. In other words, these functional systems within the MML appear to be very sensitive to tension and stress.

In passing, we can observe that within mainstream somatic therapy, such as physiotherapy, little or no attention is paid to these myofascial structures in the context of psychosomatic stress disorders. In a somewhat black-and-white way, we could claim that the physiotherapist is mainly concerned with the outer layer of larger muscle systems that are focused on movement and the deeper muscles around the spine that are responsible for stability (deep layer). Although the approach to these two layers may be appropriate and useful (e.g. Kim et al., 2015), it is often less suitable in the context of psychosomatic disorders. Sometimes, it is, in fact, even counterproductive, for example by carelessly prescribing the today somewhat hyped core-stability training. Just think of patients who already present with a muscle armour that is so rigid, they can hardly experience flexibility in their body. More specific myofascial therapies (Chaitow, 2016), such as osteopathy and myofascial release therapies, would be expected to include the MML in their approach – which they do – but many of these approaches remain very focused on structural parameters within the top-right quadrant. Interesting exceptions to this are Rolfing (from Ida Rolf) and Postural Integration (from Jack Painter),[6] which work with body experience based on the whole fascial system. Most regular body therapies treat, for example, the deep neck or gluteal muscles, but only with a view to stretching and relaxing trigger points or building up strength. What is lacking is the experiential integration in the treatment or, in terms of the Four Quadrant Model, the left side. So, despite the fact that myofascial therapists do important work with the psychosomatic body, they often lack the background theory and therapeutic framework to grasp and guide the entire dimension of psychosomatic processes (Heller, 2012). From the introduction of this book, we remember that this is precisely where BPT's work domain is situated and the integration that EBW aims to achieve. Let's first subject the MML to a further analysis from the top-right quadrant.

An anatomical view of the myofascial middle layer

In his book *Anatomy Trains*, Thomas Meyers (2014) works out a myofascial approach within the top-right quadrant. Although he indicates that his model is clinically and empirically founded rather than strictly anatomically scientific, his concept of myofascial axes is a thorough and more than commendable attempt to give therapists handles for their clinical work. Meyers (idem) first describes six myofascial axes or lines, the functionality of which lies in movement and stability. In addition, he formulates a seventh 'deep frontal line', which he calls 'the body's myofascial core' (p. 185).[7] Although not quite the same, this deep line of Meyers has a clear overlap with what we understand here as the MML. This deep frontal line turns out to be different from the other axes, as it is three-dimensionally organised and literally creates room. Think, for example, of the diaphragm or the pelvic floor. It is also typical that this deep frontal line is not responsible for specific movements (with the exception of hip flexion/adduction and breathing), but does affect all movements. It consists of dense fascia and slow-twitch fibres that support endurance rather than fast muscle action. It facilitates the good working order of the other lines, or at least makes it possible. Meyers (idem) also points out that problems of this deep line are barely visible at first and certainly not to the untrained eye. However, a dysfunctional deep frontal line also weighs heavily on the body's biomechanical proportions. For example, underlying tension in the pelvic floor can contribute to chronic irritation of the groin (adductors) or a neck region that is too tense can have a detrimental effect on the shoulder muscles, such as the *supraspinatus*. Typical for the functioning of these functional myofascial chains – and the MML in particular – is that tension can travel from one region to another, sometimes even as a result of the therapy. Often the tension then literally takes a plunge into the depths and fixes itself in the MML: 'Sometimes, tension may move from an easily accessible part, situated on the surface of the body (e.g. the shoulders) to a less accessible part (e.g. the diaphragm or the psoas)' (Heller, 2012, p. 543). Stecco (2015) points to what she calls 'myofascial expansions' that manifest themselves as connecting structures between different regions or layers: 'It becomes apparent, therefore, that for almost all of our movements, specific muscles are activated and selective portions of the deep fascia are stretched by way of specific myofascial expansions. Myofascial expansions permit reciprocal feedback between fascia and muscles' (p. 69).

If we leave Meyers' clinical-empirical approach aside, scientific research has shown that there is a great deal of evidence to support the idea of a layered myofascial body. In purely anatomical terms, the myofascial substrate effectively consists of various tissue layers that we situate briefly. First of all, there is the most superficial layer that is formed by the skin. Strictly speaking, however, this layer does not form part of the fascial tissue, since skin embryologically originates from a tissue other than fascia (*ectoderm* instead of *mesoderm*). It goes without saying that the skin is, of course, crucial from a clinical-therapeutic point of view as a contact surface for myofascial work.[8]

Under the skin, there is then a rich subcutaneous region[9] with a first 'real' fascial layer, the *fascia superficialis*. Therapeutically, in EBW, we take all these layers – skin, subcutaneous tissue and superficial fascia – together as one functional point of reference for the practice and refer to this as layer 1 (Figure 4.2). A second 'real' fascial layer, which is much denser and more rigid in nature than layer 1, can be found further down the line. This layer is the *fascia profunda* and plays a major role in the deep myofascial bodywork. Whereas the *fascia superficialis* forms a non-contiguous network, the *fascia profunda* is considered to be a body-wide and continuous envelope of muscles, organs and body cavities. This layer – together with the *epimysium* that lies just below it – is called layer 2. Therapeutically, this second layer is therefore approached as a single continuity that functionally connects various muscles and regions.

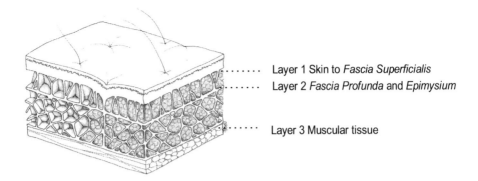

Figure 4.2 Three functional layers within the myofascial tissue

The 'real' muscle tissue lies underneath and has its own fascial tissue system that penetrates the muscle ever more deeply and finely.[10] This layer 3 therefore contains the muscle tissue as it is generally recognised because of its contractile properties. With regard to this contractile ability, it is important to note that the generated forces in layer 3 achieve their functional range to a large extent through the cooperation with layer 2. The *fascia profunda* was, after all, the dense structure that forms a body-wide connection system and can, thus, further direct the resulting forces (Stecco, 2015). This is the basis for thinking and working with myofascial chains, axes or lines.

Why is this further detail of layers important now? To answer this, we need to take a brief look at the relationship between these myofascial layers and their respective functions as receptor organs.

Thus, all of the skin, *fascia superficialis* and superficial fat layers – layer 1 in other words – not only plays a nourishing and draining role, it is mainly involved in exteroceptive abilities, such as the sense of touch. The *fascia profunda* and the underlying muscle fascia – i.e. layers 2 and 3 – are more responsible for proprioception and peripheral motor coordination[11] (Stecco, 2015).

This partly answers the question of where and how to tackle the muscle armour. After all, the depth of manual work appears to cause different effects in terms of contact with the outside world (exteroception), the sense of one's own presence in space (proprioception) and influence on the muscle function and coordination. Another dimension of perception that is at least as crucial for EBW – called interoception – relates even more explicitly to these layers, as we will discover in a moment. It should be noted that some researchers, such as Guimberteau and Armstrong (2015), go one step further and insist on considering myofascial tissue as one large network that, at specific locations and depths, densifies to a certain layer or diffuses to a certain type of tissue by the presence of certain cells. According to them, therefore, there are no demarcated layers present in the human body, only compaction and structure/functional adjustments. This vision, therefore, further encourages us to see the myofascial body as one functional whole that adapts under the influence of various external factors from the right quadrants, such as environmental stress, but certainly also left-quadrant factors, such as emotional stress. The armour as an attempt to absorb the influence of these factors is, therefore, gradually evolving from a functional adaptive substrate to a dysfunctional and rigid structure. When we mentioned a moment ago that tensions can move from superficial to deep (and vice versa) through the three myofascial layers between different regions, the scientific research of Guimberteau and Armstrong (idem) makes this very plausible. Let us revisit the three layers briefly.

In addition to the receptive functions described earlier, various neuroendocrine processes also take place within these myofascial layers, some of which are particularly interesting for the myofascial work within Body Psychotherapy and EBW, in particular. In the next section, we will return to the role of oxytocin, for example, that is released when working with a haptic touch. Here, we also mention hyaluronic acid as an important substance,[12] which is produced by specific cells in the fascia and acts as a lubricant between almost all layers of the myofascial tissue (Stecco et al., 2011; Stecco, 2015).

The absence, or disturbed presence, of hyaluronic acid is said to lead to fascial layers that become more rigid and (threaten to) adhere (Stecco, 2015) and, as such, play an important role in the development of myofascial symptoms, such as, for example, a-specific back pain. We also recognise this in the case of the 'tense patient' who sometimes 'slouches' almost visibly in his body, as if he were walking around in a T-shirt that is far too small. The effects of myofascial therapy, therefore, lie in optimising this gliding function via hyaluronic acid and, more broadly, in the draining effect on the neuroendocrine matrix via hands-on techniques (Chaitow, 2016). Another, perhaps even more important, role of fascial tissues is in their contribution to regulatory processes of a vegetative nature. We will return to this in the next section, but in essence, it boils down to the damping role of the sympathetic nervous system by facilitating the parasympathetic system. A purely practical/therapeutic consequence of the layered myofascial organisation can be found in Schleip (2003a, 2003b, 2011) and Schleip et al. (2012), who point out how best to approach these different fascial layers 1 to 3, given their specific receptors and regulatory capacity. Working with a so-called 'slow melting pressure' appears to be most effective. If we want to approach the myofascial body as optimally as possible in terms of damping, regulating, draining and interoceptive functions, we must adopt a deep, slow, melting approach to the tissue. This results in what is often referred to in myofascial therapies as tissue release.

So much for the detail. The first thing we remember here is that the clinical concept of a functional layered body also holds up from an anatomical-physiological point of view. The emphasis is on *fascia* as a dynamic, plastic, sensitive and responsive substrate that is organised body-wide from extremely subtle cellular relationships to coarser anatomical connections between all functional somatic systems and also plays a central role in neuromuscular control (Benjamin, 2009). Thus, both on a structural level (*fascia* as anatomical structure) and on a functional level (physiological processes within *fascia*), we can consider the entire myofascial tissue of layers 1 to 3 as an adaptive substrate that we can work with. We already mentioned that this adaptive character can come under a lot of

88 The tense body

pressure during trauma, in which Fogel (2009) points to a conclusion that we can only understand based on the top-right quadrant: 'Trauma memory is as much in the sensory receptors, in the skin and in the muscles as it is in the brain' (p. 259). All the more reason to subject this layered myofascial entry point and the MML in particular to further analysis, but now specifically focused on the tense body during EBW. An intriguing question here is, for example, what actually happens to the body when we work with such a haptic, listening or melting touch. Once again, we approach this from a neurobiological perspective.

> S., a 44-year-old woman, suffers anxiety and panic attacks. At the intake, I see a neatly groomed lady who looks older than her age suggests. Both her presence and her clothing seemingly deprive her of a kind of smoothness and accentuate a sense of courtesy. When she gets up in the waiting room, she looks around to see if I'm addressing her, while there is no one else sitting there.
>
> She also apologises for calling me earlier, because she 'couldn't find the way to reach the practice'. Even before I ask her anything, she hands me documents from her GP and the specialist examination, which are neatly organised. She sits on her chair a quarter turned, coat still buttoned up and handbag on her lap while she smiles somewhat uneasily. When I ask her my standard question 'Who or what brings you here', she bolts like a racehorse that only had to hear the starting shot before racing up the track. For more than ten minutes, she brings a very compelling monologue that is delivered in a very orderly way, almost rehearsed. When she looks around, she turns almost with her whole body and tells me that her neck and head have been stuck for almost her entire life. She also appears to be suffering from her neck and sleeping hands. The MML clearly presents itself during an initial examination. Many of the typical tissue structures are tense and hypertonic or conspicuously hypotonic, but always sensitive to touch and deeper palpation. A first line that stands out is that of chewing, swallowing and breathing muscles. A second dysfunctional line can be found in the iliopsoas, pelvic floor and deep adductors. In terms of the fascial organisation, it is noticeable that layer 1 feels very rigid and is not easy to grab hold of (it remains very adhesive). Rolling the skin is predominantly painful and difficult to perform. The deeper layers 2 and 3 are pressure-sensitive in the specified muscles and regions. First, we work on the superficial structures of layer 1 on the neck and chest. Tissue is mobilised in three-dimensional axes in order to cover and release the underlying fascial tissues as widely as possible. After several sessions of intensive treatment of these layers, S. feels much freer, which is clearly visible in her way of sitting and moving. The sleeping sensation in her arms is better and she is more relaxed turning her neck. What especially strikes her is that she feels less anxious and 'wrapped up'.

The body as an entry point in therapy, a neurobiological analysis

Over the previous chapters, it became clear that BPT focuses on, among other things, encouraging a positive body experience, experiencing the embodied presence in the here-and-now and stimulating a deep beneficial contact with one's own body. What is special about EBW is also the place given to hands-on bodywork (Calsius et al., 2016). More specifically, EBW often works with manual techniques on the muscle armour. It is now clear that this imprint of charged muscles lends itself well as an entry point to the patient's world of experience. But how can we better understand this scientifically? In other words, how should we see the relationship between body experience and awareness on the one hand and bodywork and the layered myofascial armour on the other? We revisit the neurobiological approach for a concise analysis.

When it comes to the link between body awareness and touch, interoception appears to be a crucial link, in addition to exteroception and proprioception. Interoception is traditionally defined as the ability to observe what is happening *inside* the body.

> *The muscular tonus and the metabolic activity of the muscle tissue are also processed interoceptibly. In this way, the experience of muscle armour is strongly related to the interoceptive observation of the actual state of the myofascial tissue.*

This may include sensations such as heat, itching, hunger, breathing, activity of abdominal organs, blushing or sweating. Recently, a more inclusive definition has been proposed, namely, an umbrella term for the phenomenological experience of the state of the body, based on multi-sensorial and multi-modal integrated processing (Ceunen et al., 2016). Interesting and at the same time very important for working with the psychosomatic body is that the muscular tonus and the metabolic activity of the muscle tissue are also processed interoceptibly (Fogel, 2009; Craig, 2002). For example, it was made clear earlier in this chapter that these two elements most definitely contribute to muscle tension, but we also understand that the muscle armour, as an experience, is strongly related to the interoceptive observation of the actual state of the myofascial tissue. The abundant interoceptive receptors in myofascial tissue appear to play an important role in this. These receptors are found in large numbers in layers 1 and 2 and partly in layer 3 (Stecco, 2015; Schleip et al., 2012). Interestingly, specific sensors have also been discovered in the skin, which react via the same interoceptive network, provided that they are stimulated by soft touch or 'light sensual touch' (Ackerley et al., 2014; Schleip & Jäger, 2012; Björnsdotter et al., 2010). In addition to this supply or afferent side of specific receptors, the skin and myofascial system – as well as the skeleton system – also appear to be largely covered by the autonomic or 'visceral' nervous system, which plays a major role in interoception (Ceunen et al., 2016), in terms of control or efferent nerve function. In summary, the entire substrate, from skin to deeper myofascial tissues, therefore appears to be vital for interoception. In other words, layers 1, 2 and 3 lend themselves as an interesting entry point to body experience and consciousness.

As far as the interoceptive relationship with body consciousness is concerned, the importance of the interaction with implicit, non-lingual (trauma) memory is also pointed out (Isnard et al., 2011; Khalsa, Rudrauf, Damasio et al., 2009; Critchley et al., 2004; Craig, 2002, 2003). Regarding this implicit memory, the renowned trauma expert Bessel Van der Kolk (2014) is formal and states that trauma is always preverbal (p. 43) and essentially relates only to brain structures of the limbic system and below (p. 95).[13] The importance of interoception, therefore, lies in being able to explore 'the physical sensations beneath these emotions: pressure, heat, muscle tension, tingling, caving in, feeling hollow and so on' (p. 101) or 'being able to perceive visceral sensations is the very foundation of emotional awareness' (p. 238). Some authors go one step further and suggest a specific role for (myofascial) tissue. in storing and activating traumatic experiences (Levine, 2014a, 2014b; Tozzi, 2014; Caroll, 2005).

As already stated in a previous chapter, Fogel (2009) referred here to a 'participatory memory'.

But how does this important interoceptive information get processed? First of all, the interoceptive route is different from that of extero- and proprioception. Whereas information about the outside world (exteroception) and about spatial position and movement (proprioception) arrives in higher, cortical, 'conscious' structures via specific pathways, the interoceptive stimulus flow follows an entirely different network. The *insula*, in particular, appears to be a central structure. Although we want to avoid too much detail, it is necessary to briefly discuss the distinction between the posterior, middle and anterior parts of this *insula* (Figure 4.3). This is translated schematically as follows. Through numerous receptors and homeostatic 'rule' systems, a massive amount of information enters the back of the *insula* from all corners of the body. Here, a first image or representation is made of the state in which the body finds itself. This first, unconscious processing is, therefore, referred to as 'a primary interoceptive image of the homeostatic afference' (Fogel, 2011). This information then goes on to the middle part of the *insula*, where it is translated from an unconscious representation to an integrated re-representation. This means that there is another representation of the first state, only this time with various brain networks involved, such as the limbic system and hypothalamus. In this way, information from the emotional memory and the metabolic state of the body is simultaneously included. In addition, Ceunen et al. (2016) point to further integration of exteroceptive, proprioceptive and somatosensory information through this part of the *insula*. They (idem) refer to the middle part of the *insula* as the core structure for interoception. Various authors, such as Craig (2003, 2009, 2011), Critchley et al. (2004), Critchley and Seth (2012) and Cameron (2009, 2001) and Cameron and Minoshima (2002) then refer specifically to the role of the front part of the *insula*, which, in collaboration with a number of precortical structures, ensures the ultimate awareness of body experience. The definition of body experience already shows the importance of this specific moment of awareness: 'Body awareness is the subjective, phenomenological aspect of proprioception and interoception that enters conscious

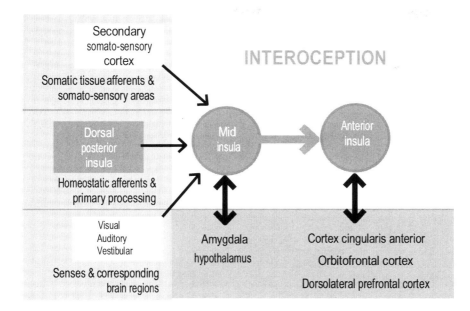

Figure 4.3 Interoception and the insula as core structure
Source: Ceunen et al., 2016, p. 11

awareness and is modifiable by mental processes, including attention, interpretation, appraisal, beliefs, memories, conditioning, attitude and affect' (Mehling et al., 2011, p. 1). As clinically relevant, we therefore remember that from the moment the unconscious 'biological' information from the body and the integrated re-representation are converted into a conscious, subjectively coloured experience, there is body consciousness or body awareness. This appears to happen in the anterior *insula*.

Researchers also point out that this conversion from unconscious to conscious results in many of the initial *stimuli* being 'lost' without this entering in the individual's awareness. As a result, body experience is always coloured. Bogaerts et al. (2010) and Bogaerts, van Diest et al. (2010) show that the personality trait 'negative affect' is such a colouring factor that strongly influences the process of awareness of interoceptive information. Patients who find it easier to experience negative states of mind or see situations as threatening are more likely to become disturbed or confused by what their bodies make them feel and, as a result, report more symptoms. Other influential factors on the ability to accurately perceive interoceptive signals appear to be age (Khalsa et al., 2009) and culture (Ma-Kellmas, 2014). In summary, the insular system can therefore be seen as the neurobiological substrate where interoceptive information from the body comes together with already present memory storage of past experiences, which leads to a pleasant, neutral or disturbing awareness of oneself as a body.

However, it is also important to stress that interoception and body awareness are not one and the same thing. In other words, however decisive interoception may be, body experience and awareness also rely on exteroceptive and proprioceptive information, such as the body schedule. That is why Ceunen et al. (2016) emphasise the phenomenological dimension that the brain constructs, regardless of the underlying sources of information. In combination with the central concept of the muscle armour, this offers an enlightening and therapeutically interesting line of thinking. By emphasising the phenomenological dimension – even apart from the individual flows of information – we understand the muscle armour mainly as that which it is in essence, namely, an experience. The patient experiences his body as tense, tight or limp and feels that it is constricted or suspended.

The answer to the previous question of how we should see the relationship between body experience and the myofascial armour is then that the armoured body *is* experience. All the more reason to see the psychosomatic conflict as working with forms and levels of awareness.

When we revisit the layered awareness process, discussed in Chapter 3, we remember the process-dynamic distinction between conceptual self-awareness (CSA), embodied self-awareness (ESA) and embodiment. From a neurobiological point of view, we could now imagine that embodiment, as an experience, corresponds to everything that happens up to and including the posterior part of the *insula*. Because before the interoceptive information can be consciously identified, it is perhaps more about what Damasio calls a 'background feeling' (2004) and Heidegger calls a 'mood' or '*Stimmung*' (1999). Once through the anterior insular network, sensory images and intuitive language (ESA) are created on the basis of the body's experience. After going through the insular route, we switch to integration with other 'higher' brain networks, and more cognitively and consciously controlled language and thinking (CSA) can emerge. When we just mentioned that body perception is always subjectively coloured by previous experiences – or in other words never complete, objective or neutral – then this has consequences for therapy. This certainly applies to touch, perhaps one of the most personally infused or idiosyncratic phenomena in therapy. Touching or, being touched activates the full spectrum of embodiment, ESA and CSA. When De Wolf (2011) sees the analytical treatment as 'a revision workshop for inadequate aspects of the inner work model' (p. 359), this certainly applies to the way in which touch is imprinted in such a work model. Explicitly linguistic, but, above all, implicitly physical memories of experiences of touch, physical contact, proximity or sexuality are often deeply ingrained and seem to be resistant to change. When it comes to early affective learning processes, developmental psychology also refers to the linguistic memory system that is compromised because the hippocampus – which provides linguistic memory – matures more slowly than the structure that is responsible for the non-lingual, procedural memory, namely, the amygdala. The latter is operational since the third prenatal trimester (Caroll, 2005), while the hippocampus does not fully function until the age of three to four years. When we previously referred to the way in which attachment patterns, affect-regulation and drive tension are stored in the developing child, this is indeed mainly, if not exclusively, done in a non-language way.

> *Pre-language software that was specific to the phase in which memory was stored, can, in therapy, be transformed using the linguistic hardware at a later stage by working with the body as an entry point and thereby leaving as much space as possible for the unconscious.*

Here is also an interesting link with touch. Soft, attentive, loving touch is not only known to the interoceptive-insular network, but also the neurobiological care, attachment and reward system. Substances, such as dopamine, vasopressin and especially oxytocin play an important role in the reduction of pain and anxiety, creating a sense of security, reducing behavioural and neuro-endocrine responses to stress and even promoting the capacity to mentalise (Morhenn et al., 2012; Nicolai, 2010; Luyten et al., 2010). Bodywork in BPT inevitably activates these neurobiological systems (top-right quadrant) that are identified around the earlier-mentioned experiences of safety, proximity, care and reward (top-left quadrant). The fact that the body is coded as an imprint for all these experiences and processes raises an interesting question in therapy. After all, how can a pre-language software, that was specific to the phase in which this particular memory was stored be transformed in therapy at a later age by the then prevailing language-controlled hardware? The answer is, therefore, that this is best done by working through the body as an entry point, leaving as much room as possible for the unconscious. The domain of BPT and, by extension, EBW, are therefore mainly aimed at working with these physical and, thus, pre-lingual layers of functioning. The theme of the unconscious, which was already discussed in Chapter 2, will be discussed in detail in the next chapter, but this time with a focus on body awareness.

In view of the importance of the interoceptive foundation for understanding body experience and, by extension, the psychosomatic request for help, we repeat here once more: when the interoceptive information from the whole body enters the back of the *insula*, our brain takes a snapshot of this. In a next phase (middle *insula*), this picture will be edited again on the basis of selection, filtering, information and noise from other networks, as well as emotional memories. Ultimately, this photo of a photo, or re-representation, leads to integration and conscious awareness, after the anterior *insula* is involved. In the case study that follows, elements that were theoretically explored in this chapter are brought to the concrete level of therapy. This reminds us that no matter how interesting and necessary these theoretical insights may be, we never treat a posterior or anterior *insula*, but always tap into the phenomenological level of the request for help, namely, that which the individual experiences.

P. (31 years) has concentration issues, a feeling of anxiety in his head and pressure on his chest. He also experiences an obsessive need for order in his home. His mother recently started a new relationship and this had taken him by surprise, which she did not understand. During the intake, P. sat on his chair, turned away, staring into the distance. While talking about his mother, he made circular movements with his hands as if he were installing something around himself, encapsulating himself. The feeling that the new boyfriend gave him, he represented with a sudden, sharp movement of his right hand right through these circles. As he did so, his voice was louder, cracking on occasions. He looked angry and then looked at me. He trembled, sighed, and after staring quietly into space for a while, he told me that the doctor told him that he was suffering from hyperventilation.

When P. shakes hands in the next session, I experience a weakness and fragility and find myself speaking with a softer and more caring voice. He sits down on the treatment table and 'nestles' against my hand that is resting on his shoulder. With his eyes closed, he starts to tell me that his mother has gone on holiday with her new boyfriend, precisely in the period that his father died.

There are a few cautious tears rolling down his face. Suddenly, he feels unwell and now he is experiencing that strong pressure on his chest again. While I place my hand on his sternum, his breathing becomes more restless and stops several times. P. indicates that something is 'in the way' in his throat. After a while, he seems to feel safer with my touch and makes circular movements again to express this. Yet, he says he is afraid to open his eyes and see my angry look. 'When you looked at me angrily before, you made sudden, sharp movements and talked about your mother's boyfriend', I say. After a long silence, he describes how, as a six-year-old, he would sit on the lap of his crying mother when father, while arguing and outraged, raised his hands in a 'brusque' manner to pull him out of there. I ask him to look at his father's gaze as he repeats and magnifies the movements with his arms. This is visibly very difficult for P.

With a soft touch, I then work from the sternum, through the neck and the floor of the mouth to cheeks and jaws. As the movements deepen and these myofascial tissues loosen, I ask P. to 'breathe into this'. We work together for minutes, focusing on the experience of my listening touch and the way his body reacts 'in depth'. His body visibly comes to rest and P. is now aware of the physical tension with which he fixes his breathing and stops his tears. He can now 'breathe them away', he says. When I ask him to associate freely, while I continue to work towards eyes and mouth, he describes how his breath penetrates deep into his mouth cavity and how this leaves a kind of 'echoing feeling'. He tells how often he still hears his dad's words as an 'echo in his head' when he had to be strong every time he was bullied at school and wanted to shout, but 'nothing came out of his throat'.

After a number of sessions of intensive, experiential bodywork, P. says that his body feels looser and freer. He says that it seems as if he is now making contact with a deep sense of relaxation in his body. I notice that his speech has become freer and more powerful. Associations, images and memories come to him more easily and he mentions how he has finally been able to tell his mother what he feels when he sees her together with her new boyfriend. In our contact, he now turns to me completely and also his gaze is calmer. 'It's no longer stuck in my throat,' he says, 'and if not, I can always breathe it away.'

Tools for therapy

- *The muscle armour, conceived by Reich as a functional-dynamic protective layer, offers conceptual and numerous therapeutic leads within EBW.*
- *Clinically, the myofascial muscle armour manifests itself as a mutual influence between various quadrants and fulcra and appears in various symptoms in daily psychosomatic practice.*
- *From a neurobiological as well as a developmental psychological and psychodynamic point of view, various facets of the muscle armour can be examined and substantiated in a scientific way.*
- *Anatomically, we distinguish three functional layers within the myofascial body that relate to specific sources of body information and manual approach in therapy: layer 1 (skin and superficial fascia), layer 2 (deep fascia) and layer 3 (muscle tissue).*
- *In addition, we also distinguish three concentric levels from the outside to the inside. For psychosomatic practice, the MML is particularly important and is related to the uroboric-pranic body (elaborated in the next chapters) from early subject development.*
- *All these myofascial layers offer effective and concrete leads to approach the difficult body in therapy. Not only what, where and why, but also how the body's work should be done, becomes clear as a result. From a neuroscientific point of view, we also understand their privileged role in the fundamental processes of body experience and awareness, as well as pre-language storage of experiences and trauma.*

Notes

1 Reich preferred the term 'discharge' to 'catharsis' (Heller, 2012, p. 467).
2 Reich is not entirely original in this respect, since Freud already wrote about this enigmatic question about the link or transition between the *psyche* and *soma*. For a more detailed reading of Freud's developing trauma theory, we refer the reader to Verhaeghe 2006. Here, we would like to draw attention to an excerpt from Freud's Q hypothesis in which we can hear the later Reichian echo resonate: 'In mental functions, there is something that displays all the characteristics of a quantity – even though we have no means of measuring it – something that can be multiplied, diminished, shifted and removed, and that spreads like a thought trail of the representations, much like an electrical charge does over the surfaces of bodies' (idem, p. 17).
3 Character armour and muscle armour are, for Reich, similar and functionally interchangeable concepts, in which muscle armour is seen on the somatic side of the spectrum and character armour on the psychological side (Reich, 1973).
4 In their review, Pavan et al. (2014) describe various stimuli and mechanisms that can lead to dysfunctional adjustments of fascial tissues and, thus, to pain. Reference is made to thickening (densification) and adhesion (fibrosis). One of the examples is adaptations of the fascia profunda of the sternocleidomastoid muscle in a headache patient.

5 Sometimes, the concentration of myofibroblasts in the *fascia thoraco-lumbalis* even turns out to be as high as in a 'frozen shoulder', which is why we speak of 'frozen lumbars'.
6 Painter, J. W. (1987). *The technical manual of deep wholistic bodywork: Postural integration*. Mill Valley: Body Mind Books.
7 Meyers (2014) considers the following myofascial structures as part of the deep frontal line: foot sole (*plantar fascia*) and deep foot muscles (*interossei, lumbricales, posterior tibialis* and toe flexors) – *popliteus* – adductor group (*magnus, pectineus, brevis, . . .*), obturator internus, piriformis – pelvic floor (*perineum, levator ani*) – *iliopsoas* – diaphragm, *mediastinum, pericardium*, anterior longitudinal ligament, *prevertebralis fascia* and pharyngeal constrictors, *raphe medianis (occiput)* – *fascia endothoracica, transversus thoracis* – *scaleni, longus capitis, longus colli, rectus capitis anterior* – infrahyoidal muscles (*sternothyroideus, sternohyoideus, omohyoideus*, etc.), suprahyoidal muscles (*mylohyoideus, digastricus*, etc.) – *masseter, temporalis* and *pterygoidei medialis* and *lateralis* (p. 187).
8 In their extensive review, Abraira and Ginty (2014) equate the richly varied sensory properties of touch with the sensitivity of the eye and point out the complex and sophisticated ability of touch to establish contact with the environment.
9 This rich subcutaneous region is further subdivided into three layers. First of all, the loose-meshed connective tissue containing the superficial subcutaneous fat tissue, then a first 'real' fascial layer, the superficial fascia, and finally again loose-meshed connective tissue containing the deep subcutaneous fat tissue.
10 Namely the *epimysium*, the *perimysium* and the *endomysium*. Whereas the outer layer (the *epimysium*) lies just below the *fascia profunda* and surrounds the entire muscle, the deepest layer (the *endomysium*) surrounds only one muscle fibre. Development of force or load arise from the contraction of a muscle fibre, whereby the force energy is successively transferred from the *endo* and *perimysium* to the *epimysium* and then passed on to the *fascia profunda*. It is especially this *fascia profunda* that directs the developed forces within larger parts of the body that are involved in specific movement.
11 The deep layer of fat between the *fascia superficialis* and *profunda* contains few nerve structures and mainly forms a boundary between these extero- and proprioceptive zones.
12 Hyaluronic cells or fasciacytes (Stecco et al., 2011) are located in the innermost layer of the *fascia profunda*. Hyaluron is present between the sub-layers of the aponeurotic fascia and between the *fascia profunda* and the underlying muscles. Hyaluronic acid is present in the muscles in the epi-, peri- and endomysium. Perivascular and perineural fascia also contain high levels of hyaluronic acid (McCombe et al., 2001; Piehl-Aulin et al., 1991; Laurent et al., 1991). Changes in the hyaluronic acid-rich matrix contribute to inflammation, pain and appear significant for changes in the pathological process. (Lee & Spicer, 2000). The role of hyaluronic acid depends partly on its biochemical composition and may even be contradictory. High-molecular chains are found in normal and 'quiet' tissue, while fragmented chains are involved in angiogenic and inflammatory processes.
13 Ceunen et al. (2016) see the importance of what happens to this 'interoceptive' flow of afferent stimuli at higher levels within the central nervous system and point to the conclusive influence of final representation.

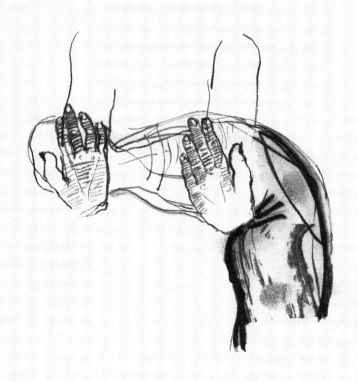

The find, 2017, drawing, pencil, conté, 42 × 28.8 cm.

5 The unconscious within experiential bodywork

In Chapter 1, we introduced Wilber's *fulcrum* concept for the first time as an important working concept within EBW. In this chapter, we want to discuss in more detail the early subject development, the way in which this leads to the formation of various bodies and how all this relates to the clinical phenomenon of muscle armour in general. Specifically in relation to the MML from the previous chapter, we pay a great deal of attention to the uroboric-pranic body. This should enable us to gain more insight into the psychosomatic body and the development of psychosomatic conflict, in particular. The latter will be discussed at length in Chapter 6. Here, it may be a good idea to start with the unconscious and establish how this relates to the development of the individual.

The unconscious has already been discussed at various times as an instrumental component within EBW. This is obviously not only the case for EBW or – by extension – Body Psychotherapy. The phenomenon of 'unconsciousness' has always intrigued mankind and has, as part of the call for consciousness, overlapped with philosophy for centuries.[1] From the Vedic era to far beyond Schopenhauer and Nietzsche (Störig, 1998), the unconscious emerges as only the unconscious can, often, many times and, above all, suddenly. In addition to neuroscience, the unconscious also found its way into psychology and psychotherapy through psychoanalysis and would never again disappear from art and literature. In this chapter we approach the unconscious mainly from its intimate relationship with the body, because this is precisely where a unique link towards BPT and EBW lies.

The unconscious as a matrix

After Freud put the unconscious on the map, psychoanalysis became a privileged interlocutor. Many later authors and analysts would attempt to describe the unconscious and to elaborate on it as a concept. Building on a Bionian and partly Merleau-Pontian lecture, Civitarese and Ferro (2015) use the metaphor of the unconscious as a field[2] that precedes the differentiation of reality in terms of form or function and point to the 'proto-mental system' in Bion.[3] In this proto-mental system, the physical and the mental are not yet differentiated (idem, p. 4).

The unconscious-as-a-field is then that from which form is created[4] and, according to these authors, has a number of interesting properties. For example, it is only visible on the basis of the effects that occur in it, it is in a constant movement of expansion and retraction, but at the same time it is delineated and acts as a container.[5] Hebbrecht (2016) adds the quality of temporality, i.e. time is not linear, but circular.[6] Within the scope of this book, we will join Wilber in looking at the unconscious-as-a-field from a development-dynamic point of view as a matrix within which the subject arises. This, therefore, precedes the development of the individual, but at the same time remains present all the time.[7] Reality is initially not yet differentiated, which is reminiscent of Heinz Hartmann's concept of 'undifferentiated matrix' (1958). The core idea that reality has not yet distinguished itself at the start of subject development, in fact, means that the consciousness of the individual at that moment is not yet differentiated. The individual cannot yet distinguish himself from his environment or from himself.

Ken Wilber (1985) describes this undifferentiated, fused state of consciousness in which the individual functions from foetus to early postnatal infant as pleromatic. He initially refers to this early field with the term 'primitive biomaterial matrix': 'Infants are simply one with their material environment and their biological mother – they make no distinction between their own physical body and the physical environment – and there are no higher levels involved in this primitive (pleromatic) fuse' (p. 138). The term 'pleromatic' refers to the fused state of being in which there is no differentiation between the foundations of later conscious reality. These foundations deal with the distinction between 'self-other-world', on the one hand, and 'time-space', on the other. Although the concepts of 'primitive biomaterial matrix', 'proto-mental system' and 'field' partly resonate with each other, in some respects they widely differ. For Wilber, the undifferentiated, pleromatic matrix from which the individual – or more specifically the consciousness – originates also forms a specific first identification for consciousness. In this way, the pleromatic field is also a very first state of being within which the young subject begins to develop. It is, therefore, the earliest stage of development in which – on closer inspection – nothing has yet developed. Through the pattern of fusion/identification, differentiation and integration processes that were described in Chapter 1 (Figure 1.7), Wilber (1999, 2000) explains in detail how the individual develops as a consciousness through various *fulcra* into higher, more complex forms of consciousness. We saw that, at the same time, the environment is becoming increasingly differentiated and the subject is constantly discovering new objects. Psychodynamically, this is referred to as object relations. For the first pleromatic level or *fulcrum*, this means that the physical environment and then the physical body will differentiate themselves from the primitive biomaterial matrix as objects. Where the subject first completely coincided (fusion) with the physical environment, it now learns to distinguish itself step-by-step (differentiation) from the environment as a physical body and discovers how it can handle this body as an object (integration). In short, this is where the physical body-self emerges.

Types of unconscious

Wilber sees the unconscious as a cradle from which reality unfolds. However, when he (Wilber, 1985) analyses the unconscious in more detail, he distinguishes five subtypes[8] and abandons the term 'primitive biomaterial matrix'. He now calls the most basic, undifferentiated unconscious 'ground unconscious'. This involves all possible depth structures that are present as potential, but have not yet been actualised. Consequently, the ground unconscious does not contain any surface structures, since these are always differentiated and taught in a certain context. A second subtype of unconscious, according to Wilber, is 'the archaic unconscious'. This includes the first and most primitive depth structures or *fulcra* that develop from the unconscious foundation. Wilber mentions these earliest *fulcra* as the *pleroma*, the uroboros and the typhon (1992, 1996).[9] Given their importance for the EBW process with a difficult body, we study these in more detail. Wilber distinguishes a third subtype of unconscious (1996) as being 'the subconscious unconscious'. This subconscious is the 'place' where those parts of reality end up that cannot be digested, processed or tolerated during subject development. We will return to this in Chapter 6.

The archaic unconscious

This pleromatic development phase in which the awakening individual learns to distinguish himself from the physical world with which he had previously coincided, is, in fact, a subphase of the first *fulcrum* and with Wilber (1992, 1999, 2000) we refer to it as *fulcrum* 1a, or F1a for short.[10] On the basis of physical and sensory-motor stimuli, the infant discovers an initial difference between what is environment and what will become 'self'. In these first few months of life, the subject comes out of his 'autistic shell', says Mahler (Mahler et al., 2000) and develops what Stern (1985) calls 'an awakening sense of self'. Clinically interesting is that the rhythm between changes appears to be the most decisive factor in this (idem). So it is not so much a specific experience in itself, but the change or movement between experiences that turns out to be decisive and instructive. For example, the back-and-forth rhythm of movements, the difference between far and near, soft and hard, light and dark, gradually result in the creation of a stable material outside world. In other words, the previous pleromatic self now experiences itself as a separate and stable physical entity (F1a). Under normal circumstances, this physical self-feeling will never disappear again. In concrete terms, this means that the individual no longer has to ask himself where his body starts and how to use his limbs. In contrast to this, the physical self of a psychotic person can be subject to experiences of fragmentation, disintegration or derealisation. *In extremis*, the subject may even disappear or merge into the environment or this environment may be so intrusive that it takes over the subject, which at that moment is in fact slipping back to pleromatic fusion.

After the pleromatic self differentiated itself from its physical surroundings, a second subphase is evident within the first *fulcrum*. Here, the subject will differentiate himself from a 'different' outside world, namely, the outside world as 'nourishment'. This sublevel of *fulcrum* 1 is what Wilber (1992, 1996) calls the uroboric self and we abbreviate it to F1b. Even though we are only here in the first months of the child's life, these *fulcra* are often crucial for a good understanding of the difficult body in therapy. We will, therefore, go a little deeper into this uroboros and subsequent typhonic *fulcrum*.

The early body in detail: pleroma, uroboros and typhon

We started this chapter with the unconscious as a field and saw that Wilber uses the term 'ground unconscious' as pure potentiality without manifestation. This means that at that moment, only space – field or matrix – is present within which consciousness can unfold itself. The first manifestation is that of the pleromatic self that distinguishes itself from the purely material environment. Remember that prior to this first development, the subject was still completely fused with its environment. So there is no differentiation in the pleromatic state and, consequently, no subject nor object or environment. More technically, the pleromatic self differentiates itself from the oceanic, proto-plasmatic and a-dual environment in which it was initially 'contained'.

In the subsequent step, the new outside world evolves from physical matter to a uroboric environment. This term, which Wilber also borrowed from the Jungian Erich Neumann, stands for the mythological uroboric snake that gradually detaches itself from the oceanic fusedness through its mouth. In Figure 5.1, we see the

Figure 5.1 The uroboros snake

Source: https://commons.wikimedia.org/wiki/File:Serpiente_alquimica.jpg.

uroboric snake that still has its tail in its mouth and is, therefore, still largely introverted.

Psychodynamically, in this phase of development, the mouth or – to put it more broadly – orality, takes precedence. The little child discovers the world through his or her mouth, for example by literally putting everything in his or her mouth and eating it. Wilber (1992) refers to the uroboric environment as a uroboric other. He describes the state of consciousness in this phase as 'a psychology of the intestines: physiology, instincts, reptilian perception and the most rudimentary discharges' (idem, p. 23).

> *Not unimportant to understand the psychosomatic clinic is the appearance of anxiety, one of the consequences associated with the gradual release (differentiation) from the uroboric environment.*

Not unimportant for understanding the psychosomatic clinic is one of the consequences associated with the gradual release (differentiation) from the uroboric environment, namely, the appearance of anxiety. This first primal anxiety is therefore an anxiety of being swallowed[11] or destroyed by the environment that is, in fact, a uroboric other. We will come back to anxiety later in this chapter. The appearance of anxiety is related to the moment when the young consciousness passes from what is called a monadic organisation to a dyadic one (and later a triadic one). So no longer a world out of one fused realm, but from then on always at least two actors in the world of the young individual, namely, the subject and the (m)other. The fused pleromatic state now changes into a dyadic or, more specifically, a symbiotic relationship. With this symbiotic-uroboric sub-stage, the first *fulcrum* is fully completed: the differentiated pleromatic self (F1a) and the uroboric self (F1b) together form *fulcrum* 1, which is referred to as the physical, sensory-motor body self: 'The pleroma-uroboros, then, stands as the archetype and perfect symbol of this primitive awareness: embedded in physical nature (pleroma) and dominated by animal-reptilian impulses (uroboros)' (Wilber, 1996, p. 26). Now that the subject has learned to distinguish itself from the physical environment and from the nourishing other (e.g. the mother figure), it has a physical body with which it no longer coincides and which can be used sensorimotorally.

The next step in subject development is *fulcrum* 2. Wilber (1992, 1996) uses the image of the mythological typhon – which is half human, half snake (Figure 5.2). Whereas the uroboric snake still had its tail in its own mouth and was, therefore, largely focused on itself, the typhon has already turned itself to the outside world. Through this new form of differentiation – in relation to the pleromatic-uroboric self, but not yet in relation to the mental self – Wilber qualifies the typhonic self as the actual body itself: 'There is the typhonic self, the self that has differentiated its body from the environment but not yet differentiated its own mind from its body. ... it is basically a body-ego, not a mental-ego' (Wilber, 1996, p. 47). As

Figure 5.2 The typhonic snake
Source: www.greekboston.com/culture/mythology/typhon/

with *fulcrum* 1, there are a number of sub-stages, namely, the axial body (F2a), the pranic body (F2b) and the image-body (F2c). Interestingly, the development of the subject as a body continues during the second *fulcrum*, with the difference that the processes of consciousness shift from focusing on 'outside' to focusing on 'inside'. For the first time an – albeit very rudimentary – inner world unfolds within the subject. This is about budding images of experience and the way in which the subject becomes aware of this. So no longer only that which takes place between the child and the outside world (the physical environment, F1a or the nourishing other, F1b), but especially that which this brings about on the inside of the subject, such as the creation of images.

> *From now on the subject consists of an outside and an inside.*

The axial body is in a sense the physical body of *fulcrum* 1 that can now be experienced on the basis of primary but stable images. Wilber (1992, 1996) refers to these as axial images: they are objects 'out there' that are only present in the present moment, because they can only exist there. As the earliest and most fundamental axial image, psychoanalysis often refers to the mother (breast). Whereas the uroboric self was still largely merged with the environment (not entirely, because that was the case with the pleromatic self) into a kind of hallucinatory experience of time and space, where the axial body-self remains in a vague, momentary passing present. The axial self, in fact, constructs a reality on the basis of groups of images

The unconscious within experiential bodywork 105

and thus arrives at a transient experience of inside and outside (Wilber (1992). From now on, the subject consists of an outside and an inside.

After stabilising axial consciousness, the pranic body unfolds.[12] This second sublevel within the typhonic stage – referred to as F2b – adds rudimentary forms of emotion that differ from the reflexes and instincts of the uroboros. These primary emotions, as Damasio (2003, 2004) calls them, are naturally highly hedonistic and focused on instant pleasure. Here, we are in the middle of the Freudian principle of lust and the polymorphic sexuality and perversity associated with it. In this sense, the principle of lust is first and foremost a body that focuses on survival and enjoyment. As the ability to hold axial images and proto-emotions expands, the axes of time and space open up in the subject's consciousness. Gradually, the image-body (F2c) emerges as the third and last level within the typhonic *fulcrum* 2. In essence, this concerns a further differentiation: 'Just as the first important axial image is that of the chest, the first important concrete image is that of the mothering' (Wilber (1992, p. 31). The difference with the previous subphase is the shift towards an 'enlarged present, in which the disorganised images of events from the past and the disordered images of future possibilities float around' (idem, p. 33). On the basis of these changes in the experience of time and emotions, a new body develops with this rounded second *fulcrum*. After the physically separated body and the oral body tuned into the nourishing environment (uroboros), the typhonic body appears. What characterises this typhonic body and what its therapeutic implications are, will be discussed in the next two chapters.

Here, we remember that from the ground unconscious, the first three depth structures of the archaic unconscious – the pleroma, the uroboros and the typhon – emerge. Together, they form the first two *fulcra* in which the self appears as a body, namely, the 'physical-sensorimotor body-self' (*fulcrum* 1 as the sum of F1a and b) and the 'phantasmic-emotional' body-self (*fulcrum* 2 as the sum of F2a, b and c) (Figure 5.3). Once we exchange this theoretical decomposition from the following chapters for a more clinical and practical approach in therapy, we will speak of the uroboric-pranic body. This is, strictly speaking, *fulcrum* 1b and *fulcrum* 2 combined. This new reference speaks more clearly and directly to the imagination regarding the core processes of this early body. More about this later.

Finally, something about a third subtype of unconscious that Wilber (1996) calls 'the submergent unconscious'. This unconscious is the 'place' where those

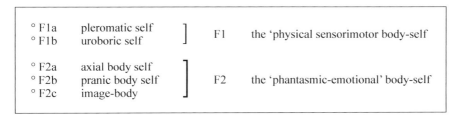

Figure 5.3 Sub-stages within the early *fulcra*
Source: Based on Wilber 1992, and 1996

parts of reality end up that cannot be digested, processed or tolerated during subject development. In the next chapter, we will see, for example, that Bion calls these parts *beta* elements. Stimuli, impressions and experiences that are evacuated by the unconscious and placed in quarantine within the submergent unconscious, according to Wilber.[13] The link with the clinic is already introduced by Ferro (2013) when he states that these *beta* elements can trigger symptoms. This statement, originally developed by Freud – 'that "something" has shifted to a way of expression where it does not belong' (Verhaeghe, 2006, p. 20) – forms a fundamental axiom within the psychoanalytical and psychodynamic approach to symptoms and contributes to the understanding of the 'hermeneutics of the body' (Mooij, 2006). Somewhat plastically worded, what has not been digested or insufficiently digested, appears in a different form, in a different place, and thus keeps the individual nicely on his toes. Given the psychosomatic importance of such 'digestive processes', we are now zooming in on their nature and relationship with the early archaic *fulcra*.

Tools for therapy

- *A Wilberian analysis sheds light on various processes, layers and manifestations of the unconscious and its fundamental role in (early) subject development.*
- *The early development of body awareness is related to the release from the fused state in which the infant finds himself and ultimately results in the appearance of the physical-sensorimotor body.*
- *After differentiation from the physical and nourishing environment, early forms of emotions, images and the experience of time appear in an environment that is propelled by (libidinous) drives and movement. This is the second fulcrum of the phantasmic-emotional body.*
- *Clinically and therapeutically, we take sub-stages together and speak of the physical-sensory body versus the uroboric-pranic body, both of which appear in the psychosomatic request for help.*

Notes

1 For a thorough philosophical consideration of consciousness, see for example *Oorspronkelijk bewustzijn* (*Original consciousness*) (Ziegelaar, 2016).
2 Hebbrecht (2016) reminds us that the field concept has been around in psychoanalytical thinking for a long time and has been developed by numerous authors, such as Freud, Klein, Winnicott, Lacan and Green, often with its own specific interpretation of the concept. When discussing this field theory, Hebbrecht (idem) reminds us of the importance that Merleau-Ponty attached to the intercorporeality that is central to preverbal and pre-symbolic communication and points to the role of the implicit memory 'in the early occurrence of traumata and the unrepressed unconscious' (p. 65). This was discussed just now in Chapter 4 and will be discussed in more detail in Chapter 6.

3 When Bion then indicates that this 'proto-mental system' of the individual is part of the 'proto-mental matrix of the group', for Civitarese and Ferro (2015) he joins in with the inter-subjective dimension that Merleau-Ponty adds to the self-as-field. An (individual) field within a (collective) field in which the former cannot be seen separately from the latter (idem, pp. 4–5).
4 The field concept of Civitarese and Ferro (2015) is reflected in Bion's 'proto-mental system': 'The proto-mental system is one in which physical and psychological or mental are undifferentiated. It is a matrix from which spring the phenomena which at first appear – on a psychological level – to be discrete feelings only loosely connected with one another. . . . Since it is a level in which physical and mental are undifferentiated, it stands to reason that, when distress from this source manifests itself, it can manifest itself just as well in physical forms as in psychological' (p. 4).
5 This capacity to contain is one of the foundations of therapy in which patients and therapists can 'emerge' during the therapeutic process.
6 Matte-Blanco (1988) sees the (Freudian) unconscious mainly as a set of structures that follow a bi-logical law with which they work partly through ordinary or traditional logic and partly through so-called symmetrical logic.
7 Junqueira and Braga (2013) refer to Bion, who also speaks of 'primordial mind' and 'primitive conscience'. This is associated with the prenatal register in which the foetus resides and the associated processes within the then available neurobiological substrate. The thalamus is the conductor and the variety of somatic, non-language impressions is stored in various sub-thalamic circuits. Given the pre- and perinatal immaturity of the brain (e.g. non-myelinated cortex, non-operational hippocampus), all experiences on a purely sensory basis are recorded in deep brain circuits. The field of perinatal psychology also offers interesting paths around these hypotheses (Glenn, 2015). A consequence is that within the proto-mental field, proto-emotions 'arise' on a purely sensory-somatic basis with the thalamus as conductor. Proto-emotions could be considered as somatic endocepts in which they represent 'something' that has been captured 'inside'. In Chapter 4, we highlighted the importance of interception for EBW.
8 The added value of Wilber's model compared to other psychodynamic models is its high level of detail and nuance by differentiating which subject processes take place within the early matrix. This specifically concerns types, i.e. no developmental stages or *fulcra*.
9 The pleroma has as its core object the physical matter, the uroboros has as its core object nourishment and the typhon emotional-sexual energies, says Wilber (1985, 1996).
10 As explained previously, here we stick to Wilbers' description of the pleroma as part of the first fulcrum. Later on in Chapter 7 we will be detailing this a bit more regarding clinical application. Then the first fulcrum will be named after the appearance of the physical 'sensori-motor' self and the pleromatic self will be assigned to the periode prior to this, i.e. from conception to first postnatal weeks.
11 This is reminiscent of the painting of Goya where Saturn ate his child.
12 Wilber deliberately uses the term *prana* to describe this level and refers to the Hindu and Buddhist meaning. In yoga, prana stands for (one of the five) vital forces and is supposed to control all biological processes. Buddhists see prana as a bound energy in contrast to the cosmic free energy called chi. See also Feuerstein (2001).
13 It is important to point out the difference between elements that have never been digested before – and therefore cannot be repressed 'afterwards' – versus experiences that were initially consciously accessible, but were taken away by circumstances below the threshold of conscious experience.

Stay II, 2014, collage on paper with rope, cloth and wood, 55 × 45 × 2.8 cm, private collection, Amstelveen.

6 The psychosomatic body within the *fulcrum* model

In previous chapters, the importance of the developmental processes within the early *fulcra*, the role of the unconscious and the emergence of body experience was already underlined. However, in order to be able to translate this to the patient with a difficult body, we need more detail. In this chapter, we will delve deeper into the psychodynamic, early subject development and the digestive processes that we already mentioned. In particular, we will look at how the psychosomatic conflict can gradually get established and what the role of anxiety can be in this. We use the *fulcrum* model as a stepping stone.[1] Whereas in this chapter, we mainly develop this roadmap in theory, in the seventh and final chapter, we arrive at a concrete therapeutic guideline, which we will call the 'development-oriented dynamics treatment template'. This can then serve as a compass when working with the psychosomatic body in therapy. Here, we first revisit the unconscious.

The unconscious in action

In Bion's works, we find a detailed analysis of the processes of the unconscious. One of these is the way in which undigested facts from the child's world of experience are converted into, for example, emotional thoughts (Brown, 2013). Bion calls these undigested facts *beta* elements and the 'digested' thoughts *alpha* elements. This transformation process is already situated within the early dyadic relationship between mother and child:

> The mother, like the mother of newly hatched chicks, must pre-masticate emotional experience through the factor of her reverie so that the internal and external stimuli affecting the baby are made into mentally 'digestible' morsels (*alpha* elements) that the infant's nascent psyche can incorporate without undue frustration.
>
> (idem, p. 14)

Freely translated, the rough and raw sensory impressions (*beta* elements) that the baby undergoes are converted into experiences (*alpha* elements) and later into thoughts because the mother does 'something' with them. This 'something the mother does' is what Bion calls the capacity for *alpha*-function or 'waking dream thought'. This ability works in a certain sense as a kind of interface between the conscious, the unconscious and the external reality:

> Our capacity to learn from experience fundamentally depends on our ability to convert the raw emotional sense impressions (*beta*-elements) into mentalisable *alpha*-elements so as to produce dream images for dream thoughts. Dream thoughts allow us to feel (mentally) our bodily emotions.
>
> (Grottstein, 2013, p. 119)

Bion places waking dream thought under *rêverie*, a concept that we came across earlier and that refers to 'the mother's capacity to develop a psychological receptor organ that is capable of absorbing, holding, digesting and transforming the baby's sensory and emotional experiences' (Stroeken, 2008, p. 166). In line with the importance of the mother's – or more broadly speaking, the first significant others in the life of the small child – ability to perform *rêverie*, Bion also points out the crucial role of the therapist's *rêverie*. We interpret *rêverie* here as the backward leaning attitude with which the therapist playfully leaves room for unconscious processes, such as associations, images or dreams. We previously situated these forms of consciousness in a different layer of functioning than, for example, concentrated thinking or explicit knowledge.

Translated to Wilber's earliest *fulcra*, a first inside/outside reality arises for the subject because the raw *beta* elements are 'premasticated' via mother's *rêverie*. In this way, the external reality (e.g. auditory and visual stimuli) and the internal reality (e.g. hunger or pain) are gradually stripped of their threatening and intrusive character, so that they can be experienced more easily. Ferro (2013) also points out, however, that certainly not all stimuli and impressions can be processed and, therefore, have to be evacuated:

> Of course, not all the clouds of sensoreality or proto-emotions can be transformed into pictograms; a certain proportion will inevitably be evacuated in the form of symptoms, acting-out, quarrelling, phobias, paranoia and so on, owing the inadequacy of the *alpha*-function.
>
> (p. 94)

From a different perspective, McDougall (1989) points to the importance of the unconscious of the mother and sees this as follows:

> With regard to early infancy, we must remember that a baby's earliest external reality is its mother's unconscious (in large part structured by her own childhood experiences and beliefs), in that this governs the quality of her presence and her ways of relating to the nursling
>
> (pp. 39–40)

According to her, the baby is not just in a dyadic field with the mother, but is embedded in the mother's unconscious and 'knows' only this reality as the first and for the time being only external reality. From the mother's point of view, the child first of all arises and exists within her subconscious. This intrinsic interweaving between the unconscious and the budding self appears to be of major clinical importance: 'This leads us to consider the presymbolic, preverbal universe as possibly providing a key to psychotic and psychosomatic potentialities' (McDougall, 1989, p. 40). We will come back to this in more detail. First we try to better understand some of these psychodynamic processes that take place within the early *fulcra*.

A psychodynamic reading of the first *fulcra*

It is the historical merit of the psychoanalytical and later psychodynamic tradition to have thoroughly mapped out the early stages of development. Their accuracy and attention to detail can also be found in the early *fulcra*, which can, therefore, be easily interpreted from a psychodynamic point of view.

With the baby's distress experience as a starting point for subject development (Kinet, 2013), we already saw that a typical dynamic is set in motion in which the small child has to focus on someone else, someone outside of it. This first Other (Verhaeghe, 2003) then turns to the baby and helps to relieve, or at least regulate, the inner tension by means of physical interaction such as caressing, cuddling, rocking and, above all, feeding. In view of this typical relationship, we regard the first Other as a uroboric Other. The child therefore appeals to this uroboric Other to relieve the tension present: the hungry baby cries, the mother latches it on the breast and the child calms down. This uroboric relationship is dyadic and symbiotic.

From a developmental psychological point of view, it forms a foundation for a stable and secure attachment (Allen et al., 2008) in which the mother's reflecting and marking presence is crucial in order to learn how to tune impressions and experiences ('affect-attunement'). For an adequate regulation and relieving of tension, it is, therefore, necessary that the uroboric Other feels sensitively what the child needs and is able to mirror this and give it back. In the fourth chapter, we already referred to the Still-Face experiment. From a Bionian point of view, we saw that the mother not only has to feel, but also has to learn to tolerate what her child does to her. For this, she needs to have sufficient *alpha*-function or *rêverie*, so that her unconscious can function as a container for everything that the baby spits out. With the digestive metaphor described earlier, we now understand how the mother's *rêverie* helps to transform indigestible impressions or *beta* elements. Through *alpha*-function, the child gradually learns to experience these impressions as feelings and thoughts. The child not only spits out that which is difficult to digest, his/her own body has to be tolerated as well. Here, too, the crucial role of mother's *rêverie* is pointed out as a protection against the flooding and threatening flow of stimuli that originate from one's own, biological body:

> Under the pressure of violent and turmoiling sensory perceptions, endangering the harmonious physical functioning (i.e. the co-ordination of the nervous,

endocrine and vascular systems) in the presence of her mother, of her mind and of the essential function of '*rêverie*', the child's mental apparatus begins to fulfil its own functions, that is recording and containment.[2]

(Ferrari, 2004, p. 44)

Junqueira and Braga (2013) allude to the immaturity of the baby's neurological system, as a result of which sensations and proto-emotions develop under the direction of the thalamus and various sub-thalamic circuits. These impressions are at times so disturbing that the child – always dependent on mother's *rêverie* – has no choice but to try to evacuate them. We also saw this dependence in a different form in the early subject who learns to identify himself within the mirror stage (Vanheule, 2005) with an image that is provided from the outside by the first Other. The child learns to discover its own body and, more specifically, its way of reacting through the uroboric Other. Despite the massive presence of physiological and physical impressions, the first self-image does not so much come exclusively from the child, but is 'digested' and 'mirrored' by the other.[3] This early identification process is, in this sense, unifying (Slatman, 2008) since the subject will gradually learn to realise 'this is me', or better put 'this is my body'. As we already mentioned, Wilber is very detailed in this and describes how this first axial image gradually evolves into an image-body in a widened present towards the end of the second *fulcrum* (F2c).

In summary, when minimal conditions are met within the field between mother and child, the ground unconscious can start to develop into the first depth structure of the pleromatic self. In concrete terms, this means that the field must be sufficiently open, safe and receptive, that the first uroboric Other must be available and at the same time have sufficient *alpha* and mirror function within which the child can be carried and tolerated.[4] In Chapter 5, we already mentioned that one of the properties of the field is the container function. This is also characteristic of the therapeutic field between patient and practitioner. A well-functioning field in therapy therefore offers – just like the development field between mother and child – the necessary space for mirroring, processing and the emergence of the first deep structures or *fulcra*, including their associated processes. In an attempt to combine some of these insights with Wilber's coat hook, we could state that physical-material (F1a), visceral 'uroboric' (F1b), axial (F2a) and pranic (F2b) *beta*-stimuli in the dyadic field are converted and mirrored in early 'editable' *alpha* images (F2c). These are becoming more and more stable and durable and can be held more and more easily: first as a physical 'sensory-motor body self' (*fulcrum* 1) and finally as a typhonic 'phantasmic-emotional' body self (*fulcrum* 2). The continuous process of fusion/identification, differentiation and integration has now brought the subject to the point where it can carry, handle and process physical and (early) emotional objects. This is a crucial moment in development, a kind of point of no return, after which the early self is born, albeit still very fragile and vulnerable. Wilber described this as a transformation process and we compared this to the climber's clicking into a grips on the wall. We'll come back to this as well.

When working with the psychosomatic body, it is interesting to remember that the self is initially formed by physical and uroboric identification processes. The subsequent typhonic body images are then the result of largely unconscious processes between mother and child in which the mother (or first Other) offers the child the possibility to incorporate the fragmented body awareness. Clinically and therapeutically, we take all these stages together as 'the uroboric-pranic body'. As already pointed out, the interconnectedness of physicality and early affective interactions also focuses on the importance of the skin and the ability to touch and be touched (Cluckers & Meurs, 2005; Anzieu, 2006). This offers therapeutic perspectives which we will translate into the concrete practice of EBW in Chapter 7.

The psychosomatic body within the *fulcrum* model

How can we situate the psychosomatic 'conflicted' body within the *fulcrum* model and the psychodynamic processes present? More specifically, how does the analysis so far help to better understand the psychosomatic body? To this end, we revisit the thesis of McDougall (1989): 'This leads us to consider the presymbolic, preverbal universe as possibly providing a key to psychotic and psychosomatic potentialities' (pp. 39–40). McDougall suggests that the pre-symbolic and pre-verbal part of the development spectrum is of key importance for understanding and explaining psychosomatic processes. This would mean that the early *fulcra* discussed earlier could determine the later development of psychosomatic symptoms. In their article on physicality and affect in psychosomatics, Meurs and Cluckers (1996) further elaborate on this path and rightly note that psychosomatics occurs at all levels of personality structure when affects – which are triggered by a particular event – cannot be processed or handled 'by the characteristic coping and defence mechanisms' (p. 71). So, as with McDougall, we are reminded of the importance of the early levels of development and the associated possibilities for processing. All levels of the personality structure correspond to all of Wilber's *fulcra*.

> *The traditional psychosomatic conflict can only arise when the mental, psychological apparatus is sufficiently operational and then takes charge of the hitherto dominant pranic body.*

Yet, Wilber (1999) seems to take a different approach and within the early *fulcra* – in line with clinicians, such as Mahler and Kernberg – he only situates the infantile autistic, symbiotic and (partly) psychotic pathologies (F1) next to those of the narcissistic borderline range (F2). For Wilber, the true psychosomatic conflict only occurs within the third *fulcrum* of the early self or newly installed ego. Here, the subject gradually acquires language and linguistic thinking and gradually learns to move into the inner world of others while mentalising. For

Wilber, this is the gradual transition to the personal 'ego' *fulcra* 4 to 6 (as opposed to the pre-personal or pre-Oedipal *fulcra* 1 to 3), where language and thinking will develop further into refined and stable abilities, such as mentalisation and later hypothetical-deductive thinking. Psychodynamically, this means that we place the individual after the third *fulcrum* in the neurotic or Oedipal developmental range, in short the ego. *Fulcrum* 3[5] is an important demarcation from pre-ego (body-emotion subject) to ego (language-thinking subject): 'With language the verbal mind could differentiate itself out of the previous body self' (Wilber, 1996, p. 99). This subject is psychodynamically referred to as an Oedipal and triangulated subject who speaks where, before *fulcrum* 3, it was a pre-Oedipal subject, consisting of body, drives and emotions.[6]

Traditionally, the psychosomatic conflict is primarily understood as an (early) neurotic conflict in which unacceptable pre-Oedipal impulses and drives must be excluded or suppressed by the neurotic defence of thought and language. In this way, psychosomatics is essentially an affect-pathology that is expressed in hysterical conversion symptoms and 'somatic' actual pathology (Meurs & Cluckers, 1996). In a certain sense, Wilber (1992, 1996, 2001) follows this way of thinking in which psychosomatics is created by the suppressive domination of the neurotic, personal ego-*fulcra* over the lower pre-personal *fulcra*. The psychosomatic conflict can, therefore, only arise at the moment that the mental, psychological apparatus is sufficiently operational and then takes control of the hitherto prevalent pranic body.[7] We follow Wilber's lead when he situates the typical psychosomatic conflict in a narrow sense within the (early) neurotic register and, thus, after the first two *fulcra*. Indeed, during the developmental dynamics of the third *fulcrum*, the early mental self begins to manifest and differentiate itself from the body and its impulses, emotions and drives (not in the least sex and aggression) by integrating all this into conceivable concepts. However, if this differentiation fails – and in Wilber's terms becomes a 'dissociation' – the individual ends up in a psychosomatic split in which the body *in extremis* can only be thought of as an object without any form of proper experience and feeling. This, sometimes mechanical, relationship can be seen, for example, in patients who only live in their heads, so to speak. The psychosomatic request for help of many patients with a difficult body is, therefore, situated in this area, where the turbulent, vital body is banished to the dungeons of the mental 'body'.

This same template of conflict/suppression dynamic is also central in the work of Wilhelm Reich, whom we introduced in Chapter 4 as the godfather of body psychotherapy. Indeed, Reich's point of view was not so far removed from Freudian theory since he too started from vegetative-biological processes and drive (*Trieb*). Nevertheless, Reich opted for an entirely individual view of the ego by specifically linking Freud's body-self to the muscular apparatus. He saw muscle tension structured as a symptom that contains both unconscious impulses and their suppression (Totton, 1998; Cornell, 2015). For Reich, too, these impulses, or drives, were forces that produce excitations from within the body, disrupt the state of the body and force the body 'to perform actions to reduce the stimuli' (Moyaert, 2014, p. 18). In the introduction, we referred to other pioneers, such as Groddeck, Ferenczi and Fenichel, who explicitly related the inability to discharge this drive tension to dysfunctional muscular tension and not just actions. We also learned that Reich (1972, 1973) developed this further into the concept of muscle armour and regards the body as an imprint of tension that has an effect on the muscle tissue, which then organises itself into dysfunctional patterns. His idea that this armoured body must be able to discharge as a body in order for the patient to be able to move emotionally was innovative in this respect. So, the body has to do something if the emotions are to be set in motion. More recently, this 'breakthrough into the vegetative realm' (Reich, 1973) has become neurobiologically founded as 'biological completion' (Payne & Crane-Godreau, 2015) and the body is regarded as a medium for affect regulation (Geuter, 2015b). Here too, explicit reference is made to the role of the muscular or myofascial system, for example in suppressing breathing, withholding anger or masking anxiety (Bloom, 2006). On the other hand, we already saw that Freud, in his early trauma theory, also took a similar course, in which 'it is necessary for mental health that this energetic occupation be discharged through: 1) the motor reactions and/or via 2) associative psychological activity.' (Verhaeghe, 2006, p. 16). Useful for therapy is that research suggests that the discharge of the myofascial muscle armour cannot be done arbitrarily. Just moving or involving random muscle groups appears to be pointless if such a discharge or 'biological completion' is to be achieved. The movement and the associated myofascial armour must form part of a meaningful approach. When this meaningful, trauma-related context is met, visualisation or 'imaginary playing-out' sometimes proves sufficient to stimulate the premotor cortex and to stimulate targeted experience in therapy (Payne et al., 2015). We will come back to this briefly in Chapter 7.

But however much the psychosomatic conflict that we are examining here in its traditional form is absolutely relevant to everyday practice within the vision of Wilber and Reich, McDougall's earlier quotation reminds us of the starting point to examine even the earliest *fulcra* as a breeding ground for psychosomatic processes in more detail.

The psychosomatic conflict within the early *fulcra*

We saw that the body does not yet exist as a separate entity within the pleromatic fusion. Only a kind of protoplasmic consciousness (Wilber, 2000, p. 612) exists, within which the physical 'sensory-motor' self still has to distinguish itself. After this differentiation of the physical-material environment comes the experience and learning of physical-nutritional stimuli (uroboros). In other words, in this very early phase, the subject already develops a rudimentary distinction between itself and the physical environment, but also between inside and outside itself through nutrition. Under optimal conditions, this exploration and demarcation leads to the experience of a 'first' own body. This uroboric body is what Bazan (2014) calls the invertebrate body, 'the sack of intestines, including the respiratory system, the blood circulation, the digestive system, the excretion device and the reproductive system' (p. 248). So when the child brings breast

118   *The psychosomatic body within the* fulcrum *model*

milk 'inside', this uroboros, invertebrate body is stimulated and gives satisfaction.[8] Bazan (2014) situates the first drive sources in this inner, invertebrate body and then describes how deficits or alarms in this body are translated into an excess of excitation that incites the outer, vertebrate body of muscles and skeleton to act (p. 249). Interesting is a review by Pluess et al. (2009) that makes an inventory of explanations of muscular tension in people with generalised anxiety. One of the possibilities that can be substantiated is to consider muscle tension as a form of coping in which the excess excitation originating from anxiety is discharged through the tension in the muscle tissue. This is, of course, fully in line with the workings and role of the muscle armour, but also with Freud's idea of shifting the energetic affect quantum (Verhaeghe, 2006).

> *Emotional tensions often manifest themselves in deeper or smaller myofascial tissues that are directly connected to functions of the uroboric-pranic, invertebrate body. This partly explains why we frequently and intensively work on the MML within EBW.*

The invertebrate body can be recognised clinically and therapeutically by two types of psychosomatic requests for help. First of all, it is striking that patients who are under long-term traumatic stress develop symptoms in this invertebrate body, such as intestinal disorders (digestion), hyperventilation (breathing), sexual dysfunction (reproductive system) or severely disrupted energy management (neuro-endocrine excretion system). Van Oudenhove (2007a, 2007b, 2010) details the neurobiological circuits that explain the harmful influence of stress on gastrointestinal complaints and explicitly points to the importance of 'body psychotherapy' (p. 69). Levine (2014b) goes one step further and states that traumatised individuals have been 'disembodied' and 'gutted' (p. 328). A second striking clinical parallel, as already mentioned in Chapter 4, is the relationship with the myofascial system that supports this uroboric-pranic, invertebrate body, namely, the MML. Deep emotional tensions often manifest themselves only in deeper, and often smaller, myofascial tissues that are directly connected to functions of the uroboric-pranic, invertebrate body. This partly explains why within EBW, we frequently and intensively work on the MML situated in the top-right quadrant substrate of this body. Typical muscles that are emphasised in many forms of bodywork and body-oriented psychotherapies are the chewing and swallowing muscles, muscular lodges in the neck, deep neck muscles, diaphragm and breathing apparatus, *iliopsoas* and the pelvic floor, including the relationship with structures in the abdominal cavity, around the spine and the deep muscle lodges of lower and upper limbs down to the sole of the foot (Totton & Edmondson, 2013; Rosen & Brenner, 2003; Painter, 1986, 1987). In some situations, the deep myofascial work becomes even more detailed and is carried out on the floor of the mouth, the inside of the oral cavity and jaw, the tongue and the roof of the mouth. This 'bucal' work is experienced as gruelling, usually involving an intense, emotional experience, and always has a powerful, liberating effect on 'oral' functions such as breathing, mouth movement and swallowing (embodied self-awareness).

Here some interesting avenues are to explore in areas such as singing, rhetorical and expressive vocal use or, more therapeutically specific, speech therapy.

If things go wrong within these very early *fulcrum* dynamics,[9] then what McDougall calls 'one body for two' will continue to exist. The body remains part of a symbiotic mother-child unit within which differentiation is not tolerated by either, which increases the risk of psychosomatic disorders (Meurs & Cluckers, 1996, p. 71). We could see it as the uroboric snake that fails to release its own head-tail (symbiosis) to become snake. On the other hand, if the process of fusion/identification, differentiation and integration does succeed, the uroboric snake lets go of its own tail and focuses on itself as the typhon of *fulcrum* 2 that symbolises the next step as half man/half snake.

The crucial process within this second *fulcrum* is the proto-emotional, phantasmic and, above all, pranic differentiation. In simple terms, from now on, the world and the subject start to live. In other words, the newly discovered world and one's own body will be vitalised. More technically, both the subject and the objects 'outside' are now occupied by this energy, which subsequently gives rise to images: first axial (F2a) and then pranic (F2b). This is how the flowing and drifting of the drive energy or *Trieb* forms the basis for the first emotions and the pranic charging or 'affecting' of the subject. However, the body itself is also vitalised as an object and becomes 'charged'. This is necessary, because 'physical unity is always implicit and confused . . . the only way to know it is to live it' (Van den Bossche, 2008, p. 152). Interestingly, Plassmann refers to this as an 'archetypal injection of vitality and enthusiasm'[10] (in Meurs & Cluckers, 1996, p. 75). This injection not only catalyses further development, but the subject ends up in a field that is charged with emotions and moves. The field is set in motion, can explode or implode and will, from now on, not only remain drive-based, but also emotional. We see this almost literally in the case of the child who is constantly starting to raise himself and moving as if he were being propelled. As we have already described, this typhonic process of vitalisation involves a first stable form of time experience: a 'widened present' in which images can be held. According to Wilber, human individualisation only really starts here, with this vitalisation. According to Henri Bergson, this combination of vitalisation and the experience of time is literally the *élan vital*. In this context, time is understood as a living time – *la dureé* – which is nothing more than 'creative driving force' (Van Dongen, 2014, p. 80).

But the process of affective injection can also ensure that within the earliest *fulcra*, and more specifically the dyadic mother-child field, things go wrong. Melanie Klein (Mitchell, 1986) introduced the concept of projective identification as a process whereby unbearable parts of the self are placed in the other beyond the boundaries of time and space.

De Wolf (2011) reminds us that, consequently, projective identification belongs to the early development phase in which anxiety is massive and overwhelming, because anxiety here is about the loss of subjectivity. So when McDougall (1989) pointed out earlier that the child's first external reality is the mother's unconscious, this also opens up to abuse on the mother's part. In that way, the mother's unconscious can pollute the dyadic field with her own unprocessed, raw material just as much. This is then, as it were, 'planted' in the child that cannot possibly handle it. In the best case, it succeeds in evacuating these intrusive elements to the outside. These kinds of overwhelming experiences are deeply traumatising and may well compromise the further process of healthy psychological development. This gives free rein to the Kleinian phantasms of aggression, sadism and haunting. At the hands of a uroboric Other who is suffocating or aggressive and (literally) in close proximity, the self of *fulcrum* 2 can get occupied with raw, dirty or destructive energy. The subject experiences the Other as dangerous, unpredictable, unreliable, taking sadistic pleasure or even cannibalistic. In this way, a deep form of suspicion towards others creeps into the world of the young subject. We also saw that it is also through this uroboric Other that the subject gets to know his body. As a result, the paranoid relationship with the world may continue on the subject's own body. Clinically, this reminds us of patients who show an extremely negative or hostile experience of their body (e.g. in case of self-harm). But equally, the psychotic body that falls apart (defragments) or overflows, can find its origin in the traumatisation of the early field by the uroboric-pranic Other. On the other hand, the dyadic field can also be corrupted by an absent or unavailable mother, as in the Still-Face experiment that was discussed earlier. In analytical terms, Green (1983) introduced the term *la mère morte* here. The subject is now left 'alone' in a field where there is hardly any differentiation and no one else is available. Here, too, the child is left to be swamped with stimuli that are impossible to digest. In short, *beta* elements of the environment, the mother and the own indigestible fragments[11] can contaminate the primary field and, thus, hinder the crucial process of fusion/identification, differentiation and integration. Returning to the psychosomatic conflict, we are not only at an earlier, but, above all, more basic level of functioning compared to the traditional psychosomatic conflict outlined earlier. The processes and structures involved have nothing to do with repression, because there is no mental, 'psychic' or neurotic structure that is strong enough to control the pranic body. Using Nietzsche's metaphor, Dionysus is still at the helm for now, while Apollo is waiting in the wings. The forces – and therefore also the symptoms – are more massive, more overwhelming, more drastic, exhausting and more frightening. The body structures and processes involved are more fundamental, more complex and literally deeper.

However, when the developmental process can be continued in a stable way, the second *fulcrum* is completed as the emotional-phantasmic self and emotional object-constancy is established. The subject knows how to distinguish himself from other emotional objects and learns to handle them. Emotional experiences can now exist and be imagined for longer. Fulfilling pleasure is one of the possibilities and the typhonic itself, or body ego, is born. Dirkx

The psychosomatic body within the fulcrum *model* 121

(2011) points out that before emotional object constancy can be achieved, there must first be physical object permanence, which means that the physical significant Other can be held, even when he is not there. With the physical and uroboric-pranic body as a foundation, the subject is now ready to explore and inhabit the mental-psychic landscape. Access to this lies in the third *fulcrum* that is completed with the conceptual object constancy. After physical and emotional object constancy, the individual can now use mental objects such as concepts and symbols. But for this progressive process of awareness, the young subject also pays a considerable price, because as we already saw in Chapter 5, anxiety now enters the stage and will continue to do so in various guises. Nicolai (2016) typifies anxiety within subject development in the following chronology: disintegration anxiety, separation anxiety, fear of loss of love, anxiety of damage and destruction, fear of conscience, fear of being rejected and fear of loss of identity. Although a further deepening is not possible within the scope of this book, it is interesting to note that Wilber (1999, 2000) points to similar anxieties when going through the various *fulcra*. From a primary anxiety of disappearing into matter (F1a) or being swallowed by the uroboric Other (F1b), over the anxiety of being abandoned by the nurturing Other (F2) to the early neurotic fear of guilt and shame (F3) and anxiety of violating social conventions (F4) to the later identity anxiety (F5) and existential crisis (F6). Anxiety is, therefore, usually present in one form or another in the patient's story, but is not always recognised as such. A challenging proposition could be to always understand the patient's request for help as a question about the relationship to anxiety (Calsius, 2012). In this sense, a request for help in its basic form is always an existential question.

> *Returning to the psychosomatic conflict, we find ourselves at an earlier, but above all more basic, level of function in comparison with the traditional psychosomatic conflict. The forces – and therefore also the symptoms – are more massive, more overwhelming, more drastic, exhaustive and more frightening. The body structures and processes involved are more fundamental, more complex and literally deeper.*

In addition to this brief interpretation of the various forms of anxiety, it is also useful to consider what anxiety does within the process of subject development.

Anxiety within subject development

We have talked a lot about the development of the subject so far. But what is the role of anxiety in this? Verhaeghe (2003) sets the tone with a challenging proposition: 'Anxiety is the driving force behind three processes of similar origin, namely, the subject development, the symbol development and the creation of human reality as such' (p. 222). Anxiety is, therefore, not just a side effect, or a consequence, of subject development, but rather a motor, a driving force. According to Verhaeghe (idem), the role of anxiety must be understood in two ways, namely, as the affective colouring of the original distressing experience and as the psychological reaction that follows the Other's absence or departure. Anxiety has a physical component as well as a relational component, since anxiety is intrinsically interwoven with the Other. This is reminiscent of the statement from the Upanishads: 'Where the other is, there is anxiety'. Anxiety is, therefore, always a anxiety of separation. So, on the one hand, the young subject is physically disturbed and, on the other, there is the Other who, although the only support, can never guarantee that there will never be distress or tension. Verhaeghe (idem) argues that the physical distress becomes psychological suffering as soon as the Other turns out to be inadequate or fails. And it is precisely this that is inevitable.

Subject development, therefore, not only implies an ongoing process of differentiation as such; it is also inevitably accompanied by the appearance – and never again disappearance – of anxiety. Important here is that when it comes to early developmental processes, these anxieties also relate to the early *fulcra* and are, therefore, a-linguistic, initially even without any image. In their most basic form, they fall back on the pleromatic fusion prior to the first differentiation with the material world. Put in Lacanian terms, we could qualify this form of anxiety as real anxiety or *jouissance* (Harari, 2001) and Bion speaks of (sub-)thalamic fear (Junqueira & Braga, 2013).[12] Either way, up to and including the second, pranic *fulcrum*, anxieties are purely physical; after all, there is nothing else available yet to defend oneself against anxiety. Clinically interesting is the insight that anxiety must be linked, or diverted, to 'something' outside the child; it is literally evacuated. This linking process is of crucial importance, so that peace can return to the child's body. We already discussed at length that this process starts in the mirror stage where the Other will help to provide early signifiers. Initially, these are actions, body language or baby language. In a later stage – from Wilber's third *fulcrum* – more and more words and language come to the fore and the anxiety is explained and understood.

Psychodynamically, there is a clinically valuable distinction at this point, namely, between psychopathological and actual pathology. As this distinction is related to the elaboration of anxiety, in case of actual pathology mental representation is not yet possible. In Chapter 3, we briefly referred to the actual pathology process in which panic is in a certain sense a kind of somatic anxiety-equivalent, the body being the anxiety. So, anxiety before or after the third 'linguistic' *fulcrum* has a fundamentally different dynamic and appearance. In the next and final chapter, we'll take this up as one of the three important turning points within the early *fulcra*: actual pathology dynamics with physical instead of mental processing versus psychopathological dynamics with sufficient mental processing.

For a more thorough exploration of this valuable dichotomy, we refer to further literature on developmental pathology versus conflict pathology (e.g. De Wolf, 2011, 2002; Cullberg, 2009). Here, we remember that during early development as uroboros, axial-pranic and image-body, the subject's first layers of identity are presented by the first Other and, at the same time, they represent a first defence against anxiety. A not insignificant clinical consequence is that the body, as an object of experience, not only forms the first fundamental layer of the later ego-identity, but also appears to be inherently connected to a primary process of anxiety regulation. This is also what the body often presents in therapy: a failing coping towards anxiety and unconscious attempts to expel the same anxiety (Calsius et al., 2013a, 2013b). The therapeutic process – and the patient in particular – therefore benefits from a therapist who wonders where anxiety appears in the story and in the patient's body.

Tools for therapy

- *Fundamental processes within the early dyadic field provide insight into digesting, mirroring and regulating the pleromatic, uroboric and pranic context in which the subject finds himself.*
- *Within these processes, the layered body emerges as the basis for the individual.*
- *When working with the psychosomatic body, we remember that the self is initially formed by physical and uroboric-pranic identification processes. The typhonic body images that follow are also the result of largely unconscious processes between child and early affective environment.*
- *The psychosomatic conflict can therefore relate to the uroboric-pranic body from early subject development, or to neurotic core processes, which are central from the third fulcrum where the mental forces want to control the body. Both registers of psychosomatic conflict are expressed through the difficult body and can be found in the myofascial armour, such as the MML.*
- *Underlying these psychosomatic processes, anxiety – intrinsically linked to the position of the Other – plays a fundamental role.*

Notes

1 For a detailed discussion of the normal and psychopathological subject development using this model, we refer the reader to Wilber 1999.
2 Ferrari (2004), in his book *From the eclipse of the body to the dawn of thought*, attempts to comprehend this difficult position of the body, distinguishing the subject, the device that registers and the object that is perceived. He conceptualises the latter as 'Concrete Original Object' and states that it is formed by the physical body and the fragmented sensations that result from it.
3 Verhaeghe (2003) recalls that 'the foundation of our identity thus amounts to an image presented by the Other, which is brought in and lays the foundation of the ego' (p. 141).
4 Bion's *alpha* function or waking dream thought is indeed not only a protective contact-barrier (Bion, 1962, p. 17), it also helps convert it into pictograms or 'narremes' and forms the basis for 'affective attunement' (Grottstein, 2013, p. 111).

124　*The psychosomatic body within the* fulcrum *model*

5　Wilber (1999) divides *fulcrum* 3 into two, one part of which is more akin to the dynamics of *fulcrum* 2 and the other, later part, is already characterised by the mentally Oedipal range of the ego. In the first part, he therefore places the borderline neurosis while the traditional, early psychoneurotic pathologies, such as hysteria, compulsive neurosis, hypochondria and phobia, belong in the more mature, second part within *fulcrum* 3.
6　Building on these authors, an important turning point will emerge around the process of triangulation or the appearance of a second crucial object figure next to the mother's object (the second Other, traditionally thought to be the father figure). This is also what McDougall means when she states that: 'Almost as powerful a factor is her relationship to her baby's father and the extent to which he is invested by her with both real and symbolic significance and affection' (p. 40). By opening the dyadic relationship, the child will be able to get out of the symbiotic dynamics with the mother and 'leave' the physical-emotional world to enter the neurotic range of development.
7　In a more mythological, anthropological and cultural-philosophical field, we recognise this characteristic psychodynamic developmental process not only in the suppression of the body, its instincts and (proto-)emotions, but also, by extension, in the suppression of everything related to the constitution of this first *fulcra*, such as the feminine, the mother, the feeling, but also the fusion, the chaos, the disappearance and the anxiety (see, for example, 'De Ontembare Vrouw' ('The Indomitable Woman') of Pinkola Estes (1996). More psychoanalytically we indeed see the shift to the linguistic, cognitive, 'symbolic-imaginary' register with an (over)appreciation of the accompanying analytical, thinking and 'mentalising' capacities. Strangely enough, even the irrational dimension of psychoanalysis (Vermote, 2010) has had a difficult time until recently.
8　In Chapter 4, we typify this process on a neurophysiological basis as 'interoceptive' and embedded in the insular network within which the body consciousness 'emerges'. Junqueira and Braga (2013) even point to the experience of swallowing and spitting amniotic fluid as a kind of priming for the later evacuation of basal emotions as in projective identification.
9　Wilber distinguishes on each *fulcrum* a possible pathological process of fixation or dissociation.
10　On a phenomenological basis, Plassmann then distinguishes four body experiences within the psychosomatic register, namely, 'the dead in the body', 'the unbounded body', 'the split body' and 'the devalued body' (Meurs & Cluckers, 1996).
11　Just as a foetus can infect the amniotic fluid with its own faeces, so too are its own retchings left undigested without any support from mother's *rêverie*.
12　This in view of her processing in (sub-)thalamic networks during the pre- and perinatal development period: 'The fetus . . . is capable of experiencing sensations as excitations in the thalamo-adrenal axis. These sensations give rise to proto-feelings which will later be nominated 'anxiety' or 'hate', that could be experienced in a primordial way, mobilising impulses to fight or flee' (Junqueira & Braga, 2013, p. 192).

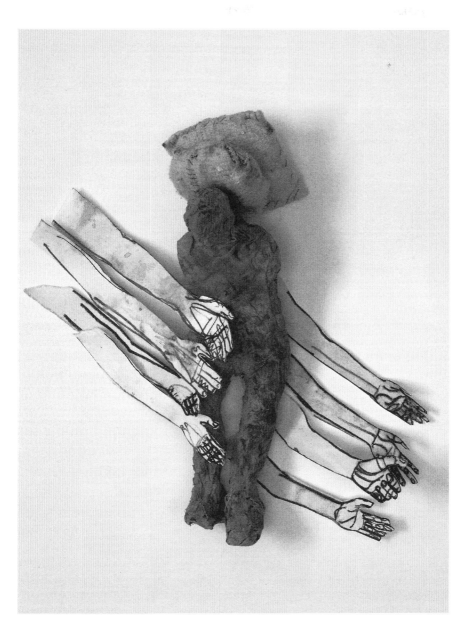

Go and stay, 2016, collage on paper, conté, papier maché, cloth, 50 × 40 × 6.4 cm.

7 The practice of experiential bodywork

In the opening reflections of this book, we already sketched out that the central topic 'A different view of the psychosomatic body' requires, first and foremost, a thorough theoretical exploration. Now that this extensive exploration of clinical concepts and theoretical frameworks is complete, we come to questions of a more practical-therapeutic nature, such as 'How do you, as a therapist, integrate the discussed material in practice and how does an EBW treatment programme proceed in concrete terms?' Or 'Which techniques are used and how do you go about using them?' These and other questions are central in this final chapter, where we home in on the practice of EBW. We start this clarification – just like the therapeutic process – with the first encounter and anamnesis and then work towards the treatment step by step. First of all, we will take a moment to think about the therapy room itself.

The therapy room

The transdisciplinary need to arrive at the integrated treatment of the psychosomatic body requires efforts in terms of not only theoretical understanding and therapeutic skills but also practical implications. Ideally, the treatment room is a tangible reflection of the dual perspective we want to adopt. Concretely, the facilities for intake, bodywork and psychotherapeutic conversation and integration are all located in one and the same room. Together with a comfortable sitting area for intake and conversation, the place for bodywork (treatment table or mattress) and sufficient space for expressive movement, are minimal requirements. Since the patient's evocative expression is central within EBW, it is necessary that the room is not only sufficiently spacious and bright, but also as soundproof as possible from other rooms, specifically the waiting room. We know from experience that physical characteristics of the treatment room, such as warmth, atmospheric lighting and a living-room feel, contribute greatly to a sense of security and safety. Treatments usually take three quarters of an hour, but can take up double that time, depending on the phase in which the therapeutic process is in. It goes without saying that patients see just one therapist and that the treatment will not be disturbed in any way by colleagues or multimedia. These rules are part of the therapeutic framework that is familiar to psychologists/psychotherapists, but often turns out to be unfamiliar to somatic therapists.[1]

128 *The practice of experiential bodywork*

First encounter and anamnesis

In the first chapter, we described the anamnesis process within EBW and pointed out the importance of the context that precedes the registration. We saw that the reason lies in the narrative of the patient that was somehow disrupted, or at least came under pressure. This then led to a situation that was difficult, or even impossible, to tolerate. The ground dynamics which the patient sets in motion, relate to his objectal foundation and are reflected in the manner of presentation (for example, very demanding) and in the relationship with the therapist (for example, seeking support in order to be able to take on family members who do not understand the disorder). Awareness of these dynamics enables the therapist to make contact with the implicit request for help that lies behind the explicit request for help. In concrete terms, the therapeutic process starts from the very first moment of contact (by telephone, in the waiting room, via the referrer, etc.) and the way in which the patient presents himself and formulates his request for help. The therapist ideally adopts the backward-leaning posture of embodied self-awareness, mind-wandering or *rêverie* and is maximally receptive and listens without judgment.

> P. jumps up when I greet him the first time in the waiting room and apologises immediately for his late arrival, but adds straight away that it will not happen again.
> Comments: As a therapist, I have the feeling that I appear strict and have admonished P. for being late, although he was actually a little early.
> When I invite E. to enter the consultation room, he takes his time to put away his mobile phone and keys in his coat pocket and slowly walks to my desk. Once there, he quietly looks around and asks me to repeat my first words, because he wasn't quite there yet. Finally, he advises me to get better signposting for the car park, so that people don't have to search for it for so long.
> Comments: I experience a somewhat uneasy feeling, as if I have to do my best and immediately have to improve a number of things in order to make E. feel good. In addition, I have the feeling that I have to prove something.
> It's S.'s mother who calls up for a first appointment. She repeats several times that it is very urgent, because S. has been feeling really bad at home for some time now. The first dates I propose, always turn out to be impossible because of practical reasons, such as appointments at the hairdresser's and the sports club. An ultimate proposal for intake is confirmed by S., who apparently has been standing next to her mother all along.
> Comments: I experience the mother as being dominant, someone who constantly takes over and fills in what her daughter's life should look like. Later on, it will turn out that mother has remarried twice, according to S., because daddy couldn't stand it anymore.

The intake usually takes up a full session and is divided into two: an anamnesis that is associative and one that is semi-structured. We always start with the

The practice of experiential bodywork 129

associative anamnesis. Key questions here are 'Who or what brings you here', 'Why now?', 'Why here?' and 'What are your expectations?' Despite the value of a fixed opening question, these questions don't have to be spoken every time, but they play a role in the background. What matters is that the patient is able to speak and is interrupted as little as possible. Some (e.g. hysterical) patients need little encouragement, while others (e.g. those suffering from depression) need more help. In the latter case, it may be useful to formulate the key questions literally. The finality of speaking is the gradual appearance of the narrative that is written down in keywords in the Four Quadrant Model (4QM). Daring to allow sufficient breaks or moments when speaking stops is an important skill that non-psychotherapists often feel uncomfortable with. Nevertheless, it is crucial that the therapist does not fill in the patient's blanks, but gives him the time to get into a rhythm (Bohlmeijer, 2012; Van Houdenhove, 2007b, 2010). In this way, we gain insight into important words and associations within the narrative. In concrete terms, the therapist gains a first insight into the themes or persons that play a role in the patient's current life, how he relates to others and tries to make sense of the world, including his own condition and request for help. As the patient continues to speak in this way, the quadrants fill up; some are overfull, while others remain remarkably empty. The practical template for the 4QM offers an additional subdivision (Figure 7.1), in which a diagonal line divides each quadrant once more. If the therapist notices certain things, such as incongruities in the story or contradictions with the body language of the patient, he notes this. What the therapist notices in terms of his own emotions, is also

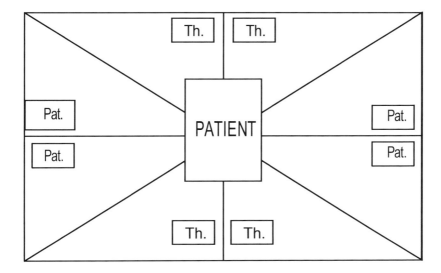

Figure 7.1 The Four Quadrant Template for anamnesis
Source: Based on Wilber, 2000, 2001a, 2006

130 *The practice of experiential bodywork*

written down here. On the other side of these diagonals is only what the patient actually expresses and says.

In the second phase of the intake – or over the course of the next session – the anamnesis change to a more semi-structured approach. Now, the therapist asks more actively for typical processes and aspects of the developmental dynamics per *fulcrum*. In order to understand the psychosomatic body thoroughly, the therapist wants to explore, for example, whether and how the patient has successfully passed the early *fulcra*. Since the third *fulcrum* corresponds to a tipping into the later self-stable *fulcra* (neurotic or Oedipal), this clinically means that the therapist wonders, among other things, whether there is sufficient ego-stability present. Typical themes that are currently being explored in the anamnesis are, for example, the way in which separation has come to pass, whether the patient can achieve mentalisation and what the general situation is with both practical and emotional self-sufficiency.[2]

Can this patient think about himself and the world he lives in, can he put himself in someone else's shoes? How does he deal with his condition and request for help? Is this something that happens to him and over which he no longer has any control, or does he understand his own part in this, his responsibility and scope for recovery? What effect does the patient have on me, what does he ask of me and how is this being staged? How can and should this person deal with pain and feelings of sorrow, powerlessness or anger? Do patterns of dependency on significant others stand out, or is there an inability to make affective connections? Are there any signs of a weak, or even absent, reality check?

All these questions come together, as it were, in the imaginary question of which Russian dolls are most prominently present and which appear to be absent. Herein lies a first sense of the development-dynamics and the place that the body occupies.

When driving off after the third session, T. became very emotional in the car, so much so that she had to pull over, because she was starting to hyperventilate quite badly. Since she couldn't reach her husband, she panicked and tried to call her doctor, but he was on a house call. She then phoned her previous therapist, who had always really been there for her. T. goes on to say how this therapist calmed her down by talking her through it.

Comment: The coping is done almost entirely by the body and out of reach of language. The anamnesis shows that T. is little separated and this is also evident in the panic-stricken search and clinging to the previous therapist who was good for her. This safe person could also easily calm her down, if only by his voice.

The therapist, however, also considers the blanks within the 4QM around significant Others who have not come up much in conversation, if at all. Specific elements, such as trauma processing, are also questioned here, including the way in which attachment figures have reacted to pain, trauma or illness. This gives the therapist a better insight into the patient's developmental processes and the current request for help can be framed within the objectal foundation and the ego-stability, if present. In this way, the therapist gains a first glimpse of the context within which the patient's psychosomatic field of tension has developed and why precisely these psychosomatic problem areas appear in the patient. Is the patient able to mentally process the tensions that occur in his life sufficiently or do they appear to stick to the body? For example, is this a patient who worries and has restless dreams (psychopathological coping), or does he suffer from hyperventilation and panic attacks (actual-pathological coping)? Do we assess this as a neurotic conflict dynamic or do we suspect psychosomatic processes from the earliest *fulcra?*

> K. tells me that after the last session (intake,) he spent two nights tossing and turning and having weird dreams. Once, he even dreamt about me as a therapist.
> The therapy room was a kind of church, maybe it was a big confessional and it seemed like I was waiting for K. in there. This dream has been preying on his mind a lot in the subsequent days.
> Comment: There appears to be transference from the first session. The patient is sensitive to this, it keeps him occupied and ponders it. A new mental process of metabolising has set in for the patient.

Naturally, the semi-structured *fulcrum* anamnesis also serves to read the body more accurately. From the physical-material body, the uroboros and pranic body, right through to the various later *fulcra* in which the body can come into focus more and more. The body appears in various ways within the narrative. Throughout the anamnesis process, the therapist also gains a sharper sense of the development-dynamics in which the body finds itself. The therapist asks himself questions such as: Are there any developmental stops?', 'Have the parents invested enough in the patient', 'Is there over- or under-regulation and what about regressive patterns?' Finally, the therapist asks himself how all this has affected the body that is speaking here.

> P. says that as a child, he was allowed to stay at home from the moment he didn't feel so well. 'Stay with me, boy' his grandmother would always say, 'you'll get better soon'. Father and mother had their own furniture store and were hardly ever at home, so he was brought up by a grandmother who lived at home.
> E. remembers that on one occasion on holiday, she threw up in the car after a visit to a Chinese restaurant. Father had blown his top and had made her clean up the mess herself. She was then only around eight years old and remembers that he was foaming at the mouth.
> When J. has a migraine, he prefers to crawl into bed in his favourite pyjamas and, as he did as a child, put the pillow over his head. The pain then gently ebbs away. He often masturbates and then feels relieved afterwards.

132 *The practice of experiential bodywork*

However, in this phase, it should not be forgotten that, in addition to current conditions and illnesses, typical information should be asked, such as relevant prior physical problems, operations, accidents or traumata (e.g. long-term medical treatments or sexual abuse) or psychiatric issues in the family. But also possible experiences and behaviours in specific periods (childhood, adolescence, pregnancy, etc.), such as stuttering, bedwetting, long-term thumb-sucking and nightmares. Finally, this phase should also be utilised – if necessary – to ask after body-related topics, such as nutrition, sports, sexuality, hygiene and medication or drug use.

In the meantime the 4QM has been supplemented and the therapist has made plenty of notes about his patient's *fulcrum* dynamics. Of course, these notes are not exhaustive, but the therapist remains alert throughout the entire therapeutic process.

In contrast to most somatic therapy anamneses, where the left quadrants only provide 'information' with which little, if anything, can be done the narrative becomes more and more evident within EBW and enhances the further therapeutic process. The therapist not only logs what the patient says and shows, but also effectively incorporates this into the treatment. If, for example, thoughts, images, meaningful movements or body reactions emerge later during conversation sessions or bodywork, the therapist can easily include these into the grid of quadrants and *fulcra*. On the other hand, the therapist can also actively contribute descriptions of events and experiences in order to facilitate, challenge or orientate the therapeutic process. In addition to this two-way cross-fertilisation, the extensive anamnestic process within EBW also serves to re-contextualise the patient and his request for help. Most patients present themselves with a de-contextualised question, usually reduced to the top-right quadrant and often because the referral was made in this way. People who suffer from panic, insecurity, tension in the neck, frantic behaviour, hyperventilation, teeth grinding or disturbing thoughts about death only want one thing, and that is to get rid of these. The sooner the better. It is crucial that the therapist takes the time for this first phase of meeting, making contact, exploring the narrative and patient re-contextualisation. The latter encompasses at least a quadrant and *fulcrum*-sensitive process. Gradually, the next anamnestic sequence will emerge, which must be understood in the same way as 'listening to the patient's story', only now from a physical point of view. While the way of recording an associative anamnesis is mostly unknown to body therapists, this first physical phase is usually unfamiliar to psychotherapists. Nevertheless, we in EBW emphasise that these two sequences involve the same techniques, namely, listening to the patient attentively and inquisitively from the first contact. Typical for the first physical contact is the reading of the body as a phenomenological entry point and the analysis of the myofascial muscle armour with a listening touch. This analysis can be done in a stand-alone sequence or can be included in the start-up of the bodywork as we will describe in a moment.

After the extensive anamnestic process, it can be decided to continue the treatment in which the three pillars of EBW – bodywork, evocative movement and room to talk are given a phased or integrated place, or not, as the case may be (Figure 7.2). Within EBW, however, we do not use a fixed pattern of therapeutic

The practice of experiential bodywork 133

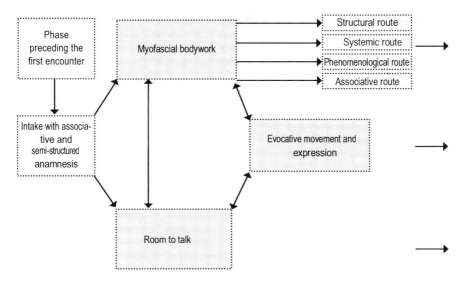

Figure 7.2 Therapeutic flowchart EBW

phases. It may well be the case that after the anamnesis, we first engage in dialogue before we can move on to physical exploration. Reasons for this may be that patients first need some time to prepare for the bodywork, to feel sufficiently safe or just want to know what it all involves first. So we work with the necessary number of 'verbal' sessions, until the patient feels sufficiently comfortable. It is also interesting to note that some patients prefer to start with bodywork and seem to keep the verbal aspect at bay, sometimes because this can also feel unsafe, or they simply do not have the energy for it. As far as the bodywork itself is concerned, the therapist has about four angles he can start from, depending on whether these are more in line with his own background, deontological framework and therapeutic expertise.

In this sense, these four access routes can also be considered somewhat prototypical, some of which will be easier for body therapists to handle, such as the structural and systemic route, which requires a certain degree of manual skill. Psychotherapists often have more affinity with the phenomenological and associative route. On the other hand, experience shows that additional training and supervision in body psychotherapy offer excellent opportunities to cross over and train as a therapist in the language and skills of neighbouring entry points. For example, psychologists/psychotherapists are usually surprised by the refinement of bodywork and the power that goes with it. After some time, they also overcome their initial unfamiliarity with physical contact and bodywork and integrate the muscle armour as an access route. In principle, none of these 'access roads' are perfect, as they can all connect in a specific way to the body that has shown

134 *The practice of experiential bodywork*

itself up to that point. On the other hand, as this classification is to some extent also didactic, experienced therapists will be able to integrate various aspects of it effortlessly and partly unconsciously into their treatment.

Four access routes to the body in experiential bodywork

The structural route

The starting point here is a well-defined diagnosis. Through body reading and listening touch, the therapist reads and listens to the body – and in particular specific regions – in order to map the presence of dysfunctional structures or zones.[3] These are often parts of the myofascial armour where the body is specifically in trouble. Within EBW, this route leads to a specific structure that will be explicitly addressed in the treatment, for example with myofascial release techniques for the three layers (Chapter 4).

Reading the body and the listening touch reveal that the diaphragm of a patient with hyperventilation problems is very tense, which means that both breathing and emotional expression are compromised. This myofascial region not only blocks the expansion of the chest, but also constantly creates an unpleasantly tight and anxious feeling, as a result of which the patient begins to 'hold back' even more. Before being able to continue working on body experience, it is necessary to first release this part of the muscle armour.

A patient is referred by the liaison psychiatrist because 'she can't keep her food down'. Since she also experiences severe discomfort when swallowing, she underwent extensive somatic examinations beforehand, but always without results. The gastroenterologist was, therefore, clear in his opinion that nothing was wrong and that it was probably a psychological issue. This patient met with severe neglect in childhood and, for some years now, has been trapped in a destructive relationship with a dominant man who regularly reminds her of her dependent position with a firm hand. In consultation with her psychiatrist, we only focus on the swallowing problem during EBW and opt for the structural route. Clinical research indicates that there is a lot of tension around the jaws and the throat lodge, whereby the swallowing movement is visibly hindered by the increased myofascial tonus. We build up gradually, first working externally on the structures around the jaw and later via the oral cavity. At the neck and throat lodge, the three layers we discussed are released, from superficial to deep, in which deep strokes along the swallowing apparatus and the floor of the mouth are combined with breathing and vibration exercises. After the structural route, this patient – who at first barely spoke – came to be more vocal ('I don't want to keep it in anymore') and indicates that she is thinking about leaving her partner ('I really don't swallow everything he does anymore').

The systemic route

In contrast to the approach of a specific structure in the previous treatment route, the therapist uses a fixed template of examination and treatment. Here, the therapist does not 'look for' a certain dysfunctional structure or region, but applies a systemic approach in which the same step-by-step plan is followed each time.[4] In practical terms, for EBW, this means that the various structures that belong to one particular systemic template (muscle armour) are all included in the treatment. In a certain sense, this is the most protocol-based approach. A typical systemic route is the one for the uroboric armour in which all the myofascial structures involved are systematically treated – in this case the MML. However, other parts of the patient's muscle armour may also be affected, such as specific myofascial axes in the lower or upper limbs that are related to reaching, grabbing, standing firm or running off.

Myofascial core structures of the uroboric system that require a depth release are the mouth, jaw and chewing muscles, neck and swallowing apparatus (hyoidal musculature), deep neck muscles, the mediastinal region, the diaphragm and breathing apparatus, the iliopsoas and other (myo-)fascial structures in the abdominal cavity, deep gluteal muscles and pelvic floor, together with myofascial lodges in deep in the legs and arms.

These are all addressed as a whole in a single treatment without the patient having to specifically feel pain in any of these structures.

During the eighth session, the therapist works with the complete myofascial armour around the feet and legs while the patient lies down and speaks with his eyes closed. He explains in detail the burden he has been carrying in that region since his adolescence, when his stepbrothers came on the scene. Guided by the words and images that the patient uses, the therapist goes deep into the tissue, sometimes with a relentless pressure that causes the patient to stop talking. By working on physical tissue structures, such as the soles of the feet and the inside of the thighs with release techniques at those moments, strong emotions come to the fore that would otherwise remain under the radar. Certainly when the therapist treats several regions at the same time and then goes over all the core structures again, the patient undergoes a very intense feeling of discharge 'from the inside out'.

Precisely because these two routes start from the explicit myofascial bodywork, which often takes up several sessions, it is important to allow sufficient time for speaking during the sessions. After intensive bodywork, patients often feel the need to talk about their experience. It is, therefore, a good idea to provide the necessary time for this in the same session. This speaking usually occurs very organically after the therapist has stopped the bodywork and sits next to the patient. For the same reason, it is recommended that the therapist always starts the bodywork sessions by asking if the patient wants to share anything. The reason for this can be that the patient may want to share something related to the previous session or the time between the sessions. We have seen before that the time between sessions

136 *The practice of experiential bodywork*

is often a fertile period in which the unconscious shows itself and the narrative continues to crystallise. Think, for example, of ensuing reactions of the body (tired, heavy or even a bit flu-like, but equally full of energy and light), of social interactions that suddenly 'change' or of creative processes, such as dreams, in which the body can speak just as much.

The phenomenological route

This route is still somewhat in line with the previous two, but appears much less 'somatic'. The importance of the narrative, the role of the associative anamnesis and how the subject relates to himself, the Other and the world have been pointed out several times. Now we want to listen to the physical manifestation of this. This is how the body can either appear in one or other signifier (word, theme, image) – literally or not – or it returns as an association within the narrative. In concrete terms, this means that here, we tune into the meaningful dimension of the body and actually start working with it. So, in a way, we do not take into account the way in which the body presents itself in its physical dimension, nor the dysfunctional structures or regions of the muscle armour.

So no specific tests either. On the contrary, we start from the way the body is experienced and appears within the story, the narrative dimension. Therefore, this access route is not a somatic-structural route, but a distinct phenomenological-hermeneutical and dialectical approach. Here, we manipulate body parts, structures or regions in the way that they are experienced as meaningful or at least appear associative within the narrative. This can be done through touch and deep tissue work, but also through evocative exercises, such as those of 'breathing together' or 'speaking consciously', which are described hereafter. In a sense, this is a pleasant and helpful way for patients to gain access to their difficult bodies, as the therapist gets to work on what the patients shared.

A patient shares that he feels unsteady on his feet and often feels constricted at the knees. Another patient complains of light-headedness and 'having a bellyful of all this misery'. We contact the body as it appears here, i.e. the legs and knees or the head and the abdomen, and get to work, for example, with grounding exercises and deep, powerful exhalation.

A patient is referred by the GP with burn-out. There are no other specific physical symptoms; on the contrary, until recently, this patient exercised up to five times a week in addition to holding down a busy job as a representative, a second job in the weekend as a waiter and renovating his house after the birth of the third child. He realises that he has been overdoing things for months and feels that he has spent all his energy, but to his surprise he can't sleep at night. 'Could this have something to do with the fact that I always want to keep everything under control', he wonders.

We start working with the signifier 'keeping control' and work with powerful breathing work and vibrate with legs and arms from a standing position. The patient notices that this is the very first time that he really feels what it's

> like to let go. While he notices how his body reacts, he explains how he has 'sat down' with another psychologist to talk about the impossibility of letting go. Now he stands up and just feels what it does to him, what it is like to surrender to the rhythm and the undoseability of the movements his body makes, such as shaking and vibrating. Then he lies down on the mat and starts looking for words to describe what all this does to him. He stumbles upon the word 'absorption', 'absorbing', 'acceptance' . . . he thinks that he has to absorb everything, but also that he has to do it for everyone else. While he leans backwards on the mat, he continues to engage in association and talks about his desire to be fully submerged once more: 'In a very hot bath, or by my wife, perhaps during sex . . . in a way, I miss my parents too (both died), because when I went there on a Sunday evening, I really felt accepted . . . at home.'

The associative route

This route seems to bear a striking resemblance to an analytical approach in which the free association of the patient is central. At the same time, it is also very removed from it, because the free association is simultaneously integrated in a process of touching and eventually bodywork, which is not done within a psychoanalytical setting. Nevertheless, of the four routes, this seems to be the closest to 'talk therapy'.

Specifically, the therapist sits next to the patient and makes contact with the patient's body, preferably in a lying position, but it can also be in a sitting position. Initially, it is just a listening touch with which the therapist explores the patient's body and, at the same time, invites him to speak. The patient can simply say what comes to mind. He often picks up on themes that have been touched upon during the anamnesis or he may wish to add new information. Usually, this is done in a rational manner of speaking, which we have previously called conceptual self-awareness or CSA. The patient mainly speaks about himself, as if he is reporting on the situation. When the therapist notices that the patient is starting to feel more comfortable, he invites him to close his eyes and continue speaking, without the need to avoid silences. The patient now gradually enters a deeper level of contact with his own physical presence, also known as embodied self-awareness or ESA. Speaking becomes more associative and, therefore, more expressive. The interesting thing about this approach is the continuous contact the therapist maintains with the patient's body, which creates a kind of real-time monitoring of deeply physical processes, sometimes vegetative and usually unconscious in nature. This is the level at which Damasio situates somatic markers, Depestele speaks of pre-implicit knowledge and, according to Reich, the subtle, vegetative currents of the muscle armour occur. At the same time, there is a reciprocity with speaking to the patient in which the contact of the therapist interferes with the free association. In this way, the touch can be experienced as supportive and helpful, but also as unfamiliar or even confusing and threatening. In principle, this is the basic template of this route, the patient speaks while the therapist remains in contact with the body.

138 *The practice of experiential bodywork*

As this process progresses over the course of several sessions, this contact can gradually evolve into touches in which the therapist invites, facilitates and, where necessary, challenges the body. It goes without saying that this makes the process more intense, that the patient stays more in the intermediate layer of ESA and that the body and its signifiers come to the fore more. Just as in an analytical process of free association, the patient can discover meaningful aspects or dimensions in his own words. What is unique about EBW is that during this insightful process, the patient is in constant contact with his own body, the physical aspect is present and that it is precisely from here that the words can be nourished and enriched. Of the four routes discussed, the associative route is also the one that is the most accessible and the least 'demanding' of patients. No intensive bodywork, no challenging experiences or movements, not having to speak to the therapist while sitting down, but just being allowed to lie down and perhaps talk. Very often, when we think of patients who are deeply depleted, are in a severe depression or have undergone a severe trauma, this route is the only viable one.

A 19-year-old student calls on the advice of the student counselling service of the university where she is studying. She feels insecure and anxious that she will fail her exams for the second time. Having already had several sessions at a Mental Health Centre and eighteen sessions of 'relaxation therapy' with the physiotherapist, the EBW-therapist proposes to work via the associative route. He takes a seat next to her, puts his hand on her abdomen and invites her to continue speaking. Having talked about her home situation for a while, she stops and notices that it is actually easier to lie like this with her eyes closed and to talk than when she had to sit in front of her previous psychologist. The therapist's contact with her abdomen catches her attention and suddenly she remembers that as a child, she often suffered from abdominal pain and that her mother put her hand on her belly while she was lying on the sofa. The patient continues to talk about her mother's overprotection, her father who was strict but fair, and her parents' unsuccessful marriage, which was compensated for with a great deal of material luxury and abundance. Studying law was also a typical expectation that had to be fulfilled, she confesses, and she starts sobbing.

Working with a listening touch: a phenomenological analysis

Making deep, felt contact with the patient's body is a basic premise in EBW. Here, we consider the actual practice of this touch and adopt a phenomenological approach for this purpose.

The central question here is how working with a listening touch can be built up throughout the EBW process.

A typical structure and phasing of myofascial tissue work (Figure 7.3) always starts with establishing contact from maximum receptivity. The therapist places his hand on the patient and simply waits. This waiting is not a passive waiting, but rather an opening up of contact with the patient in a sensitive manner. When Bion

Sequence	Phenomenological description	Feels like...
1. Maximum receptivity	Listening to the tissue	'*melts like butter*'
2. Progressive depth	Direction	'*dog on a leash*'
3. Imaginary enlarging of tissue direction	Inertia	'*dancing with the tissue*'
4. Taking and exploring tissue	Rhythm	'*resonate with the tissue*'
5. Maximum creativity	Experiential image in therapist and evocative language in patient	

Figure 7.3 Phenomenological description of myofascial bodywork within EBW

(1976) states that 'the purest form of listening is without any memory or desire', he touches on the very core of the phenomenological attitude that we also strive for in EBW. In this phase, we let the patient's body come to us from a backward leaning, receptive posture without judgment or further analysis. It's about 'not putting anything onto the body'. The experience of the therapist in this first phase of maximum receptivity is as if his hand melts in butter where is hand touches the patient's body. In this moment when the therapist allows the tissue to come to life, a feeling of depth is created in which the therapist's hand melts deeper, without actually going deeper into the tissue. The therapist explores this depth as a space in which the tissue shows itself in a certain direction of movements. Initially, this is the movement of the tissue under the influence of breathing. Then, the therapist tries to establish contact with the subtler expression that arises from the various tension lines that manifest themselves in the body and that determine the freedom of movement of the tissue. In a certain sense, this is a first contact with the muscle armour. Without moving, the therapist follows this tissue expression, much like a walker would follow his dog wherever he goes. The only thing the therapist does is to keep contact with the leash to which the dog is attached. This second phase adds direction to the listening contact.

By sinking deeper into the tissue and following the intrinsic direction of the tissue, a feeling of inertia arises in which the tissue develops and the therapist gets to know the subtle build-up of tension of the myofascial armour. This third phase is also phenomenologically a turning point, since the therapist – who until now was receptive and following – is more active in the dyadic, listening tissue contact. He does this by increasing the experience of movement of the tissue as an image. The expression of the tissue in depth and direction is magnified by the therapist in an imaginary way. For example, if the therapist observes that the patient's sternum does not rise by inhalation, he will lower it deeper and deeper in his mind, as if it were sinking through the patient's body to the ground. Through this visualisation, the therapist gradually takes the tissue with him in a direction and depth of his choice. So the therapist takes over here. From now on, the therapist starts to work on the myofascial structures in an actual and visible way and, where necessary, to go deep into the tissue. In this phase, he explores all directions, including those that prefer not to leave the body – and thus induces a field of tension between their own contribution and tissue expression. Phenomenologically, this creates a sense of rhythm that we could see as a result of resonance and resistance within the myofascial tissue as armour.

Whereas in the first phase, the therapist started from maximum receptivity, the fifth and final phase ends from maximum creativity and optimal resonance:

> With listening touch, there is a resonance that develops between the practitioner's hand and the client's body. This resonance creates an intersubjective awareness that goes both ways. The client can feel more deeply into herself and the practitioner can open to the possibility of feeling both her own and the client's experiences.
>
> (Fogel, 2009, p. 224)

The dyadic process between therapist and patient now takes place from ESA in both the therapist and the patient and brings up experiential images and evocative language, respectively. In the case of the therapist, a physically palpable experiential image emerges in which the tissue expresses itself. This could be the image of the body as a concrete bunker or a dead, disintegrated old tree. On the patient's side, we see the emergence of expression in evocative (body) language. These can be words or images, but also movements, attitudes or emotional catharsis. Although there is no specific duration for these five phases, the final phase does require sufficient preparatory work. Phase three and especially phase four usually take a lot of time and involve the typical bodywork within EBW. This does not alter the fact that the first two phases are of decisive importance in order to be able to start.

The development-dynamic treatment template

In Chapters 5 and 6, we discussed in detail the early developmental *fulcra*, which resulted in increasing object constancy and a growing stability of the 'I' experience. In addition to the traditional psychosomatic conflict, we have come to know the uroboric and pranic body in relation to dysfunctional psychosomatic processes, such as panic and depression, stress and burn-out, but also trauma and physically unexplained symptoms. Within EBW, this development-dynamic thinking is not only important for a better conceptual understanding of dysfunctional, psychosomatic processes, but also serves as a concrete template for the therapeutic structure and approach.

This affords the *fulcrum* model a practical application as a development-dynamic treatment template (DDT) (Figure 7.4) and is worked out as a concrete therapeutic guideline. In view of its central importance, and after a detailed explanation, we illustrate the possibilities of this DDT on the basis of a concrete case study.

Fulcrum	Sub-level	Characteristics	Questioning during EBW
Fulcrum 0 Pleromatic body	Fusion	No differentiation between subject and object	Is there de-realisation or are there fading boundaries in relation to physical reality? Is it a question of merging, fragmentation or massive, overwhelming anxiety?
Fulcrum 1 Sensorimotor body	Matter	First manifestation in the world as simple, physical matter. The subject as an object is born and can begin to react to an environment from which it can only distinguish itself physically.	How does the tissue feel like matter-wise? Rigid, hard, dry, cold, empty, absent? Or rather soft, well-fed, warm and present?
	Sensation	From here on, the physical organism is increasingly irritable on the basis of simple to complex receptor activity.	How does the tissue react to stimuli? Sympathetically, parasympathetically; are there tender points, exaggerated reflex reactions or is the tissue rather soft and does it react in balance? What about tonic immobility?
	Perception	The stimulation of the organism so far (matter plus sensation) now progressively leads to rudimentary forms of sensation that can be held for a short period of time. The uroboric body is now the foundation for the first inside-outside experiences with the Other and the world.	Can the patient experience basic contact as present, on the surface or deep? Does he feel that he is being touched in the contact? Does 'inside' feel different from 'outside' for the patient?
Fulcrum 2 Vital-phantasmic body	Pranic body	The sensorimotor body is now being vitalised and comes into motion from within and no longer just as an 'action-reaction' to external stimuli. Stimulation and flow characterise the pranic body that after the uroboric nutrition of nutrients and breathing gets acquainted with libidinous charge and stimulation. The subject is born and can now begin to feel himself.	Is there already a charge and current in the patient's body; or should it be facilitated sooner? Is the armour perhaps too much charged? Does the patient feel what happens when his pranic body is stimulated? Does the body allow itself to be vitalised or is it blocked off?
	Proto-emotional phantasmic body	Libidinous tensions move the subject (e-movere) but are not yet fully fledged emotions. However, the energetic charge of the pranic body creates images or fantasies around ecstasy, fusion or grandiosity, but also aggression, disgust and anxiety.	What happens to the patient during the pranic charge? What experience images does he bring? How does the body speak here? Is there anxiety that threatens regression? Or does the patient dare to surrender and arise from this specific body being?

Figure 7.4 Development-dynamic treatment template

Source: Based on Wilber 1992, 1996, 1999, 2000

Fulcrum	Sub-level	Characteristics	Questioning during EBW
Fulcrum 3 Early mental thinking	Symbolic thinking	Where the sensations in F1 were still purely perceptual and could only be held for a short period of time, the vitalisation of the body in F2 for the creation of phantasmic images and libidinous occupation of objects that can remain present for an extended period of time. The symbolic thinking of F3 creates a whole new force that is much more mental. After the pictorial thinking (shape of a tree), the subject can now think in images that refer to something as a symbol (t-r-e-e refers to the shape and the appearance of the tree in the reality of a tree). The early mental self is born. The subject can now begin to think	Is there room for words and language in therapy? What is typical about these early signifiers? Can the patient already deal with ambivalent feelings and experiences, for example during bodywork?
	Conceptual thinking	Symbolic thinking can only refer to something while concept thinking is the beginning of thinking that means something and integrates previous forms of thinking (e.g. multiple symbols). Language starts with pictographic and symbolic thinking, but now a new dimension emerges in which language – and thus the entire linguistic world – acquires meaning. Yet this is only the beginning of mental-cognitive thinking; thinking about thinking is not yet an issue.	Can the patient start talking about his experience (i.e. not only from inside his experience)? Can he take an outside viewpoint in relation to his physicality?. Can he put himself in the position of what the body offers and says?

Figure 7.4 (Continued)

Three, two, one ... go! Getting started with the development-dynamic treatment template

Sublevel 'matter' and 'sensation'

A normally functioning body requires at least a physiological capacity for irritability. This means a combination of the sublevels 'matter' and 'sensation' of *fulcrum* 1[5] from the DDT. The first way of being is through this irritable body, which can manifest itself as a hyper- or hypo-irritability. This only concerns receptor sensitivity as a purely sensory activity and the way in which the body reacts to it. Think, for example, of the baby's reflex arm movements or reactions of the enteric intestinal nervous system to stimuli from the outside world. At the same time, this is also the sensory-motor body with which the patient can move rudimentarily without the intervention of higher brain structures, an instrumental body involved in procedural actions. In therapy, this is the purely somatic level that can be translated into interventions such as tissue release, manipulations, mobilisations or even strength exercises.

When, for example, an osteopath frees up the deep fascias of the gluteal muscles or a physiotherapist stretches the sciatic nerve in the lower limb, then in a certain sense they only have to rely on this sub-level where the body (matter) is stimulated in a specific way (sensation).

Sublevel 'perception'

From the next sublevel of 'perception' within *fulcrum* 1 onwards, more happens in therapy. To the simple actions of the sensory-motor body, a perceptual or proto-experience image is now added. The patient is now able to perceive the touch, the movement, as well as the corresponding internal sensations. We speak of a proto-experiential image, because it concerns a set of sensations that are combined only in the present moment. This experience is coherent, but at the same time hallucinatory in nature. So it is certainly not a concept, not even a pictorial image.

This addition of a brief 'perceptual' image of what is happening in the body completes the first *fulcrum* of the sensory-motor body. Matter plus sensation plus perception equals the first *fulcrum* of the physical self in therapy.

In concrete terms, this is the level that enables the patient to experience warmth or depth, for example, when the therapist touches the patient manually. The warmth is experienced in a deeply sensory way and is clear in that sense, but this perception as an experience cannot be sufficiently identified, localised or expressed in words. The patient can – at best – be in it.

Using the DDT, the therapist can easily check whether this *fulcrum* 1-body has been sufficiently developed and is reflected in the patient's functioning. When the therapist makes contact with a listening touch, he touches this material-sensory body, which normally reacts instantaneously and unconsciously. On a physiological level, this happens, for example, via the vegetative nervous system, where the tissue either 'melts' and relaxes (parasympathetic) or hardens and starts to sweat (sympathetic activation). Stimulating the first two sublevels has a certain effect beyond the patient's control. The patient then begins to experience that these sensations do something to his body. This is the third subphase of perception. But no matter how self-evident it may seem, perception is not obvious for every patient. The path from the stimulus of 'warmth' to experiencing the 'deep, relaxing touch' is often the first point where the patient gets stuck. He feels that he is being touched in a sensory way, but that is all he feels. In the case of severe trauma – think for example of the concept of tonic immobility (Chapter 4) – it is even possible that the touch is simply not felt. The patient is disconnected from his body, sometimes even depersonalised and always isolated from his own world of experience.

However, if perception works, the sensory-motor and the uroboric body will appear. When the little baby drinks from the mother's breast and ingests the warm, nourishing milk (sensory-motor), hallucinatory perceptions of what this does to the body are created (proto-experiential images). Warmth, glow, stimulation of the mouth and throat, sensations in the abdomen, but also sensations of satisfaction are accompanied by early perceptions that can hardly be contained. After the sensory-motor body, the therapist uses the DDT to determine the extent to which the uroboric body is present and available to the patient. Together with the skin as a sensory organ, the patient's uroboric system provides insight into the fundamental experiences of the outside and inner world. This may include deep breathing, swallowing and chewing movements, but also reactions to bodywork on the abdomen. We have previously compared this with Bazan (2014) as the invertebrate sack of intestines and described how this oro-anal system subsequently directs tension and excitations to the vertebrate or myofascial system. From these uroboric processes of breathing, swallowing, spitting and digesting, the consciousness process takes a step to the next level, where the vitalisation of the pranic body is central.

Sublevel 'pranic body'

We have now reached the second *fulcrum* within the DDT. The underlying energetic processes have a compelling biological or neuro-endocrine basis, but are, at the same time, more than that. Drive, libido, bio-energy, *élan vital*, kundalini, chi or pneuma are just a few of the terms that, through cultures and philosophies, refer to the category of life energies that make the somatic body vital. What will later develop into willpower, desire or enthusiasm, starts as bodily biological energy and tilts at the beginning of the second *fulcrum* towards a pranic dynamic, characterised by propelling, floating and erecting. The little child is now moving, fired from the inside, and will soon be getting up, before invariably exploring the world in a upright position.

In the patient, this pranic phase can hardly be overestimated and forms a common thread throughout numerous psychosomatic therapies. In the practice of

EBW, we notice that patients – for example in case of depression – are often stuck here and their own physical flow can no longer be experienced, if at all. The contact with the body has become nothing but a mechanical instrumental relationship between the owner and the thing-body. We also referred to 'cerebral' types that live mainly in their heads or to the clinical concept of disembodiment. At this level, we also see people getting stuck in the other direction and lose themselves completely in the suction effect of vital forces.[6] These people are overwhelmed and have to contend with tantrums, outbursts of anger or difficulties with impulse control, for example.[7] We also used the term hyperembodiment in this context.

When people have become disconnected from their own bodies, we in EBW focus on the pranic body with deep rhythmic breathing and pelvic tilt, deep, slow release of the uroboric muscle armour, often supplemented by accelerated movements of arms and legs.[8] Typically, patients then tell us that they tremble, get very hot, get light-headed or start to perspire. Uncontrolled movements, such as shocks and tremors, hyperventilation or emotional outbursts, are also common at this stage. These strongly organically driven symptoms usually come to the fore when the patient moves away from the phase of tonic immobility. As a result, his body begins to react more sympathetically (Fogel, 2009; Levine, 2014a, 2014b). The question why we often refer to the uroboric body in therapy with a difficult body, can easily be clarified from the DDT. This phase precedes that of the pranic body. Working in a development-dynamic way implies that, as a therapist, we can sense which Russian dolls have already grown sufficiently and which are asking for help or are simply still premature. This often means that we go back a level within the DDT and work with the possibilities of the body available there.

This is clarified in the extensive practical example 'Working with the DDT that follows after this paragraph.

An interesting relationship that we cannot elaborate on in detail here is the relationship between automutilation and the discharge of the pranic energy in the body. Here, too, we see this reverse dynamic move to a previous level within the DDT. When people can no longer cope with this pranic tension (e.g. provoked by a context of abandonment, failure or frenzied anger), they go back to the previous *fulcrum* of the physical self. By carving and cutting into the biological body, they stimulate the most basic layers of matter and sensation (sensory-motor body F1ab) and thereby induce a deep perception that, as a hallucinatory experience (F1c), briefly satisfies (sometimes compared to an orgasm) and takes away the tension. So, 'something' is regulated and reduced (Van Camp, 2012). From a psychoanalytical point of view, it is stated that automutilants, by cutting, try to anchor themselves in their bodies and thus in the world here and now: 'By self-injury, one seems to confirm the limits of the self . . . and to strengthen self-coherence' (Van Gael, 2012, p. 36). This, too, can be explained from the DDT perspective.

Sublevel 'proto-emotional, phantasmic body'

Once this energetic, driving and erecting body appears, the second *fulcrum* moves to the next subphase in which the early mental field is injected with this pranic energy and phantasmic images arise. Due to their originally rough, raw somatic energies, these images are often the scene of aggressive, sadistic, devouring or haunting experiences. In line with Melanie Klein's paranoid-schizoid stage (Mitchell, 1986; Meurs, 2004), patients at this stage experience the Other (e.g. the therapist) as threatening, too close or unreliable. Opening up to the pranic-vital stimulation of the body during therapy can lead to the patient being overwhelmed by physical sensations, movements and deep perceptions (*fulcrum* 1), as well as primarily physical emotions and primeval fantasies (*fulcrum* 2). It goes without saying that the therapeutic framework, including the therapeutic relationship, must guarantee that this process can be absorbed, tolerated and channelled as and when necessary.

Sublevel 'concepts and symbolic thinking'

Slowly but surely, the early mental field of *fulcrum* 3 unfolds and the first clear forms of thinking emerge. Whereas in the pranic phase of the second *fulcrum*, pictographic forms are still central, the third *fulcrum* is characterised by symbolic and conceptual thinking. The patient's world of experience is also gradually becoming more expressive (language-wise) and what can be thought of now refers to something (symbolic) or means something (conceptual). In the previous chapter, we saw that this also changes the patient's perception of anxiety. Anxiety can mean something from *fulcrum* 3 onwards; it becomes a signal anxiety.

We saw that prior to this moment, anxiety is only what it is, namely, physical excitation and reaction (*fulcrum* 1) plus physical drive and propulsion (*fulcrum* 2a) and all this possibly surrounded by raw phantasmic images that stick around mercilessly (*fulcrum* 2b). So from the third *fulcrum* onwards, our patient can gradually come to speak and think about something that could be meaningful, but that has not yet shown itself to be so. On the other hand, the DDT clearly reminds us that this thinking also has its origin in the somatic register of non-language processes. This insight is by no means strange. Freud already called this the primal unconscious and Bion referred to the somatic register of *beta* elements. Lacan speaks of the biological body as the real versus the symbolic-imaginary body as the mental. According to Depestele (2004), there is a similar ontology that starts with pre-implicit knowing: 'The unconscious is the body. Not just the physiological body – which is also referred to as the reduced body – but the body that is meaning-potential and that attempts to make sense of things' (p. 114).

Three early turning points

For the assessment of the psychosomatic request for help and, thus, the therapeutic process, it is important to note that the DDT essentially shows three crucial turning points within early subject development. A *first turning point* takes place from a fused, undifferentiated state to a form of materialisation in which the world distinguishes itself as the physical Other. The *second turning point* is very crucial within EBW. Here, the material-sensory body object from F1 is vitalised and, thus, essentially subjectified. In a certain sense, the subject only really comes into play here. When Mahler (Mahler et al., 2000) talks about the birth of the individual who leaves his symbiotic and autistic shell, this happens within the DDT from F1 to F2. Psychodynamically, this is also the development sequence in which the narcissistic energy starts to properly course through the subject. Subsequent linguistic concepts such as flow, change and propulsion are introduced here on the turning point between an energetic and phantasmic dimension. The subject no longer only works in the field of senses and perception, but now really feels from within what is pulling, pushing and propelling unsatisfactorily. These experiences are no longer separate from divergent images and scenarios in which the pranic-narcissistic impulses take shape without really being identifiable (phantasms). From a therapeutic point of view, the *third turning point* should be even less underestimated, given the bridging function to the subject's language-thinking capacity. Whereas *fulcrum* 1 was matter and barely a body, and *fulcrum* 2 was body, but barely thinking, *fulcrum* 3 is already a thinking subject, albeit young, but nevertheless stabilised. The subject is no longer endlessly pushed or mercilessly flooded, but can use early linguistic thinking to get a handle on what is happening to and within him. In the previous chapter, the importance of this turning point was worked out in more detail in relation to anxiety.

In practice, we recognise the psychosomatic patient who puts all his efforts into language and thinking (fulcrum 3 up to 5). This is the patient who also experiences himself as someone who thinks a lot, likes to know and understand things or sometimes has something to say and explain. We then clearly feel how much the patient invests in the language-cognitive defence of CSA or what is also referred to as the symbolic-imaginary aspect according to Lacan.

Although we cannot dwell on the traditional psychopathologies here, such as hysteria and obsessive-compulsive neurosis (Cullberg, 2009), these often turn out to be successfully characterised by propelling or cramped, inhibited speech. Working with speech with the patient is, therefore, a powerful awareness exercise within EBW when it turns out that the third *fulcrum* and turning point are significant. In therapy, we sometimes liken this exercise of 'conscious speaking' with wine tasting, in which the sommelier allows a small amount to go through his mouth and throat and thus makes deep contact with all the facets of wine. In the same way, we want to teach the patient to make room to make contact with their own speaking, to taste deeply and to arrive at a more conscious presence in speaking.

> Speaking about the inner experience while in a state of mindfulness . . . allows the therapists to share in the inner processes of their clients. Psychodynamically, this increases the probability that previously implicit or procedural memories can be consciously experienced and subsequently stored as explicit memories.
>
> (Gottwald, 2015, p. 134)

Exercise conscious speaking

E. is a civil engineer and considers herself to be a reasonable and, above all, rational kind of person. An old rivalry with her sister once led her to choose to study engineering, although this was not really her thing. E. was quite talented musically and would have preferred to attend a music academy. However, as an industrial engineer in architecture, her father had set up a decent-sized company in one generation and E. felt that Dad wanted one of his two daughters to take over the business one day. The fact that her sister finally followed her passion and is now not only happy, but above all successful, continues to prey on her mind. From the very first meeting, E.'s speech struck me as unbridled twitter that conjures up the image of a continuous text without punctuation or capitals. In the early days of the therapy, there were occasions when I had to explicitly ask her to take a break and allow a silence. This was almost impossible and led to questions such as 'Why is this necessary?', 'What is the point of this' or 'Am I doing it right, now?'

During the exercise of 'conscious speaking', E. sits with her eyes closed and breathes in and out deeply several times. Then she starts speaking again, but this time more from an ESA, at which point I ask her to actually lean back a bit. The first thing E. notices is the urge she feels to start speaking. She laughs a little awkwardly, because she can hardly contain the urge, that's how much she likes to talk. In the next sequence, she starts to speak, but at my request she does so from a tender place and at a slower pace. Right away, not only her timbre changes, but also her facial expressions. She now lets the words swirl around in her mouth more before sharing them. After a few sessions and the necessary 'homework', E. indicates that she much prefers to speak this way and that it even calms her down. She is now also more in touch with the movement and meaning of the words that arise: 'It reminds me of a poetry and storytelling evening that I enjoyed so much from my high school days. The poets spoke so beautifully and softly and also thoughtfully . . . it was almost music!' Later on, E. will tell that since that evening, she has dreamt of the music academy.

Let us now clarify the therapeutic scope and clinical richness of the DDT as a whole by means of a concrete case study.

Practical example of working with the DDT

B. is a 31-year-old man who suffers severe migraines that have made his life a misery for years. The doctor's referral contains references to severe trauma in his childhood. In addition, he suffers from terrifying nightmares and has fainted at work several times in recent months. He works as a police officer in Brussels, where the occupational physician advises him to have his neck unblocked, because no structural or neurological problems could be identified in his X rays. B. makes a very tense and restless impression at our first meeting. He sits twisted on his chair and is constantly moving his right leg up and down, without being aware of this. He talks fast and I have the feeling that he is trying to keep a close eye on both me and the treatment room. The anamnesis is difficult, in which B. constantly asks what exactly is going to happen in the treatment. There is little room for speaking and an inner exploration of experiences and thoughts seems to be completely out of the question. We decide to continue with the physical anamnesis of body reading and listening touch. B's body may tell us more.

When B. is lying on the table and I touch his head and neck, I notice an extremely hardened and tense musculature.[9] It feels like his neck is wrapped in thick steel cables that I associate with 'reinforced concrete'. B. has his eyes wide open and occasionally looks up to keep an eye on me: 'You never know what you might get up to suddenly', he says. When I ask him what he means by that, he says that I might throttle him, since my hands are so close to his neck. Then, when I ask him if he thinks this could be a realistic scenario in which I, as a therapist, squeeze a patient's throat, he says, 'Of course not, but . . . you never know, I'd better be on my guard.' He adds that in his job as a policeman, he also has to be constantly 'uptight', 'especially with the terrorist threat these days.' Later, he will tell me how he spilled the popcorn and coke over his girlfriend at the cinema once when she touched him unexpectedly. He flew off the handle, walked out and then regretted his reaction later. B.'s sensory-motor 'irritable' body (F1) clearly reacts on a vegetative-sympathetic level.

Wherever I make contact, the skin becomes red, sweaty and the myofascial tissue tightens immediately. Whenever I just indicate that I would like to gently move his neck, it locks completely and no movement at all is possible. His whole torso then becomes one rigid block of tension. I even notice that as I keep in touch with his body, his hands are tight fists and his abdomen contracts. I catch myself thinking that he might hit me unexpectedly with his fists. At the moment, we are at the first fulcrum of matter plus sensation within the DDT and B. is unable to make contact with deeper sensations associated with the physical contact. His body is purely action-response at the receptor level, B. here is only a sensory-motor body that reacts violently.

However, so far we have been able to capture elements that refer to processes at other DDT levels of which B. is unaware. Phantasms full of threats, destruction and aggression are shown to me, in which the world is a deeply unsafe place and the Other is totally unpredictable and unreliable. Out of the blue, this Other can strangle and destroy you. . . . The fantasy of the threatening Other also extends to me as a therapist. However, B. cannot get in touch with it, partly because the developmental step that precedes the fantasies of F2 is not yet possible. We first work on the perception level and teach B. to make contact with sensations that take place in his body while stimulating the sensory-motor body. In concrete terms, simple instructions, such as closing the eyes and turning attention inwards, are initially almost impossible for him. After all, you have to keep an eye on the world all the time, because you never know. . . . We therefore agree that he can keep his eyes open if this gives him more peace of mind and start with a simple contact exercise. For this, I sit next to B. who is lying on his back and I put my hand on his abdomen (sitting behind him is too threatening as he won't be able to see me). Through superficial breathing, B. gradually manages to locate my hand; he now feels where my hands are on his body. Through my hand contact, he feels for the first time how his abdomen is moving and reacting. I myself notice that I am not allowed to deepen my listening touch for the time being, because this generates too many stimuli. So I literally stay on the surface.

After a while, B. indicates that he feels warmth and notices that this calms him down, but at the same time that he finds it disturbing, since this means that he is now less alert ('You'll send me off to sleep next!'). Gradually, we work all over the body and initially, we stimulate on a proprioceptive level by establishing obvious contact and using slow movements. We saw how our listening touch has a profound effect on the interoceptive system that partly underlies the body experience. For some patients such as B., however, this can result in an excess of depth perception and can, therefore, be experienced as overwhelming and threatening. Occasionally, B. even spontaneously closes his eyes and his breathing becomes noticeably deeper. In this phase, it is tempting to actively question the patient about his experiences. Although this is, in itself, not wrong and sometimes even called for, especially with anxious patients whom we want to anchor in the here and now, there is a danger that the patient will only speak from his CSA. Speaking in this way is more a kind of reporting, a speaking about. On the other hand, it is important that the patient is able to stay in the newly discovered contact and speak from there. The early thinking of fulcrum 3 may already be well established, it often anxiously guards the pranic body. After a number of sessions, we move towards fulcrum 2 by intensifying the breathing work and progressively combining it with rhythmic pelvic tilts. In practice, we work on the floor and place B. on a large mattress in a space with sufficient freedom of movement.

Combining deep breathing with movement from the pelvis and abdomen, often acts as a catalyst for vitalising the pranic body. B. indicates that his arms and face are starting to tingle and he becomes light-headed (hyperventilation); he is also getting warm all over his back. As I urge him to persevere, he says that he feels like he is losing all control and aborts the exercise. It is possible that the dosage and build-up at this moment was not sufficiently attuned to what he could handle and that the experience was too overwhelming, too threatening. One session later, B. does manage to maintain the deep, rhythmic breathing work and experiences that the dreaded loss of control decreases when he continues to breathe and relies on me as a therapist and himself as a body. When I see B. again a week later, he tells me that he has felt remarkably warm throughout the week and was able to fall asleep more easily (he often lay awake for hours and had nightmares several times). His body does indeed feel warmer and softer and gives the impression of being more relaxed.

The next sequence is the one in which we want to open the phantasmic and proto-emotional parts from the pranic fulcrum 2. For this, I return to B.'s very first contact with his head and neck and now I sit behind him. The first moments are not easy and B. in a certain sense regresses to his purely reactive sensory-motor body. Suddenly, it is no longer possible to close his eyes and breathing is controlled and superficial. Working on the neck is charged in such a way that it immediately activates a fantasy of threat and chase. Unlike the first time, I can continue to reach him and he has the capacity to tolerate me – at least for the time being – at his neck. I opt for deep tissue work on his uroboric body that just precedes the pranic body. The myofascial armour with which the uroboric system takes shape, is processed in a number of sessions with deep tissue contact. I treat the uroboric armour with listening touch and slow melting pressure. Initially, it is very difficult for B. to stay in ESA, but continuing to offer support points and verbal guidance works wonders. He learns to make contact with the uroboric armour that prevents him from growing into his pranic body. During this work, typical symptoms occur that can be associated with deep bodywork at the uroboric level. Sweating, cramping of face and neck, uncontrolled swallowing and gasping for breath, but also vomiting are part of this for B. After a number of sessions, the work on this part of the armour becomes calmer and more stable and we continue to shift it into the uroboric body. Through the sternum and diaphragm, we take the breathing apparatus with us, not forgetting the intercostal muscles (we had already tackled the breathing musculature in the neck). An important part of the uroboric body is also located in the abdomen and pelvis.

These areas require a specific approach that we are not going to elaborate on here. In terms of myofascial structures, the iliopsoas and perineum are of crucial importance to be able to release the uroboric armour.

After about eight sessions, we complete this early fulcrum work and in B. we focus on stimulating the pranic body. For this, we use deep, rhythmic breathing work and combine this with more intensive myofascial work of the armour. More than ever before, the body has become vitalised and fantasies occur, but at the same time B. is able to make and keep better contact with his body during the treatment. As a result, he remains more grounded, is less overwhelmed and experiences a more body-own confidence that he has never known before. When we gradually leave more room for silence in the sessions, B. arrives at verbal communication that is new to him; it is more of an expression of feelings. He starts talking about his father who was always drunk and aggressive, beating them all at home whenever he felt the urge. B. witnessed countless instances of his father beating his mother and then continuing to act out his aggression on the children, often with his belt. B. shows me the scars he has on his lower back. It strikes me that his voice is much softer than before and he even closes his eyes now and then while talking about his father. We are about a dozen sessions and about three months into the treatment and B. can now be present in space, tolerate me as a therapist and has sufficient confidence to close his eyes. Given the seriousness of the developmental stops in B.'s case, the work so far has, in a way, been pretherapy for what is yet to come. Eventually, he will attend EBW sessions for almost two years.

The uroboric armour and the myofascial middle layer

In Chapters 5 and 6, it became clear that the early *fulcra* can have a major impact on psychosomatic problems and that the uroboric-pranic body affects this. In Chapter 4, we introduced the MML as the top-right quadrant substrate that corresponds with the uroboric-pranic body. Just because EBW focuses on the psychosomatic

152   The practice of experiential bodywork

field, the uroboric-pranic body/MML is very instrumental in therapy. Here, we briefly consider the specific myofascial bodywork around this structure, which, in a way, is a further elaboration of the systemic route described earlier. This bodywork is almost always combined with evocative movement, for example the exercise 'breathing together' and 'sounds', which we describe in the next paragraph.

The therapist sits behind the patient, who is lying on his back, and rests his hands on his face. With deep, slow strokes (as they are called in Postural Integration), the therapist works layer by layer until he notices that he is deep in the tissue. These movements can be performed with fingertips, thumbs, palm, forearm or even elbow, depending on the structure or location where work is done.

Under 'slow melting pressure', the tissue relaxes and any sensitive or tender points present are released. While the therapist explores the uroboric muscle armour, it is important to make clear-cut 'connecting' movements. We have already explained that specific stimulation of the myofascial tissue ensures that the patient learns to explore and feel his body 'from the inside out'. These deep connecting movements come from deeper interoceptive brain networks of emotion, body regulation and basic forms of self-awareness (embodiment and ESA). It is as if the therapist's hands tell the patient 'look, this is your face, your mouth, your throat, . . . and together they form one powerful whole'. Painter (1986) clearly describes this as: 'Individuals need to be confronted by their armour, but at a rate which gradually allows time to assimilate and explore what is happening' (p. 111).

We also saw that the armour here comprises the MML core structures, such as the masseters (m. masseter, m. temporalis and muscles around the jaw joint), the swallowing breathing apparatus around the neck, throat and mouth, then the region around the chest and the diaphragm, the abdomen and the hip flexors below it (m. iliopsoas), deep buttocks and adductors, and finally the pelvic floor. Each time, the melting touch on the uroboric armour is combined with working from ESA and is gradually supported with vitalisation of the pranic body through breathing or sound vibrations. Sometimes, it is advisable to stimulate the pranic charge extra by inviting the patient to stamp his foot or thump the mattress with his fists. As the first two fascial layers have become softer and more accessible, the manual pressure focuses on the third, actual muscle layer. Characteristic here are the bi-manual touches in which the body is continuously processed in rhythmic-organic movements which, at times, have a fairly deep and intense effect on the muscle armour. In practice, the therapist uses a scale of 1 to 10, with which the patient can indicate the intensity of the experience: 5 stands for a reasonable pressure that does not hurt while 10 stands for an intolerable painful pressure. At the most intensive moments, it is possible to go up to 8, but usually the touches range between 3 and 7.

Experiential movement or bodywork in motion

Until now, reference was mainly made to examples of hands-on interventions, such as the deep myofascial bodywork and the listening hand touch. Although an essential pillar within EBW, manual bodywork is only one of the three, in addition to 'evocative movement' and 'room to talk'. Like other forms of body psychotherapy, EBW also works with experiential movements and exercises. These can be integrated during the myofascial work but usually take place in a hands-off set-up in the therapy room or on the mattress. Space for awareness and expression are central to this. This expression is indicated by the term 'evocative language' in contrast to what Fogel (2009) calls 'evaluative language', which is more based on CSA. As with the manual bodywork techniques, this part of EBW is, therefore, situated as much as possible within the patient's ESA field:

> In evocative language, words are chosen to resonate in felt experience. If words 'reach us' they are felt as 'true', 'deep' and 'powerful. Words – evocatively spoken from the practitioner's own embodied self-awareness – can enhance and amplify feelings.
>
> (idem, p. 248)

Experience-oriented movements and evocative language can, in a certain sense, be seen as a conscious replay from the procedural memory, so that a new or corrective set of experiences can overwrite the absent or existing ones. This implies an awareness process from ESA ('being fully present') so that the intero-, extero- and proprioceptive learning history of failed, interrupted or jammed movements and postures can be adjusted. As stated earlier, researchers indicate that even imaginary movements, such as visualisation, can be sufficient. On the other hand, the muscular activation cannot be random. In concrete terms, this means that not any movement or posture is active in therapy, but only those that relate meaningfully to the original context of tension or trauma. So when a patient often had to hold back as a child in order not to retaliate to his authoritarian and aggressive father, it does not help to train his arm muscles in the gym, but deep discharge is only possible in exercises such as hitting a punching bag during therapy:

> Profound shifts seem to occur when the activity responds to movement that was interrupted in the precipitating event. It is very unlikely that ordinary voluntary vigorous exercise, even if it used those muscles, would have brought about comparable results.
>
> (Payne et al., 2015)

Therapists and researchers, such as Peter Levine, Pat Ogden, Bessel Van Der Kolk and Peter Payne, underline the role of the top-right quadrant in their respective trauma theory and associated therapies, in which context we already pointed out that a jammed or incorrectly programmed biophysical cascade causes a great deal of distress. Van Der Kolk (2014) goes even one step further, claiming that 'the emotions and physical sensations that were imprinted during the trauma are experienced not as memories but as disruptive physical reactions in the present' (p. 204). Logically, the trauma must therefore be approached within this dimension, as a result of which therapeutic interventions have a strong experiential slant (i.e. top-right and top-left quadrant). 'In order to regain control over your self, you

154 *The practice of experiential bodywork*

need to revisit the trauma' (idem, p. 208). Re-performing specific movements and postures, but also more behavioural therapeutic techniques, such as desensitisation or exposure, are therefore part of the therapeutic repertoire. The fact that this must be done within an optimal, safe context with maximum space for awareness and expression (left quadrants), in turn, means that it concerns evocative, catharsis-sensitive processes that seek to raise awareness and not 'mere' movement or behaviour. 'At the core of recovery is self-awareness', says Van der Kolk (idem, p. 208).

Very often, however, patients are not ready for these explicit and sometimes violent forms of discharge and the therapist has to take a few steps back within the DDT. The first step is to focus on fundamental experiences, such as security, safety and support, until the patient feels ready for the next step. This is illustrated by the exercise 'breathing together', which is often used in people with anxiety, depression or trauma. Breathing is one of the earliest movements we undergo and discover.

It is not an action that we consciously perform; on the contrary, we breathe spontaneously. What's more, breathing happens automatically and does not require any effort. However, breathing freely and quietly is one of the most recurrent stumbling blocks for the patient, and many symptoms are expressed through breathing. Breath is, therefore, often one of the first indicators of disturbance of the vegetative control system in the case of psychosomatic dysfunction or trauma (Geuter, 2015b; Victoria & Caldwell, 2013). Philosopher and analyst Luce Irigaray (2009) points out that breathing in our Western culture is very neglected and invites us to learn from Eastern traditions where it is more common to be aware that 'life and breathing are one and the same' (p. 104). Irigaray, who distinguishes two forms of breathing – a feminine/natural and a masculine/cultural – sees yoga as a connecting practice that helps cultivate conscious breathing. The following exercise also helps the patient first of all to reconnect with the naturalness of their own breathing in all its facets of rhythm, depth and security. Van der Kolk (2014) – himself a great advocate of yoga – explicitly points out how rhythm, movement and chanting can help with recovery after trauma (p. 100).

'Breathing together' exercise

The patient lies on his side on a large soft surface, pulls up his legs and rests his arms and head against the raised legs (foetal position). In the case of very vulnerable patients or in case of a need to retreat, the therapist places a large blanket over the patient. He himself sits alongside the patient on the floor and places his hands on the patient's side, preferably head and pelvis. As the patient breathes calmly and deeply, the therapist is silent and supports breathing with his hands by following the movements of chest, abdomen, pelvis and head with a listening hand. This 'breathing together' is made even more explicit by the fact that the therapist breathes in and out audibly with the patient. This is often experienced as very supportive ('containment'). The patient is then invited to breathe deeper and faster, while the therapist holds

> him in the broadly possible grip and offers tangible support (literally 'holding'). In a subsequent sequence, the intensive breathing frequency is slowed down, guided by the therapist, who slows down his breathing, both audibly and noticeably, and takes the patient into this rhythm. Once the breathing is sufficiently calm and slow, the therapist slowly takes the blanket away from the patient and guides him in reconnecting with the outside world of the therapy room. Opening the eyes and beginning to speak mark the end of the exercise, after which the patient is given the time and space to express his experiences and share them with the therapist. In a next step or session, the patient goes through the same build-up, but now from a sitting position, hugging his knees. When sitting in this position, you can also work with a blanket and the therapist kneels behind the patient. If necessary, the evocative process of breathing in this exercise can be supported by the therapist gently rocking the patient. The therapist must be able to properly hold the patient and make sure that the patient does not fall over unexpectedly. Here, too, breathing is increased in depth and rhythm in a first moment and then slowed down again from breathing together.
>
> A final step that follows the previous sitting position adds to the experience of breathing-together the important dimension of learning to raise oneself up, to open up to the world and to breathe independently. Where in both previous sequences, breathing-together was central, with emphasis on the automatic experience of being breathed, being allowed to surrender to it and thus being able to stay in breathing, we now help the patient to 'emerge' from breathing. The therapist still sits behind the patient and places one hand on the sternum and the other hand on the lower back or the sacrum. From these support points, the therapist progressively accompanies an upward movement in which the back is stretched, the chest opens (thanks to the first hand) and the back and abdomen are brought forward (thanks to the second hand). At the same time, the patient is invited to express his breathing in a more powerful and dramatic way, through movements such as opening, raising up and growing big. Whereas until then, breathing-together was central, the patient now discovers how he can, and may, breathe alone without having to give in to feelings of safety and fullness.

This exercise of breathing-together is often combined or supplemented with the exercise 'sounds', which is more focused on the pranic level. In essence, what we call 'sounds' here is an ancient method of creating sounds and vocal vibrations through deep, rhythmic breathing. From meditative mantras to the recitation of texts or the emission of breaths and cries in Eastern martial arts, it is always about facilitating, stimulating and confronting the body from its pranic level. From a neuroscientific point of view, this stimulation can be taken literally and the terms interoceptive and partly proprioceptive afference are used in this context. Put simply, the body is stimulated 'from within' by numerous specific receptors. In Chapter 4, we described how this information is then processed in an insular network in the brain, which is firmly anchored in the emotional memory and the control systems for body and metabolism. On the other hand, the link between sound and awareness is also psychologically 'primeval', in the sense that

156 *The practice of experiential bodywork*

a baby literally learns from the inside by making connections between objects in the outside world and their meaning through his own body:

> The baby learns the felt connection between the exteroceptive sensation (a color, a sound, a tactile impression) of an object to be named, with the interoceptive sense of how it feels to make the sound of that name and hear oneself making it, and the body schema awareness of knowing which parts of the body need to be moved to create the sound and action related to the object, like grasping or pointing.
>
> (Fogel, 2009, p. 245)

'Sounds' exercise

Initially from a supine position and later from a slightly bent position, the patient places the hands on his abdomen (the first time it often helps to put a hand on his throat or sternum). The eyes are closed and the patient establishes contact with himself and the room he is in from ESA. With his mouth half open, he now breathes in and out quietly, in particular when breathing out spontaneously, much like a balloon deflating.

The patient becomes aware of how the breath caresses the oral cavity and throat and thus finds its way to the chest, abdomen and finally arrives in the pelvis. Progressively, this exercise builds itself up on the basis of visualisations and feedback from one's own hands on the abdomen, chest or pelvis. In the next sequence, the breathing is increased in rhythm and depth, and the breathing becomes more and more audible. Initially this sounds like a strong exhalation, but by playing with the oral cavity and throat as a sound box, they become more and more clear sounds. These basic vibrations are now also very clearly felt by the patient and make the entire uroboric sleeve vibrate from mouth to pelvic floor. If desired, rhythmic movements can be added with the pelvis and eventually the entire torso. With a small adjustment, this exercise can also be done in a sitting, or even standing, position.

A patient testifies about working with breathing:

What I also remember very well is how my breathing felt at the time. It felt as if my lungs were filling up with oxygen deeper than ever before, right down to its smallest branches, just as if oxygen was reaching places it had never reached before. It felt as if my whole torso was breathing, as if every fibre of it was absorbing oxygen, as I got deeper and deeper into/within myself. Never before have I breathed in such a conscious and intense, deep way. It was as if the deep relaxation had suddenly created more space (which was probably literally the case) and that the oxygen reached, fed, and penetrated every cell in my (torso).

What also stayed with me is how smoothly the practice with sounds went in the days after the double treatment. My entire torso resonated and vibrated without any effort and it sounded so deep that I could hardly comprehend it myself. My torso functioned as one large bass instrument and there was not the slightest resistance or cramping that stopped the vibration.

The body in transference

A specific topic that we address – albeit briefly – is the possible role of the body within processes of transference and countertransference. In the introductory chapter, we already touched on ethical dilemmas surrounding touch in psychotherapy (Ogden et al., 2006; Tune, 2005), which rightly pointed to possible pitfalls or dangers, including misinterpretation as a reward or sexual advances and, thus, in a broader sense (counter)transference:

> Touch – even well-considered, boundaried, therapeutic touch – may evoke transference if the therapist is uncomfortable or unskilled, if the patient has poor ego strength, if the therapeutic alliance is weak, or if the connection resulting from touch exceeds the working intimacy in the therapeutic relationship.
> (Ogden et al., 2006, p. 201)

In that case, Cornell (2015) refers to 'touch enactment' (p. 51) and the possible provoking of regression. On the other hand, these authors also point out possible advantages for the therapeutic process. In the final analysis, Body Psychotherapy – and therefore the full application of touch and bodywork – can only be done after thorough training and within a clear deontological framework, such as in accordance with the guidelines of the European Association for Body Psychotherapy (EABP, 2012).

Given these strict conditions, the process of somatic (counter)transference in Body Psychotherapy is even put forward as a valuable therapeutic instrument (Cornell, 2015; Reich, 1973; Soth, 2005; Totton, 1998). In essence, somatic (counter)transfer is the same as (counter)transference in the classical sense, in that it activates and projects previously installed patterns, but including the physical substrate of the interaction (Soth, 2015).[10] Two levels can be distinguished here. The first level deals with the physicality of the first impressions that the therapist perceives in the patient and in himself, such as the patient's body language and physical appearance or the therapist's physical sensations and internal experiences as a reaction to the encounter within a broader emotional pattern of reaction (Quinodoz, 2003). The second level of physical (counter)transference is situated in a deeper and more meaningful layer of physical interaction:

> It may be the analyst who feels in himself the bodily experience that accompanied the patient's unconscious affect, in which case he will be able to help the patient attend to this sensation, to progress from the sensation to bodily experience, and thence to its emotional meaning
> (idem, pp. 103–104)

This second level is therefore more specific and focuses on the somatic attunement between the patient and therapist. Reich initially saw this as a kind of unconscious imitation. Later, the following terms were being used: vegetative identification (Blumenthal, 2001), organic transference (Stattman, in Heller, 2012), dyadic resonance (Hart, 2008) or somatic resonance (Cornell, 2015). Bloom (2006) refers to this state of being with the term 'embodied attentiveness' and states that it increases the therapist's sensitivity to unconscious affects in the patient. This state of being is also characteristic of working with touch and movement within Body Psychotherapy. Unlike the traditional concept, the patterns of (counter)transfer now also consist of somatic structures, such as muscular or visceral tissue and associated neurophysiological processes of hypertonia, contraction or secretion.[11] To understand this intrinsically physical foundation of somatic (counter)transference, Schore (2003) refers to the early object relationships that are recorded neuromuscularly and continue to function as an unconscious, incorporated work model. This almost literal interweaving between body, charge and early object relations is in line with the previously described Reichian concept of muscle armour.

> When E. talks about her mother, she presses her thumb into her index finger and pushes her feet forward. She describes this as 'piercing' and 'squeezing'. When I ask her to enlarge this movement, she is reminded of her mother who always gave her a 'pinch in the neck' when E. annoyed her. This often happened, usually resulting in bruising. It was cowardly and sneaky', says E., 'the pinching felt like she really wanted to pinch me to death, to get rid of me'. She closes her eyes and notes that she often braced her feet as well, just as she is sitting opposite me. E. now moves vigorously with her arms and feet as if she wants to free herself from a grip. Initially, she refers to this as 'anger and resistance', but after that, she mainly feels anxiety. During the further experiential bodywork through posture, deep breathing and expression, her gaze indeed becomes more anxious. In myself, I perceive a vague feeling of sadness, an image of a child in panic, distraught. But as the session progresses, I sense a somewhat anxious feeling in my stomach, as if something is contracting and can explode at any moment, which happens a few minutes later. Suddenly E. makes herself big and shouts 'I might pinch you back, maybe even in your throat'. Then she drops down into the chair, somewhat surprised about her outburst, says nothing for minutes, while she presses her thumb deep into her index finger.

Working with children in experiential bodywork

Body psychotherapy and working with children go hand in hand. Body, touch and movement naturally belong in the realm of children and, together with play, form the core of their language. Often, these are even the only possible or available ways of accessing their inside (left quadrants), especially in smaller children. In line with body psychotherapy, EBW also offers starting points for working with children. Here are just a few examples.

> S. is a 5-year-old boy with a family history of serious neglect in the early years of life. S. also spent almost a year in an institution, where his biological parents barely came to visit him. He shows a disorganized attachment. The children's therapist indicates that S. is not able to play; all he does is create a mess and chaos and displays a lot of unsafe behaviour. During the team meeting, she describes some examples from recent sessions. 'S. and I are police officers and we have to fight the crooks together. When S. accidentally bumps his head against a table, I want to come to his aid, but he immediately gets

angry and shouts: "Don't touch me! Leave me alone! I hate you!" A minor pain stimulus is all that's needed to render S. uncontrollable and to make him fall apart, at which point the therapist suddenly shifts from playmate to "someone to hate". A few sessions later, I try to make a start on body contact through play, but this remains very difficult and precarious. I have the feeling that this boy has no skin and I have to tread very carefully.

By the way, he can only manage brief moments of play, if he has first wrapped himself in a "strong" suit, such as a Spiderman outfit, a Superman outfit or a policeman's jacket. When things get very tense, he even puts on two outfits on top of each other.

Here, we recognise elements, such as the process of projective identification, in which unbearable parts end up projected in the other, and Bick's 'second skin'. Interesting is to see how S. works with multiple layers of clothing in order to protect himself when things get too tense. Based on the DDT, we understand on the one hand that S., through the pain stimulus and the associated hostile objectal foundation, shifts down to a lower fulcrum, in which the Other is either kind and good, or just plain bad. On the other hand, in the DDT, we also see that during the game, S. 'rises up' to the third fulcrum of the early self (triadic), which is just above the level at which he largely functions, namely, the 'magical' fulcrum 2 (dyadic), where things went wrong in terms of secure attachment. This fulcrum to which he rises (metaphor of the wall climber) involves early mythical identification processes, peopled with heroes like Spiderman and Superman, but also father figures like his own daddy, whom he never saw again.

Within EBW, we could start by getting S. to experience basal contact warmth by simply placing hands on his torso (if necessary, S. can wrap himself in a fleece blanket the first few times). The next step is to work with variations on breathing-together. Here too – if necessary – an intermediate step can be taken in which S. first does this exercise with a doll in play therapy and he can pretend to be the therapist.

D. is a 14-year-old boy and registers with the diagnosis of conduct disorder. Father is a drug addict and does not feature in his life. When D. is asked to draw a person, he does so in a somewhat infantile way, resulting in a figure with a penis and breasts. 'This is a man who is also a woman', he explains. A little later he says: 'And I'm going to have my dad's name tattooed here' (points to his arm). Earlier in the session, he had said how he hates his father and is disgusted by him. The ambivalence is thus inscribed in his body. The boy's personal hygiene was always a struggle at home. He comes to the session with grubby nails and an unwashed face.

Working with D. is complex and requires meticulous cooperation with the child psychologist. The share of EBW consists of a combination of working with the meaningful body (phenomenological route) around the arm where the tattoo should be and deep tissue work on feet and legs (structural route). In the next phase, we will address the anger and disgust by working with visualisation and evocative exercises. When we happen to mention 'capoeira' in passing during a session, D. appears to prick up his ears. A few weeks later, he has made a start and thinks 'it's so cool to learn those tough capoeira moves to music . . . they also have tattoos there, but not of their dads, so I'm not sure yet what I'm going to do with that'.

The pranic body in everyday life

Looking at the body from a development-dynamic perspective within EBW can easily be visualised with a set of Russian dolls that transcend and encompass each other. At the same time, we have pointed out that this holarchical back-and-forth dynamic is part of the natural process of subject development. In concrete terms, this means that all these levels (or Russian dolls) can come to the fore, depending on the context. Moreover, being able to make contact with this variety of developmental elements within ourselves is part of a healthy and resilient identity. For example, let's look at the pranic body in our everyday lives. Let's take sexuality. The merging, but also passionate dimension of sexuality requires the involvement of the pleromatic, uroboric and pranic bodies, respectively. The *quasi* physical boundary-blurring aspect, the search for contact with erogenous zones and stimuli, as well as the libidinous charge of the excited body sum up healthy sexual interaction between people. Conversely, if a person cannot 'descend' to these basic levels of (self-)experience and for example is not able to descend past the third *fulcrum* of early neurotic, mental identifications, then this often forms a breeding ground for sexual problems. Some people find it difficult to surrender or allow the Other to come close; orgasm or ejaculation fail or are premature and in general, sexuality is mainly experienced from the head. The body is something that is difficult to connect with.

Also in sports. Take, for example, the workout at the gym. The pranic body provides a vitalising propulsion, whereby the body is literally pumped up and 'grows'. At the same time, we also pointed at the narcissistic dimension of this pranic energy. This driving narcissism is also part of the vibe and self-experience during intensive power training (how different would it be without mirrors in the gym?). At the same time, exciting, driving or tribal music boosts pranic energy, allowing athletes to push their limits. Maintaining this pranic body results in previous levels becoming apparent. The deeper level of perception within the DDT can be recognised, for example, in the feeling of fullness and deep warmth that athletes experience when they are properly 'charged'. The uroboros is evident in the grunts/shrieks produced during peak exertions, in gulping down fluids in between, but also in the basal process of being stimulated by movements and breathing, as well as in sweating and trembling. Intensive exercise also has something hallucinatory – just think of runner's high – and causes an immersion in the moment (axial images in the enlarged present). On the other hand, there is also a tendency for the body, movement and environment to 'pleromatically' coincide. The access to these different bodies thus provides a necessary substrate for expressing important parts of being human. Unlimited merging, deep satisfaction and grandiose power are also part of who we are and what we sometimes need.

The psychosomatic body in therapy: a four-quadrant approach

At the start of this book, we immediately underlined the value of adopting a transdisciplinary approach towards the patient. In addition to the specific therapeutic interpretation around integrated Experiential Bodywork, this means on a conceptual level that the four quadrant approach from the anamnesis is extended to the process of treatment. This does not in any way imply that the therapist assumes responsibility for all these quadrants; on the contrary, everyone should stick to what they're good at. But how can we understand a four quadrant approach in concrete terms?

As outlined in Chapter 1, we can situate EBW on the intersection between the top-right and left quadrant, with body and lived body alternating as substrate in the treatment. The therapist guides the patient from a dual perspective through a process of experience 'from the inside out'. We could call it 'inside-out learning'. But a 4QM requires more than just bodywork, evocative movement or conversation therapy. When it comes to a psychosomatic request for help, the perspective of physical movement is often desirable as well. There is no doubt that exercise and sport are vital for healthy functioning. Sport, says Van den Bossche (2008), helps us tap into the evolutionary legacy of the hunter-gatherer in every one of us, who still has a head start compared to the mere few centuries of more sedentary life. Many patients (including anxiety, depression, trauma or burn-out) would indeed benefit enormously from regular physical movement and the positive effects of many forms of movement are now also scientifically substantiated. Physical training is, therefore, rightly at the heart of the physiotherapist's treatment.

But no matter how important this treatment is, the bar within body psychotherapy is set a little higher, or at least in a different way. For example, working with sports movement within EBW in an integrated manner mainly means working with vitalising forms of movement. Experience shows that people with psychosomatic disorders often feel anything but vital, are not able to listen to what their bodies are saying, and often have a weak body schedule, whether or not with a wrong body image. Sometimes, they are overwhelmed by their physical sensations (hyper-embodiment) or they experience their bodies as an object (dys-embodiment):

> In both cases, they are unable to distinguish between the different sensations. Nor are they able to determine what they should do. Sensations are inhibited and are chaotic. When overwhelmed, they can't distinguish nuances, causing them to overreact. If they shut themselves off, they become numb and entangled in a web of inertia
>
> (Levine, 2014b, p. 328)

Zeiler (2010) also mentioned a spatio-temporal contraction, which means that these people are stuck in their bodies as a cramped point in time and space.

This has many practical implications for therapy. After all, when these patients start exercising, for example, they do so from a relationship they have with their bodies which is anything but optimal: insufficiently felt, often with a weak body scheme, thing-like mechanically, tired and empty, in short, lacking vitality.

Logically, this implies the need for re-vitalisation and, in EBW terms, this means working on the pranic level of *fulcrum* 2. Without a doubt, there are many forms of therapy that offer this, such as psychomotor therapy, postural integration, the Feldenkrais method or bioenergetics. It should be noted, however, that almost all of these approaches – albeit unwarranted – fall outside the mainstream or are in any case insufficiently known to patients and referring physicians. The negative consequence of this is that many patients start working with forms of movement that – at that moment in their recovery – are far from suitable. The *conditio sine qua non*, therefore, consists, first and foremost, of bringing the patient back into contact with his own physicality (embodiment) via an 'inside-out learning' from ESA.

Specifically, in EBW we activate the patient's pranic charge, breathing and felt sense. Levine (2014a) describes the felt sense as sometimes vague, always complicated and always changing: 'It (the felt sense, JC) moves, shifts and transforms continuously. It can vary in clarity and intensity and, therefore, enables us to change our understanding' (p. 79). It is also interesting that Levine (idem) links the felt sense to the importance of working with interoceptive perception and (physiological) rhythms. The second level of the pranic body within the DDT corresponds to many of the therapies mentioned earlier, but also to forms of movement, such as yoga and tai-chi, in which attention, breathing, movement and rhythm are central. A special place is reserved for expressive and modern dance, and certainly also for certain forms of Eastern martial arts. Original forms, such as Shaolin Kung-Fu, were intended to support monks in their often hard, meditative work (Reid & Croucher, 1986). In order to train their bodies, they started working with the sensory-motor and pranic *fulcra*. Perseverance, power generation and control, concentration building and explosive discharge through movement and sound are all variations on the pranic theme.[12] Many of these martial forms of movement emphasise the importance of a powerful posture and a well-lived, resilient centre line that runs from the pelvis through the spine to the crown. Here, too, as the left (experience) and the right quadrant (body) are integrated, the pranic aspect kicks in. Within EBW, we therefore regularly work with forms of movement derived from Eastern martial arts.[13]

But no matter how much a 4QM approach stimulates the psychosomatic patient to work in a sporty and vital way in their top-right quadrant, this does not offer a complete picture either. Sometimes, patients get stuck in their lower-right quadrant, such as in the case of divorce, dismissal, bankruptcy or debts, and very much need intervention and guidance from actors in this field, such as Public Social Welfare Centres, employment agencies, career counselling, debt mediation or divorce counsellors.

Very often, this is also intertwined with negative processes in the lower left quadrant and referral to family, systemic or relational therapists is necessary.

But a psychosomatic problem can also be anchored in personality problems, abuse or family influences (see e.g. Gilleland et al., 2009) or the widespread 'work-stress' (see e.g. Nakao, 2010). Sometimes, people fall on hard times with hardly any support or social network, as a result of which all quadrants have to be addressed simultaneously, preferably within a professional setting, such as hospital admission or day therapies. In this case too, a transdisciplinary

The practice of experiential bodywork 163

perspective deserves its place and the pranic-vitalising approach described earlier is desirable.

> *If we flesh this out in concrete terms, we could support the psychosomatic body by stimulating the four quadrants as follows (based on Wilber, 2001):*
>
> - *Top-right quadrant:*
>   *aerobic training, such as start-to-walk (run, swim, etc.); pranic exercises such as bioenergetics, chi-gong; experienced posture and movement as in yoga; stimulating rhythmic movement, such as free dance, capoeira or Wing Chun; nutrition/diet and a healthy biorhythm*
> - *Bottom-right quadrant:*
>   *engaging in sports together; joining clubs for hobbies and leisure; going back to work, adapted or not, as the case may be*
> - *Bottom-left quadrant:*
>   *sharing and discussing experiences from, for example, Gestalt exercises, mindfulness or other quadrants in group; joining encounter groups; couples therapy*
> - *Top-left quadrant:*
>   *creative expression following pranic bodywork; artistic expression, such as painting, music or writing; working with dreams; forms of introspection*

Notes

1 Another typical example is the importance of the punctual beginning and end of each session, even if the patient or therapist would like to make an exception.
2 In a certain sense, the questions used here in the anamnesis resemble those in the Attachment Biographical Interview.
3 However, it is not possible to test indiscriminately here. Many physiotherapists and manual therapists, as experts of the biomedical body in the top-right quadrant, implicitly approach the body only as an object to be treated. This is not what is meant here. Precisely to avoid this pitfall, we use both listening touch and body reading within EBW to feel the various layers of the myofascial system and to literally bring the therapist to a specific region (e.g. the pelvis) or tissue structure (e.g. the deep fascia of the neck), which requires attention. Having said that, there are a lot of body therapists who are trained in this sensitive expertise and who provide powerful work from a similar view of the human being. Usually, these are therapies that are more centrally located within the therapeutic spectrum of the introduction.
4 This approach is not unusual in experience-based body therapies. For example, the treatment within bioenergetics (Löwen, 1996; Löwen & Löwen, 1993) and Postural Integration (Painter, 1986, 1987) is related to specific zones which, in terms of sequence and intervention, are fixed in advance from a clear therapeutic vision. Rolfers and some osteopaths also work on the basis of such a systematic approach.
5 As stated earlier we knowingly distinguish here between a pleromatic self in *fulcrum* 0 and a sensorimotor self in F1. What is referred here as 'matter' and 'sensation' is in fact the pleromatic self that started in the prenatal realm of physical matter. Initially this is an archaic and proto-plasmatic self which is not differentiated from any surroundings. Once differentiation starts, based on reflexive and later on progressively more sensorimotor interaction with the physical world/other, the first sub-phase of

fulcrum 1 kicks in. At that moment this still is a very rudimentary way of reacting and moving. So the first sub-phase here is based on the sublevels 'matter' and 'sensation'. The second and last sub-phase of F1 goes a bit further and is about bodily perceiving. Here the previously mentioned uroboric self is involved. The typhonic realm will get involved once the second fulcrum is reached by the evolving self. In this way Wilber's pleroma-uroboros-typhon is actually still present in the DDT.

6 Based on Nietzsche, we could say that these people are overwhelmed by the Dionysian aspect and cannot offer enough Apollonian counterweight to anchor themselves in the propelling and ecstatic experience of the pranic. 'The Dionysian aspect is a sense of the unity of creativity and destruction with a preference for the vital, the endless, the monstrous, the frequent, the uncertain and the terrible' (IJsseling, 1999, p. 20).

7 Wilber situates the broad category of borderline pathology here.

8 An interesting application of this is found in Bercelli (2010), who successfully works with large groups of trauma victims in developing countries where he collectively gives them numerous exercises around trembling and shaking.

9 Core structures are first and foremost the neck lodge, neck and face. The sternocleidomastoid, hyoidal musculature, *scaleni* group and suboccipital musculature are addressed in a first session and the *masseter, temporalis* and pterygoid muscles and mouth muscles in a second session.

10 Soth (2005) even points out that physical (counter)transference can be seen as pleonastic. Since drive has biological roots, transference can only be physical.

11 Somatic (counter)transference can also appear as a form of primitive communication, as in projective identifications (Bloom, 2006).

12 At the same time, it would be both incomplete and incorrect to state that the physical training of these monks was aimed solely at the lower *fulcra* of grounding and discharge. Much of their bodywork was aimed at integrating the higher *fulcra* of thought. This connecting work can be found in Wilber's (1999, 2000) work as a sub-stage of the sixth *fulcrum* and is symbolised by the centaur.

13 This connecting element forms the core of yoga, a term that etymologically comes from the same tribe (yuj) as the word 'yuj', which connected the oxen so that the cart could be pulled (Heller, 2012; Feuerstein, 2001).

In retrospect

A word about therapists, time and future.

At the start of this book, we talked briefly about terminology and language. Throughout the book, we referred to 'the therapist'. However, we failed to identify them in concrete terms: is it a psychotherapist or a body therapist? We described experiential bodywork as layered work, straddling body and mind. We formulated fairly strict transdisciplinary criteria and referred to various non-negotiable elements, such as an adequate therapeutic framework. On the other hand, it was already made clear in the introduction that there is still a lot of undeveloped – partly unexplored – land, but insufficiently framed, both legally and deontologically. By definition, it is impossible to attribute pioneering work to one movement, let alone one person (after all, before Columbus, the New World was already inhabited), but that does not mean that it is all just the same, on the contrary.

For me personally, given the context and uniqueness we have described in this book and given existing therapeutic practice and expertise, the integrated work with a difficult body tips in favour of psychotherapists. The privileged role of body psychotherapy was more or less obvious from the introduction, but deserves a mention nevertheless. In addition, the Achilles heel of many regular body therapies requires a revival: however powerful and sophisticated the arsenal of body-oriented techniques, such as deep tissue work and evocative movement, is – which it is without a doubt – the appropriate psychotherapeutic framework is lacking, as are the necessary psychological background and the much-needed phenomenological-hermeneutic approach in order to be able to work with the things that come into motion during therapy to a sufficient degree. Even just being a sounding board for spontaneous stories that may bubble up, or catharsis, is not an easy task. The following quotation from Ulfried Geuter (2015b), underlines this importance once again:

> Fundamental and determining patterns of body experience and self-experience, of emotional awareness and affect regulation are acquired as a child in early interaction and dialogue. In order to understand patients and their suffering, as well as various phenomena that can occur in therapy, it is necessary to unlock those experiences from their life history that have moulded their current experience and behaviour. To this end, it is very important to have

> sufficient insight into developmentally psychological coherence and processes. This is also necessary when inviting patients into therapy to express early and pre-verbal sensorimotor movement patterns and experiences such as clinging, hiccups or shouting and ranting.
>
> (p. 210, translation JC)

The clinical psychologist or psychiatrist – both in their capacity as psychotherapists – is, however, handed the timely task of finally learning how to work with the patient's body and with their own.

So even though Satellite Navigation says that the final destination for psychologists is closer than for (most) body therapists, they still have a fair bit of travelling to do. And as with a SatNav, it is advisable to keep your eye on the road yourself.

This brings us to the future, about which we can be somewhat brief. There is still quite a bit of work to be done in the area of training, research and legal support for body psychotherapy and integrated bodywork on an international scale. But the good news is that there is a lot of enthusiasm and that crucial steps have already been taken for some decades (see, e.g., European Association for Body Psychotherapy or United States Association for Body Psychotherapy).

Finally, from future to time, and thus back to practice. We shouldn't kid ourselves: working with psychosomatic or trauma related problems – that is, a 'difficult' body – takes time. Of course, much depends on the criterion of 'recovery', but it is often a long road, which sometimes cannot be travelled to the end. So, time turns out to be a difficult partner, or at least the way in which we as therapists wish to deal with it. In attempts to achieve an optimal marriage of convenience between psychologists and policymakers, for example, we work with indicative numbers for treatment. However, this almost fetish-like obsession with seeing how quickly things can be fixed does not apply to working with a difficult body. Not that this means that people cannot be helped in a few sessions, certainly not. Sometimes, it really is nothing short of a miracle to come into contact with your body for the first time or to release carefully stored physical tension. Only, it is difficult to predict. The body as the manifestation of the unconscious does not (so easily) allow itself to be squeezed into a predetermined straitjacket. I myself have been able to help people move forward in a few sessions or weeks in a limited number of cases. Many of them really needed more time (months) and, occasionally, I see people for a few years. At least, that is my experience. Working with a psychosomatic or trauma related 'conflicted' body, as it happens within Experiential Bodywork and body psychotherapy, requires a subtle interplay of kairological time – beautifully brought to life by Joke Hermse (2014a) – and the chronological time that adds structure to our day-to-day activities. We have also talked extensively about the importance of leaning back in therapy. Here, we can now add the need for slowing down, and with Ordine (2017) perhaps even the value of the futile aspects in therapy. It would lead too far to add nuance to these statements, but as already mentioned in 'Some opening reflections', we refer once more to various inspiring, but especially to 'inappropriate'[1] views in numerous essays, manuscripts and manifestos (see for example De Dijn, 2014; Ordine, 2017; Verhaeghe, 2009; Hermse, 2014, 2017).

Because averse to time pressure, deaf to cries of efficiency and reluctant to the idea of controllability, the body is in the meantime simply coasting along quietly, and it is not only the patient who will have to learn to get used to this . . .

Note

1 I borrow the tantalizing term 'inappropriate' from Philip Brinckman, who is currently working on his promising book *Tijd voor Onaangepast Onderwijs* (*Time for inappropriate education*), in which a critical, but above all, clear analysis is central, which I feel is also clearly rooted in transdisciplinary thinking. On a final note and with his permission, I would dare to speak of 'time for inappropriate therapy'.

Bibliography

Abbott, R. D., Koptiuch, C., Iatridis, J. C., Howe, A. K., Badger, G. J., & Langevin, H. M. (2013). Stress and matrix-responsive cytoskeletal remodeling in fibroblasts. *J. Cell. Physiol.*, *228*(1), 50–57.

Abraira, V. E., & Ginty, D. D. (2013). The sensory neurons of touch. *Neuron*, *79*(4), 618–639. doi:10.1016/j.neuron.2013.07.051

Abu-Hijleh, M., Dharap, A. S., & Harris, P. (2012). Fascia superficialis. In R. Schleip, T. W. Findley, L. Chaitow, & P. Huijing (Eds.), *Fascia: The tensional network of the human body* (pp. 19–23). London, New York and Oxford: Churchill Livingstone Elsevier.

Ackerley, R., Backlund Wasling, H., Liljencrantz, J., Olausson, H., Johnson, R. D., & Wessberg, J. (2014). Human C-tactile afferents are tuned to the temperature of a skin-stroking caress. *The Journal of Neuroscience: The Official Journal of the Society for Neuroscience*, *34*(8), 2879–2883.

Adamec, R. (1990). Does kindling model anything clinically relevant? *Biological Psychiatry*, *27*(3), 249–279. doi:10.1016/0006-3223(90)90001-I

Afari, N., Ahumada, S. M., Wright, L. J., Mostoufi, S., Golnari, G., Reis, V., & Cuneo, J. G. (2014). Psychological trauma and functional somatic syndromes: A systematic review and meta- analysis. *Psychosom. Med.*, *76*(1), 2–11. doi:10.1097/psy.0000000000000010

Allen, J. G., Fonagy, P., & Bateman, A. W. (2008). *Mentaliseren in de klinische praktijk*. Amsterdam: Nieuwezijds.

Allison, E., & Fonagy, P. (2016). When is truth relevant? *Psychoanalytic Quarterly*, *85*, 275–303. doi:10.1002/psaq.12074

Alma, H. A. (2005). *De parabel van de blinden: Psychologie en het verlangen naar zin*. Amsterdam: SWP.

American Psychiatric Association. (1980). *Diagnostic and statistical manual of mental disorders III*. Washington: APA.

American Psychiatric Association. (2001). *Beknopte handleiding bij de Diagnostische Criteria van de DSM-IV-TR. Bureau-editie*. Lisse: Nederlandse vertaling Swets & Zeitlinger.

Anzieu, D. (2006). *Le Moi-Peau*. Paris: Dunod.

Apkarian, A. V., Sosa, Y., Sonty, S., Levy, R. M., Harden, R. N., Parrish, T. B., & Gitelman, D. R. (2004). Chronic back pain is associated with decreased prefrontal and thalamic gray matter density. *J. Neuroscience*, *24*(46), 10410–10415.

Atarodi, S., & Hosier, S. (2011). Trauma in the mind and pain in the body: Mind-body interactions in psychogenic pain. *Human Architecture*, *9*(1), 111–131. Accessed via http://scholarworks.umb.edu/human architecture

Bar-Levav, R. (1998). A rationale for physical touching in psychotherapy. In E. Smith, P. Clance, & S. Imes (Eds.), *Touch in psychotherapy*. London: The Guilford Press.

Barsalou, L. W., Simmons, W. K., Barbey, A. K., & Wilson, C. D. (2003). Grounding conceptual knowledge in modality-specific systems. *Trends Cogn. Sci.*, *7*(2), 84–91. doi:10.1016/S1364-6613(02)00029-3

Bartels, A., & Zeki, S. (2004). The neural correlates of maternal and romantic love. *NeuroImage*, *21*, 1155–1166.

Bassal, N. (2015). The Norwegian tradition of body psychotherapy. In G. Marlock, & H. Weiss (Eds.), *The handbook of body psychotherapy and somatic psychology* (pp. 62–70). Berkeley, CA: North Atlantic Books.

Bazan, A. (2007). *Des fantômes dans la voix: Une hypothèse neuropsychoanalitique sur la structure de l'inconscient*. Psychologie. Université Lumière – Lyon II, 2009. Français. Retrieved from HAL Id: tel-01519179 https://tel.archives-ouvertes.fr/tel-01519179

Bazan, A. (2010). Betekenaars in hersenweefsel: Bijdrage tot een fysiologie van het onbewuste. In M. Kinet, & A. Bazan (Eds.), *Psychoanalyse en Neurowetenschap: De geest in de machine*. Antwerp and Apeldoorn: Garant.

Bazan, A. (2014). Neuropsychoanalyse: geschiedenis en epistemologie. *Tijdschrijft voor Psychoanalyse*, *20*, 245–255.

Bechara, A., & Naqvi, N. (2004). Listening to your heart: Interoceptive awareness as a gateway to feeling. *Nat. Neurosci.*, *7*, 102–103.

Beck, D., & Cowan, C. (2004). *Spiral dynamics: Mastering values, leadership and change*. Hoboken, NJ: Blackwell Publishing.

Bedi, U. S., & Arora, R. (2007). Cardiovascular manifestations of posttraumatic stress disorder. *J. Natl. Med. Assoc.*, *99*(6), 642–649. Accessed via www.ncbi.nlm.nih.gov/pmc/articles/PMC2574374

Benjamin, M. (2009). The fascia of the limbs and back – a review. *J. Anat.*, *214*, 1–18.

Bercelli, D. (2010). Neurogenes Zittern: Eine körperorientierte Behandlungsmethode für Traumata in grossen Bevölkerungsgruppen. *Trauma und Gewalt*, *2*(4), 148–157.

Berlucchi, G., & Aglioti, S. M. (2010). The body in the brain revisited. *Exp. Brain. Res.*, *200*, 25–35.

Bermond, B., Vorst, H. C. M., & Moormann, P. P. (2006 [2012], January). Cognitive neuropsychology of alexithymia: Implications for personality typology. *Cognitive Neuropsychiatry*, *11*, 332–360.

Bianchi-Berhouze, N., Cairns, P., Cox, A., Jennett, C., & Kim, W. W. (Eds.). (2006). On posture as a modality for expressing and recognizing emotions. *Emotion and HCI workshop at BCS HCI London* (pp. 74–80). Retrieved from https://scholar.google.be

Bick, E. (1968). The experience of the skin in early object-relations. In E. Briggs (Ed.), *Surviving space: Papers on infant observation*. London: Karnac Books.

Bick, E. (1986). Further considerations on the function of the skin in early object-relations. In E. Briggs (Ed.), *Surviving space: Papers on infant observation*. London: Karnac Books.

Bion, W. (1962). *Learning from experience*. London: Karnac Books.

Bion, W. (1976). *Penetrating silence*. Published in the Complete Works of W.R. Bion. Vol. 15 (pp. 31–44). London: Karnac Books. Retrieved from https://books.google.be/books

Björnsdotter, M., Morrison, I., & Olausson, H. (2010). Feeling good: On the role of C fiber mediated touch in interoception. *Experimental Brain Research*, *207*, 149–155.

Blakeslee, S., & Blakeslee, M. (2007). *The body has a mind of its own: How body maps in your brain help you do (almost) everything better*. New York: Random House.

Bloom, K. (2005). Articulating preverbal experience. In N. Totton (Ed.), *New dimensions in body psychotherapy*. Maidenhead: Open University Press.

Bloom, K. (2006). *The embodied self: Movement and psychoanalysis*. London and New York: Karnac Books.

Blumenthal, B. (2001). The psychotherapist's body. In M. Heller (Ed.), *The flesh of the soul: The body we work with* (pp. 153–160). Bern, Switzerland: Peter Lang.

Bob, P. (2008). Pain, dissociation and subliminal self-representations. *Consciousness and Cognition, 17*(1), 355–369. doi:10.1016/j.concog.2007.12.001

Bogaerts, K., Van Diest, I., & Van den Bergh, O. (2010). Interoceptie, symptoomperceptie en gezondheidsklachten. In B. Van Houdenhove, P. Luyten, & J. Vandenberghe (Eds.), *Luisteren naar het lichaam. Het dualisme voorbij* (hoofdstuk 6). Leuven: Lannoo Campus.

Bogaerts, K., Van Eylen, L., Li, W., Bresseleers, J., Van Diest, I., De Peuter, S., & Van den Bergh, O. (2010). Distorted symptom perception in patients with medically unexplained symptoms. *Journal of Abnormal Psychology, 119*(1), 226–234.

Bohlmeijer, E. (2012). *De verhalen die we leven: De narratieve psychologie als methode.* Amsterdam: Boom.

Bovin, M. J., Jager-Hyman, S., Gold, S. D., Marx, B. P., & Sloan, D. M. (2008). Tonic immobility mediates the influence of peritraumatic fear and perceived inescapability on posttraumatic stress symptom severity among sexual assault survivors. *J. Trauma Stress, 21*(4), 402–409. doi:10.1002/jts.20354

Bovin, M. J., Ratchford, E., & Marx, B. P. (2014). Chapter 3. Peritraumatic dissociation and tonic immobility: Clinical findings. In F. Ulrich, U. Lanius, S. Paulsen, & F. Corrigan (Eds.), *Neurobiology and treatment of traumatic dissociation: Towards an embodied self* (pp. 51–67). New York: Springer. Accessed via https://books.google.be

Braeken, M. A., Jones, A., Otte, R. A., Nyklicek, I., & Van den Bergh, B. R. (2017). Potential benefits of mindfulness during pregnancy on maternal autonomic nervous system function and infant development. *Psychophysiology, 54*(2), 279–288. doi:10.1111/psyp.12782

Braeken, M. A., Kemp, A. H., Outhred, T., Otte, R. A., Monsieur, G. J., Jones, A., & Van den Bergh, B. R. (2013). Pregnant mothers with resolved anxiety disorders and their offspring have reduced heart rate variability: Implications for the health of children. *PLoS One, 8*(12), e83186. doi:10.1371/journal.pone.0083186

Bremner, J. D., Southwick, S. M., & Charney, D. S. (1999). The neurobiology of posttraumatic stress disorder: An integration of animal and human research. In P. A. Saigh, & J. D. Bremner (Eds.), *Posttraumatic stress disorder: A comprehensive text* (pp. 103–143). Needham Heights, MA: Allyn & Bacon.

Breslau, N., & Kessler, R. C. (2001). The stressor criterion in DSM-IV posttraumatic stress disorder: An empirical investigation. *Biol. Psychiatry, 50*(9), 699–704. doi:10.1016/S0006-3223(01)01167-2

Briere, J., & Scott, C. (2015). *Principles of trauma therapy: A guide to symptoms, evaluation, and treatment* (2nd edition). Washington, DC: Sage Publications.

Brown, L. J. (2013). The development of Bion's concept of container and contained. In H. B. Levine, & L. J. Brown (Eds.), *Growth and turbulence in the container/contained Bion's continuing legacy*. London and New York: Routledge.

Brunia, C. (1999). Neural aspects of anticipatory behavior. *Acta Psychol., 101*(2–3), 213–242. doi:10.1016/S0001-6918(99)00006-2

Buffington, C. A. T. (2009). Developmental influences on medically unexplained symptoms. *Psychotherapy and Psychosomatics, 78*, 139–144.

Bulhof, I. N. (1995). *Van inhoud naar houding: Een nieuwe visie op filosoferen in een pluralistische cultuur*. Kampen: Kok Agora.

Bullington, J. (2009). Embodiment and chronic pain: Implications for rehabilitation practice. *Health Care Analysis, 17*, 100–109.

Büntig, W. E. (2015). The work of Wilhelm Reich (Part I). In G. Marlock, & H. Weiss (Eds.), *The handbook of body psychotherapy and somatic psychology* (pp. 71–82). Berkeley, CA: North Atlantic Books.
Bushnell, M. C., Ceko, M., & Low, L. A. (2013). Cognitive and emotional control of pain and its disruption in chronic pain. *Nat. Rev. Neurosci., 14*, 502–511.
Calsius, J. (2012). Existentiële bewustwording en angst: Kanttekening rond ontwikkeling en verticaliteit. In T. Jorna (Ed.), *Mag een mens eenzaam zijn? Studies naar existentiële eenzaamheid en zingeving* (pp. 81–98). Amsterdam: SWP.
Calsius, J. (2017a). Het lichaam als mogelijke toegangspoort in psychotherapie. *Tijdschrift voor Psychoanalyse, 2*.
Calsius, J. (2017b). Het lichaam, een unheimliche gast in therapie? *Tijdschrift voor Klinische Psychologie, 47*(3), 56–71.
Calsius, J., Alma, H., & Pott, H. (2013a). Doorheen de angst. Fenomenologische analyse van vijf existentiële structuurmomenten. *Tijdschrift Cliëntgerichte Psychotherapie, 51*(3), 226–242.
Calsius, J., Alma, H., & Pott, H. (2013b). Het lichaam doorheen een existentieel bewustwordingsproces: Mogelijk of niet? *Tijdschrift Cliëntgerichte Psychotherapie, 51*(4), 297–313.
Calsius, J., Courtois, I., Feys, P., Van Asch, P., De Bie, J., & D'Hooghe, M. (2015). "How to conquer a mountain with multiple sclerosis". How a climbing expedition to Machu Picchu affects the way people with multiple sclerosis experience their body and identity: A phenomenological analysis. *Disabil. Rehabil.*, 1–7. doi:10.3109/09638288.2015.1027003
Calsius, J., De Bie, J., Hertogen, R., & Meesen, R. (2016). Touching the lived body in patients with medically unexplained symptoms: How an integration of hands-on bodywork and body awareness in psychotherapy may help people with alexithymia. *Front Psychol., 7*, 253. doi:10.3389/fpsyg.2016.00253
Cameron, O. G. (2001). Interoception: The inside story-a model for psychosomatic processes. *Psychosomatic Medicine, 63*, 697–710.
Cameron, O. G. (2009). Visceral brain-body information transfer. *NeuroImage, 47*(3), 787–794.
Cameron, O. G., & Minoshima, S. (2002). Regional brain activation due to pharmacologically induced adrenergic interoceptive stimulation in humans. *Psychosom. Med., 64*, 851–861.
Carman, T. (2008). *Merleau-Ponty*. London and New York: Routledge Philosophers.
Caroll, R. (2005). Neuroscience and the law of the self. In N. Totton (Ed.), *New dimensions in body psychotherapy* (pp. 13–29). Maidenhead: Open University Press.
Carrion, V. G., Weems, C. F., Ray, R. D., Glaser, B., Hessel, D., & Reiss, A. L. (2002). Diurnal salivary cortisol in pediatric posttraumatic stress disorder. *Biological Psychiatry, 51*(7), 575–582. doi:10.1016/S0006-3223(01)01310-5
Ceunen, E., Vlaeyen, J. W. S., & Van Diest, I. (2016). On the origine of interoception. *Front. Psychol., 7*, 743. doi:10.3389/fpsyg.2016.00743
Chaitow, L. (Ed.). (2016). *Fascial dysfunction: Manual therapy approaches*. Edinburgh: Handspring Publishing.
Cipolletta, S. (2013). Construing in action: Experiencing embodiment. *Journal of Constructivist Psychology, 26*, 293–305. doi:10.1080/10720537.2013.812770
Cipolletta, S., Consolaro, F., & Horvath, P. (2014). When health is an attitudinal matter: A qualitative research. *Journal of Humanistic Psychology, 54*, 391–413.
Civitarese, G., & Ferro, A. (2015). *The analytic field and its transformations*. London: Karnac Books.

Cluckers, G., & Meurs, P. (2005). Bruggen tussen denkwijzen? In M. Kinet, & R. Vermote (Eds.), *Mentalisatie*. Antwerp: Garant.

Cooper, M. (2008). *Existential therapies*. Los Angeles and London: Sage Publications.

Cornell, W. F. (2015). *Somatic experience in psychoanalysis and psychotherapy: In the expressive language of the living*. London and New York: Routledge.

Courtois, I., Cools, F., & Calsius, J. (2015). Effectiveness of body awareness interventions in fibromyalgia and chronic fatigue syndrome: A systematic review and meta-analysis. *Journal of Bodywork and Movement Therapies, 19*, 35–56.

Craig, A. D. (2002, August). How do you feel? Interoception: The sense of the physiological condition of the body. *Nature Reviews. Neuroscience, 3*, 655–666.

Craig, A. D. (2003). Interoception: The sense of the physiological condition of the body. *Current Opinion in Neurobiology, 13*, 500–505.

Craig, A. D. (2004). Human feelings: Why are some more aware than others? *Trends Cogn. Sci., 8*, 239–241.

Craig, A. D. (2009). How do you feel now? The anterior insula and human awareness. *Nature Reviews: Neuroscience, 10*(January), 59–70.

Craig, A. D. (2010). The sentient self. *Brain Struct. Funct., 214*, 563–577.

Craig, A. D. (2011). Significance of the insula for the evolution of human awareness of feelings from the body. *Annals of the New York Academy of Sciences, 1225*, 72–82.

Creed, F., Henningsen, P., & Fink, P. (2011). *Medically unexplained symptoms, somatisation and bodily distress: Developing better clinical services*. Cambridge: Cambridge University Press.

Critchley, H. D. (2009). Psychophysiology of neural, cognitive and affective integration: fMRI and autonomic indicants. *Int. J. Psychophysiol., 73*, 88–94.

Critchley, H. D., & Seth, A. (2012). Will studies of macaque insula reveal the neural mechanisms of self-awareness? *Neuron, 74*, 423–426.

Critchley, H. D., Wiens, S., Rotshtein, P., Ohman, A., & Dolan, R. J. (2004). Neural systems supporting interoceptive awareness. *Nature Neuroscience, 7*(2), 189–195.

Csikszenmihalyi, M. (2008). *Flow: Psychologie van de optimale ervaring*. Amsterdam: Boom.

Cullberg, J. (2009). *Moderne psychiatrie: Een psychodynamische benadering*. Amsterdam: Ambo.

Damasio, A. (2003). *Looking for Spinoza: Joy, sorrow and the feeling brain*. New York and San Diego: Harcourt Books.

Damasio, A. (2004). *Het Gelijk van Spinoza*. Amsterdam: Wereldbibliotheek.

Damasio, A., & Carvalho, G. B. (2013). The nature of feelings: Evolutionary and neurobiological origins. *Nat. Rev. Neurosci., 14*, 143–152.

Davis, M., Walker, D. L., Miles, L., & Grillon, C. (2010). Phasic vs sustained fear in rats and humans: Role of the extended amygdala in fear vs anxiety. *Neuropsychopharmacology, 35*(1), 105–135. doi:10.1038/npp.2009.109

De Dijn, H. (2014). *Vloeibare warden: Politiek, zorg en onderwijs in de laatmoderne tijd*. Kalmthout: Pelckmans-Klement.

De Gucht, V., Fischler, B., & Heiser, W. (2004). Personality and affect as determinants of medically unexplained symptoms in primary care: A follow-up study. *Journal of Psychosomatic Research, 56*, 279–285.

De Gucht, V., & Heiser, W. (2003). Alexithymia and somatisation: A quantitative review of the literature. *Journal of Psychosomatic Research, 54*, 425–434.

De Haan, S. (2012). Fenomenologie van de lichaamservaring. In D. Denys, & G. Meynen (Eds.), *Handboek Psychiatrie en Filosofie*. Utrecht: De Tijdstroom.

Dehue, T. (2012). Over de (on)wetenschappelijkheid van de DSM, een wetenschapstheoretisch perspectief. In D. Denys, & G. Meynen (Eds.), *Handboek psychiatrie en filosofie* (hoofdstuk 3). Utrecht: De Tijdstroom.
Denk, F., McMahon, S. B., & Tracey, I. (2014). Pain vulnerability: A neurobiological perspective. *Nature Neuroscience, 17*(2), 192–200.
Denys, D., & Meynen, G. (2012). *Handboek psychiatrie en filosofie*. Utrecht: De Tijdstroom.
Depestele, F. (2000). De therapeutische ruimte vanuit experiëntieel perspectief. *Tijdschrift Cliëntgerichte Psychotherapie, 38*(4), 237–262.
Depestele, F. (2004). Het lichaam vóór de 'gevoelde zin'. In G. Lietaer, & M. Van Kalmthout (Eds.), *Praktijkboek gesprekstherapie. Psychopathologie en experiëntiële procesbevordering.* Utrecht: De Tijdstroom.
Depestele, F., Korrelboom, K., de Wolf, T., & Snijders, H. (2003). Fasering en process: Een experiëntieel, gedragstherapeutisch en psychoanalytisch perspectief. In S. Colijn, J. A. Snijders, & R. W. Trijsburg (Eds.), *Leerboek integratieve psychotherapie*. Utrecht: De Tijdstroom.
De Wolf, M. H. M. (2002). *Inleiding in de psychoanalytische psychotherapie: Ontwikkeling, psychopathologie, diagnostiek en behandelvormen*. Bussum: Coutinho.
De Wolf, M. H. M. (2011). *Psychoanalytische behandelingen: Onderbouwing, uitleg en toepassing van diverse behandelvormen*. Bussum: Coutinho.
Dirkx, J. (2011). Hysterie. In J. Dirkx, M. Hebbrecht, A. W. M. Mooij, & R. Vermote (Eds.), *Handboek psychodynamiek*. Utrecht: De Tijdstroom.
Donadio, V., Liguori, R., Elam, M., Karlsson, T., Giannoccaro, M. P., Pegenius, G., & Wallin, B. G. (2012). Muscle sympathetic response to arousal predicts neurovascular reactivity during mental stress. *The Journal of Physiology, 590*, 2885–2896.
Downing, G. (2015). Early interaction and the body: Clinical implications. In G. Marlock, & H. Weiss (Eds.), *The handbook of body psychotherapy & somatic psychology*. Berkeley, CA: North Atlantic Books.
Driessen, E., Cuijpers, P., de Maat, S. C. M., Abbass, A. A., de Jonghe, F., & Dekker, J. J. M. (2011). De effectiviteit van kortdurende psychodynamische psychotherapie bij depressie: Een meta-analyse. In P. Luyten, W. Vanmechelen, & M. Hebbrecht (Eds.), *Depressie: Actuele psychoanalytische benaderingen*. Antwerp and Apeldoorn: Garant.
Duddu, V., Husain, N., & Dickens, C. (2008). Medically unexplained presentations and quality of life: A study of predominantly South Asian primary care population in England. *Journal Psychosomatic Research, 65*(4), 311–317.
EABP. (2012). *Body psychotherapy competencies*. Retrieved from www.eabp.org
Engel, G. L. (1980). The clinical application of the biopsychosocial model. *The American Journal of Psychiatry, 137*, 535–544.
Fenton, B. W. (2007). Limbic associated pelvic pain: A hypothesis to explain the diagnostic relationships and features of patients with chronic pelvic pain. *Med. Hypotheses, 69*(2), 282–286. doi:10.1016/j.mehy.2006.12.025
Fenton, B. W., Brobeck, L., Witten, E., & Von Gruenigen, V. (2012). Chronic pelvic pain syndrome- related diagnoses in an outpatient office setting. *Gynecol. Obstet. Invest., 74*(1), 64–67. doi:10.1159/000336768
Ferrari, A. (2004). *From the eclipse of the body to the dawn of thought*. Eastbourne: Free Association Books.
Ferro, A. (2013). Vicissitudes of the container-contained and field theory. In H. B. Levine, & L. J. Brown (Eds.), *Growth and turbulence in the container/contained Bion's continuing legacy*. London and New York: Routledge.

Feuerstein, G. (2001). *The yoga tradition: Its history, literature, philosophy and practice*. Arizona: Hohm Press.

Field, T. (2010). Touch for socio-emotional and physical well-being: A review. *Developmental Review*, *30*, 367–383.

Field, T., Deeds, O., Diego, M., Hernandez-Reif, M., Gauler, A., Sullivan, S., & Nearing, G. (2009). Benefits of combining massage therapy with group interpersonal psychotherapy in prenatally depressed women. *Journal of Bodywork and Movement Therapies*, *13*(4), 297–303.

Fink, P., & Schröder, A. (2010). One single diagnosis, bodily distress syndrome, succeeded to capture 10 diagnostic categories of functional somatic syndromes and somatoform disorders. *Journal of Psychosomatic Research*, *68*, 415–426.

Fogel, A. (2009). *The psychophysiology of self-awareness*. New York: W.W. Norton.

Fogel, A. (2011). Embodied awareness: Neither implicit nor explicit, and not necessarily nonverbal. *Child Development Perspectives*, *5*(3), 183–186.

Fonagy, P., Luyten, P., & Allison, E. (2015, October). Epistemic petrification and the restoration of epistemic trust: A new conceptualization of borderline personality disorder and its psychosocial treatment. *J. Pers. Disord.*, *29*(5), 575–609. doi:10.1521/pedi.2015.29.5.575

Forman, M. D. (2010). *A guide to integral psychotherapy: Complexity, integration, and spirituality in practice*. New York: SUNY Press.

Foudraine, J. (1997). *Bunkerbouwers: Een hartstochtelijk pleidooi voor de psychotherapie*. Amsterdam: Ambo/Anthos.

Frances, A. (2014). *Saving normal: An insider's revolt against out-of-control psychiatric diagnosis, DSM-5, big pharma, and the medicalization of ordinary life*. New York: HarperCollins Publishers.

Freud, S. (1988 [1923]). *Het Ik en het Es: Psychoanalytische Theorie 3* (pp. 9–82). Meppel and Amsterdam: Boom.

Friedman, M. J. (2016). *PTSD history and overview*. Accessed on 11 April 2016 via www.ptsd.va.gov/professional/PTSD-overview/ptsd-overview.asp

Fuchs, T. (2001). The tacit dimension. *Philosophy, Psychiatry, & Amp.; Psychology*, *8*, 323–326.

Fuchs, T., & Schlimme, J. E. (2009). Embodiment and psychopathology: A phenomenological perspective. *Current Opinion in Psychiatry*, *22*, 570–575.

Gameiro, G. H., da Silva Andrade, A., Nouer, D. F., & Ferraz de Arruda Veiga, M. C. (2006). How may stressful experiences contribute to the development of temporomandibular disorders? *Clin. Oral Investig.*, *10*(4), 261–268. doi:10.1007/s00784-006-0064-1

Gard, G. (2005). Body awareness therapy for patients with fibromyalgia and chronic pain. *Disability and Rehabilitation*, *27*(June), 725–728.

Gauriau, C., & Bernard, J. (2002). Pain pathways and parabrachial circuits in the rat. *Exp. Physiol.*, *87*(2), 251–258. doi:10.1113/eph8702357

Gellhorn, E. (1956). Analysis of autonomic hypothalamic functions in the intact organism. *Neurology*, *6*(5), 335–343. Accessed via www.neurology.org

Gellhorn, E. (1964). Cardiovascular reactions in asphyxia and the postasphyxial state. *Am. Heart J.*, *67*, 73–80. doi:10.1016/0002-8703(64)90400-4

Gellhorn, E., & Hyde, J. (1953). Influence of proprioception on map of cortical responses. *J. Physiol.*, *122*(2), 371–385. doi:10.1113/jphysiol.1953.sp005007

Gendlin, E. T. (1969). Focusing. *Psychotherapy: Theory, Research and Practice*, *6*(1), 4–15. Retrieved from www.focusing.org/gendlin/docs/gol_2048.html

Gendlin, E. T. (1993). Three assertions about the body. *The Folio*, *12*(1), 21–33. Retrieved from www.focusing.org/gendlin/docs/gol_2064.html

Gendlin, E. T. (2008). *Focussen: Gevoel en je lijf*. Haarlem: De Toorts.
Gendlin, E. T., & Olsen, L. (1970). The use of imagery in experiential focusing. *Psychotherapy: Theory, Research and Practice*, 7(4), 221–223. Retrieved from www.focusing.org/gendlin/docs/gol_2066.html
Germain, A., Buysse, D. J., & Nofzinger, E. A. (2008). Sleep-specific mechanisms underlying posttraumatic stress disorder: Integrative review and neurobiological hypotheses. *Sleep Med. Rev.*, 12(3), 185–195. doi:10.1016/j.smrv.2007.09.003
Geuter, U. (2015a). The history and scope of body psychotherapy. In G. Marlock, & H. Weiss (Eds.), *The handbook of body psychotherapy and somatic psychology* (pp. 22–39). Berkeley, CA: North Atlantic Books.
Geuter, U. (2015b). *Körperpsychotherapie: Grundriss einer Theorie für die klinische Praxis*. Berlin, Deutschland: Springer.
Gilleland, J., Suveg, C., Jacob, M. L., & Thomassin, K. (2009). Understanding the medically unexplained: Emotional and familial influences on children's somatic functioning. *Child Care Health Dev.*, 35(3), 383–390. doi:10.1111/j.1365-2214.2009.00950.x
Galliéron, E. (2005). *Het eerste gesprek in de psychotherapie*. Maastricht: Gianni.
Glas, G. (2002). *Angst: Beleving, Structuur, Macht*. Amsterdam: Boom.
Glenberg, A. M. (1997). What is memory for: Creating meaning in the service of action. *Behav. Brain Sci.*, 20(1), 41–50. doi:10.1017/S0140525X97470012
Glenn, M. (2015). Prenatal and perinatal psychology: Vital foundations of body psychotherapy. In G. Marlock, & H. Weiss (Eds.), *The handbook of body psychotherapy & somatic psychology* (pp. 332–343). Berkeley, CA: North Atlantic Books.
Goehler, L. E., Lyte, M., & Gaykema, R. P. (2007). Infection-induced viscerosensory signals from the gut enhance anxiety: Implications for psychoneuroimmunology. *Brain Behav. Immun.*, 21, 721–726.
Goldstein, D. S. (1983). Plasma catecholamines and essential hypertension: An analytical review. *Hypertension*, 5(1), 86–99. Accessed via http://hyper.ahajournals.org
Gorostiaga, A., Balluerka, N., Guilera, G., Aliri, J., & Barrios, M. (2017). Functioning in patients with schizophrenia: A systematic review of the literature using the international classification of functioning, disability and health (ICF) as a reference. *Qual. Life Res.*, 26(3), 531–543. doi:10.1007/s11136-016-1488-y
Gottwald, C. (2015). Neurobiological perspectives on body psychotherapy. In G. Marlock, & H. Weiss (Eds.), *The handbook of body psychotherapy and somatic psychology* (pp. 126–147). Berkeley, CA: North Atlantic Books.
Grabe, H. J., Frommer, J., Ankerhold, A., Ulrich, C., Gröger, R., Franke, G. H., & Spitzer, C. (2008). Alexithymia and outcome in psychotherapy. *Psychotherapy and Psychosomatics*, 77, 189–194.
Graves, C. (1970). Levels of existence: An open system theory of values. *Journal of Humanistic Psychology*, 10, 131. doi:10.1177/002216787001000205
Graves, C. (2004). *Levels of human existence*. Santa Barbara: ECLET Publishing.
Green, A. (1983). *Narcisme de vie, narcisme de mort*. Paris: Editions de Minuit.
Groot, A. E., & Klostermann, J. E. M. (2009). *'Daar botst het weten.' Interdisciplinair en transdisciplinair onderzoek binnen Wageningen UR*. Wageningen: Alterra.
Grottstein, J. S. (2013). Dreaming as a 'curtain of illusion'. Revisiting the 'Royal Road' with Bion as our Guide. In H. B. Levine, & L. J. Brown (Eds.), *Growth and turbulence in the container/ contained: Bion's continuing legacy* (pp. 107–128). London: Routledge.
Gu, X., Hof, P. R., Friston, K. J., & Fan, J. (2013). Anterior insular cortex and emotional awareness. *J. Comp. Neurol.*, 521, 3371–3388.
Guilbaud, O., Corcos, M., Hjalmarsson, L., Loas, G., & Jeammet, P. (2003). Is there a psychoneuroimmunological pathway between alexithymia and immunity? Immune

and physiological correlates of alexithymia. *Biomedicine and Pharmacotherapy*, 57, 292–295.

Guimberteau, J-C., & Armstrong, C. (2015). *Architecture of human living fascia: The extracellular matrix and cells revealed through endoscopy*. Edinburgh: Handspring Publishing.

Gupta, M. A., & Gupta, A. K. (2012). Chronic idiopathic urticaria and post-traumatic stress disorder (PTSD): An under-recognized comorbidity. *Clin. Dermatol.*, 30(3), 351–354. doi:10.1016/j. clindermatol.2012.01.012

Gupta, M.A., Lanius, R.A., Van der Kolk, B. (2005). Psychologic Trauma, Posttraumatic Stress Disorder, and Dermatology. *Dermatology Clinical* (23) 649–656.

Gyllensten, A. L., Skär, L., Miller, M., & Gard, G. (2010). Embodied identity – a deeper understanding of body awareness. *Physiotherapy Theory and Practice*, 26(7), 439–446.

Häfner, M. (2013). When body and mind are talking: Interoception moderates embodied cognition. *Experimental Psychology*, 60(4), 255–259.

Halvorsen, L. A. (2014). *Understanding peritraumatic dissociation: Evolution-prepared dissociation, tonic immobility, and clinical dissociation* (Ph.D. dissertation). Antioch University, New England. Accessed via http://aura.antioch.edu/etds/88

Han, J. S., & Neugebauer, V. (2004). Synaptic plasticity in the amygdala in a visceral pain model in rats. *Neurosci. Lett.*, 361(1–3), 254–257. doi:10.1016/j.neulet.2003.12.027

Harari, R. (2001). *Lacan's seminar on "Anxiety"*. New York: Other Press.

Hart, S. (2008). *Brain, attachment, personality*. London: Karnac Books.

Hartmann, H. (1958). *Ego-psychology and the problem of adaptation*. New York: International Universities Press.

Haugstad, G., Haugstad, T., & Kirste, U. (2006). Posture, movement patterns, and body awareness in women with chronic pelvic pain. *Journal of Psychosomatic Research*, 61, 637–644.

Hebbrecht, M. (2010a). *De droom: Verkenning van een grensgebied*. Utrecht: De Tijdstroom.

Hebbrecht, M. (2010b). Een nieuwe Ferro. Bespreking van Antonio Ferro (2008). Mind works, technique and creativity in psychoanalysis: The new library of psychoanalysis. London Routledge. *Tijdschrift voor psychanalyse*, 16(1), 48–50.

Hebbrecht, M. (2016). Veldtheorie à la Ferro. Bespreking van Antonio Ferro & Giuseppe Civitaverese. The analytic field and its transformations. London: Karnac Books. *Tijdschrift voor Psychoanalyse*, 21(1), 64–66.

Heerkens, Y. F., de Weerd, M., Huber, M., de Brouwer, C. P., van der Veen, S., Perenboom, R. J., & van Meeteren, N. L. (2017). Reconsideration of the scheme of the international classification of functioning, disability and health: Incentives from the Netherlands for a global debate. *Disabil. Rehabil.*, 1–9. doi:10.1080/09638288.2016.1277404

Heidegger, M. (1999). *Zijn en Tijd*. Amsterdam: Sun.

Heimer, L., & Van Hoesen, G. W. (2006). The limbic lobe and its output channels: Implications for emotional functions and adaptive behavior. *Neurosci. Biobehav. Rev.*, 30(2), 126–147. doi:10.1016/j.neubiorev.2005.06.006

Heller, M. (2012). *Body psychotherapy: History, concepts and methods*. New York: W.W. Norton.

Henningsen, P. (2016). *Classification of bodily distress syndromes: Somatic symptom disorders in primary care*. Symposium East London: NHS Foundation Trust.

Henningsen, P., Zipfel, S., & Herzog, W. (2007). Management of functional somatic syndromes. *The Lancet*, 369, 946–955.

Herbert, B. M., Herbert, C., & Pollatos, O. (2011). On the relationship between interoceptive awareness and alexithymia: Is interoceptive awareness related to emotional awareness? *Journal of Personality*, 79, 1149–1175.

Herbert, B. M., & Pollatos, O. (2012). The body in the mind: On the relationship between interoception and embodiment. *Topics in Cognitive Science, 4*, 692–704.

Hermse, J. (2014a). *Kairos: Een nieuwe bevlogenheid*. Utrecht, Amsterdam and Antwerp: De Arbeiderspers.

Hermse, J. (2014b). *Stil de tijd: Pleidooi voor een langzame toekomst*. Utrecht, Amsterdam and Antwerp: De Arbeiderspers.

Hermse, J. (2017). *Melancholie van de onrust*. Amsterdam: Boom.

Hinz, B., Phan, S. H., Thannickal, V. J., Prunotto, M., Desmoulière, A., Varga, J., . . . Gabbiani, G. (2012). Recent developments in myofibroblast biology: Paradigms for connective tissue remodeling. *Am. J. Pathol., 180*(4), 1340–1355.

Holstege, G. (2014). The periaqueductal gray controls brainstem emotional motor systems including respiration. *Prog. Brain Res., 209*, 379–405. doi:10.1016/B978-0-444-63274-6.00020-5

Horwitz, A. V., & Wakefield, J. C. (2007). *The loss of sadness: How psychiatry transformed normal sorrow into depressive disorder*. New York: Oxford University Press.

Huber, A., Suman, A. L., Biasi, G., & Carli, G. (2009). Alexithymia in fibromyalgia syndrome: Associations with ongoing pain, experimental pain sensitivity and illness behaviour. *Journal of Psychosomatic Research, 66*, 425–433.

Huijing, P. O., & Langevin, H. M. (2009). Communicating about fascia: History, pitfalls and recommendations. *International Journal of Therapeutic Massage and Bodywork, 2*(4), 3e8.

IJsseling, S. (1999). *Apollo, Dionysos, Aphrodite en de anderen*. Amsterdam: Boom.

Irigaray, L. (2009). *Tussen Oost en West: Van singulariteit naar gemeenschap*. Amsterdam: Ten Have.

Isnard, J., Magnin, M., Jung, J., Mauguire, F., & Garcia-Larrea, L. (2011). Does the insula tell our brain that we are in pain? *Pain, 152*(4), 946–951.

Ivbijaro, G., & Goldberg, D. (2013). Bodily distress syndrome: The evolution of medically unexplained symptoms (Editorial). *Mental Health in Family Medicine, 10*, 63–64.

Jackson, J. L., & Passamonti, M. (2005). The outcome among patients presenting in primary care with a physical symptom at 5 years. *J. Gen Intern Med.*, (20), 1032–1037.

Jung, C. G. (1995a). *Archetype en onbewuste*. Rotterdam: Lemniscaat.

Jung, C. G. (1995b). *De held en het moedertype*. Rotterdam: Lemniscaat.

Jung, C. G. (1999). *Herinneringen Dromen Gedachten. C.G. Jung een autobiografie*. Rotterdam: Lemniscaat.

Jung, R. (1981). Postural support of goal-directed movements: The preparation and guidance of voluntary action in man. *Acta Biol. Acad. Sci. Hung., 33*(2–3), 201–213. Accessed via http://europepmc.org

Junqueira De Mattos, J. A., & Braga, J. C. (2013). Editors' introduction to chapter 8. Primitive conscience: A glimpse of the primordial mind. In H. B. Levine, & L. J. Brown (Eds.), *Growth and turbulence in the container/contained Bion's continuing legacy*. London and New York: Routledge.

Kegan, R. (1982). *The evolving self: Problem and process in human development*. Cambridge: Harvard University Press.

Kegan, R. (1994). *In over our heads: The mental demands of modern life*. Cambridge, MA: Harvard University Press.

Khalsa, S. S., Rudrauf, D., Damasio, A. R., Davidson, R. J., Lutz, A., & Tranel, D. (2008). Interoceptive awareness in experienced meditators. *Psychophysiology, 45*, 671–677.

Khalsa, S. S., Rudrauf, D., Feinstein, J. S., & Tranel, D. (2009). The pathways of interoceptive awareness. *Nat. Neurosci., 12*, 1494–1496.

Khalsa, S. S., Rudrauf, D., &Tranel, D. (2009). Interoceptive awareness declines with age. *Psychophysiology*, *46*(6), 1130–1136.

Kim, H. J., & Yu, S. H. (2015). Effects of complex manual therapy on PTSD, pain, function, and balance of male torture survivors with chronic low back pain. *J. Phys. Ther. Sci.*, *27*(9), 2763–2766.

Kinet, M. (2005). Poëzie en psychoanalyse, muze en mentalisatie. In M. Kinet, & R. Vermote (Eds.), *Mentalisatie*. Antwerpen and Apeldoorn: Garant.

Kinet, M. (2013). *Psychopathologie van het hedendaagse leven: Vier verhandelingen*. Antwerp and Apeldoorn: Garant.

Kinet, M., & Bazan, A. (2010). *Psychoanalyse en neurowetenschap: de geest in de machine*. Antwerp: Garant.

Kinet, M., & Vermote, R. (Eds.). (2005). *Mentalisatie*. Antwerp: Garant.

King, J. A., Mandansky, D., King, S., Fletcher, K., & Brewer, J. (2001). Early sexual abuse and low cortisol. *Psychiatry and Clinical Neurosciences*, *55*(1), 71–74. doi:10.1046/j.1440-1819.2001.00787.x

Kleinstauber, M., Withoft, M., Steffanowski, A., Marwijk, H., Hiller, W., & Lambert, M. J. (2014). Pharmacological interventions for somatoform disorders in adults. *Cochrane Database of Systematic Reviews*, *11*.

Kooiman, C. G., Bolk, J. H., Brand, R., Trijsburg, R. W., & Rooijmans, H. G. (2000). Is alexithymia a risk factor for unexplained physical symptoms in general medical outpatients? *Psychosomatic Medicine*, *62*(26), 768–778.

Kooiman, C. G., Bolk, J. H., Rooijmans, H. G. M., & Trijsburg, R. W. (2004). Alexithymia does not predict the persistence of medically unexplained physical symptoms. *Psychosomatic Medicine*, *66*(12), 224–232.

Kregel, J., Coppieters, I., DePauw, R., Malfliet, A., Danneels, L., Nijs, J., Cagnie, B., & Meeus, M. (2017). Does conservative treatment change the brain in patients with chronic musculoskeletal pain? A systematic review. *Pain Physician*, *20*(3), 139–154.

Krout, K. E., Belzer, R. E., & Loewy, A. D. (2002). Brainstem projections to midline and intralaminar thalamic nuclei of the rat. *J. Comp. Neurol.*, *448*(1), 53–101. doi:10.1002/cne.10236

Kuchinad, A., Schweinhardt, P., Seminowicz, D. A., Wood, P. B., Chizh, B. A., & Bushnell, M. C. (2007). Accelerated brain gray matter loss in fibromyalgia patients: Premature aging of the brain? *J. Neuroscience*, 27(15), 4004–4007.

Lacan, J. (2004). *Le Séminaire livre X. L'angoisse*. Paris: Editions du Seuil.

Ladd, C. O., Owens, M. J., & Nemeroff, C. B. (1996). Persistent changes in corticotropin-releasing factor neuronal systems induced by maternal deprivation. *Endocrinology*, *137*(4), 1212–1218. doi:10.1210/endo.137.4.8625891

Lakoff, G., & Johnson, M. (2003). *Metaphors we live by*. London: The University of Chicago Press.

Lamprecht, F., & Sack, M. (2002). Posttraumatic stress disorder revisited. *Psychosom. Med.*, *64*(2), 222–237. Accessed via http://journals.lww.com/psychosomaticmedicine

Langevin, H. M., & Huijing, P. A. (2009). Communicating about fascia: History, pitfalls and recommendations. *Int. J. Ther. Massage Bodywork*, *2*, 3–8.

Langfeld, H., & Rellensmann, D. (2015). Genealogy of body psychotherapy: A graphic depiction. In G. Marlock, & H. Weiss (Eds.), *The handbook of body psychotherapy & somatic psychology*. Berkeley, CA: North Atlantic Books.

Larun, L., Brurberg, K. G., Odgaard-Jensen, J., & Price, J. R. (2016). Exercise therapy for chronic fatigue syndrome. *Cochrane Database Syst. Rev.*, *12*, CD003200. doi:10.1002/14651858.CD003200.pub6

Laurent, C., Johnson-Wells, G., Hellström, S., Engström-Laurent, A., & Wells, A. F. (1991). Localization of hyaluronan in various muscular tissues: A morphologic study in the rat. *Cell Tissue Res.*, *263*(2), 201–205.

Layne, R. D., Weihs, K. L., Herring, A., Hishaw, A., & Smith, R. (2015). Affective agnosia: Expansion of the alexithymia construct and a new opportunity to integrate and extend Freud's legacy. *Neuroscience and Biobehavioural Review*, *55*, 594–611.

LeDoux, J. (1998). *The emotional brain*. London: Phoenix.

Lee, D., Lee, L. J., & McLaughlin, L. (2008). Stability, continence and breathing: The role of fascia following pregnancy and delivery. *Journal of Bodywork and Movement Therapies*, *12*, 333–348.

Lee, J. Y., & Spicer, A. P. (2000). Hyaluronan: A multifunctional, megaDalton, stealth molecule. *Curr. Opin. Cell Biol.*, *12*(5), 581–586.

Leichsenring, F., Luyten, P., Hilsenroth, M. J., Abbass, A., Barber, J. P., Keefe, J. R., & Steinert, C. (2015). Psychodynamic therapy meets evidence-based medicine: A systematic review using updated criteria. *Lancet Psychiatry*, *2*(7), 648–660. doi:10.1016/S2215-0366(15)00155-8

Leijssen, M. (2001). Lichaamsgerichte interventies in de psychotherapeutische hulpverlening: waardevol en ethisch verantwoord? *Maandblad Geestelijke Volksgezondheid* (3), 195–217.

Leijssen, M. (2004). Kenmerken van een helende innerlijke relatie. In G. Lietaer, & M. Van Kalmthout (Eds.), *Praktijkboek gesprekstherapie: Psychopathologie en experiëntiële procesbevordering*. Utrecht: De Tijdstroom.

Leijssen, M. (2009). *Tijd voor de ziel*. Tielt: Lannoo Campus.

Leijssen, M. (2010). Focussen. In M. Gundrum, & N. Stinckens (Eds.), *De schatkist van de therapeut: Oefeningen en strategieën voor de praktijk*. Leuven: ACCO.

Leisner, S., Gerhardt, A., Tesarz, J., Janke, S., Seidler, G. H., & Eich, W. (2014). Childhood abuse experiences and chronic low back pain. Direct and mediated effects of childhood abuse in different pain dimensions of nonspecific chronic low back pain. *Schmerz*, *28*(6), 600–606. doi:10.1007/s00482-014-1487-2

Levin, S. M., & Martin, D. C. (2012). Biotensegrity: The mechanics of fascia. In R. Schleip, L. Chaitow, T. W. Findley, & P. Huijing (Eds.), *Fascia: The tensional network of the human body: The science and clinical applications in manual and movement therapy* (pp. 137–142). Edinburgh: Elsevier.

Levine, P. (1977). *Accumulated stress, reserve capacity and disease* (doctoral thesis). University of California, Berkeley. Accessed via www.traumahealing.org

Levine, P. (2005). Panic, biology and reason: Giving the body its due. In N. Totton (Ed.), *New dimensions in body psychotherapy* (pp. 30–39). Maidenhead: Open University Press.

Levine, P. (2014a). *De tijger ontwaakt: Traumabehandeling met lichaamsgerichte therapie*. Haarlem: Altamira.

Levine, P. (2014b). *De stem van je lichaam: Trauma's helen met je lichaam als gids*. Haarlem: Altamira.

Lewis, R. (2007). *Robert Scaer's neurobiological model for PTSD and psychosomatic illness*. Accessed via www.bodymindcentral.com

Linden, M. (2017). Definition and assessment of disability in mental disorders under the perspective of the international classification of functioning disability and health (ICF). *Behav. Sci. Law*, *35*(2), 124–134. doi:10.1002/bsl.2283

Liptan, G. L. (2010). Fascia: A missing link in our understanding of the pathology of fibromyalgia. *Journal of Bodywork and Movement Therapies*, *14*(1), 3–12.

Lovero, K. L., Simmons, A. N., Aron, J. L., & Paulus, M. P. (2009). Anterior insular cortex anticipates impending stimulus significance. *NeuroImage*, *45*(3), 976–983.

Löwen, A. (1996). *Handboek bio-energetica*. Utrecht: Servire.
Löwen, A., & Löwen, L. (1993). *Bio-energetische oefeningen*. Utrecht: Servire.
Lutz, A., McFarlin, D. R., Perlman, D. M., Salomons, T. V., & Davidson, R. J. (2013). Altered anterior insula activation during anticipation and experience of painful stimuli in expert meditators. *NeuroImage, 64*, 538–546.
Luyten, P. (2014). Persistente somatische klachten: Nieuwe inzichten vanuit de dialoog met de neurowetenschappen. *Tijdschrift voor psychoanalyse, 21*(4), 266–276.
Luyten, P., & Fonagy, P. (2011). Depressie en de onlosmakelijke band tussen fenomenologie, theorie en techniek: De centrale rol van mentalisatie en gehechtheid. In P. Luyten, W. Vanmechelen, & M. Hebbrecht (Eds.), *Depressie: Actuele psychoanalytische benaderingen*. Antwerp and Apeldoorn: Garant.
Luyten, P., & Kempke, S. (2010). Psychodynamische factoren bij functionele somatische symptomen en syndromen. In B. Van Houdenhove, P. Luyten, & J. Vandenberghe (Eds.), *Luisteren naar het lichaam: Het dualisme voorbij* (hoofdstuk 5). Leuven: Lannoo Campus.
Luyten, P., Lowyck, B., Vermote, R., & Fonagy, P. (2010). De neurale basis van mentalisatie: implicaties voor de conceptualisatie en behandeling van de borderline persoonlijkheidsstoornis vanuit een psychodynamisch kader. In M. Kinet, & A. Bazan (Eds.), *Psychoanalyse en neurowetenschap: de geest in de machine* (pp. 155–188). Antwerp: Garant.
Maes, F., & Sabbe, B. G. C. (2014). Alexithymie bij fibromyalgie: prevalentie. *Tijdschrift voor Psychiatrie, 56*(12), 798–806.
Mahdi, S., Viljoen, M., Massuti, R., Selb, M., Almodayfer, O., Karande, S., . . . Bolte, S. (2017). An international qualitative study of ability and disability in ADHD using the WHO-ICF framework. *Eur. Child Adolesc. Psychiatry*. doi:10.1007/s00787-017-0983-1
Mahler, M. S., Pine, F., & Bergman, A. (2000). *The psychological birth of the human infant: Symbiosis and individuation*. New York: Basic Books.
Ma-Kellmas, C. (2014). Cross-cultural differences in somatic awareness and interoceptive accuracy: A review of the literature and directions for the future. *Frontiers in Psychology, 5*. doi:10.3389/fpsyg.2014.01379
Mangwana, S., Burlinson, S., & Creed, F. (2009). Medically unexplained symptoms presenting at secondary care: A comparison of white Europeans and people of South Asian ethnicity. *Int. Journal Psychiatry Med., 39*(1), 33–44.
Marlock, G. (2015). Body psychotherapy as a major tradition of modern depth psychology. In G. Marlock, & H. Weiss (Eds.), *The handbook of body psychotherapy and somatic psychology*. Berkeley, CA: North Atlantic Books.
Marlock, G., & Weiss, H. (2015a). The field of body psychotherapy. In G. Marlock, & H. Weiss (Eds.), *The handbook of body psychotherapy and somatic psychology* (pp. 1–19). Berkeley, CA: North Atlantic Books.
Marlock, G., & Weiss, H. (Eds.). (2015b). *The handbook of body psychotherapy and somatic psychology*. Berkeley, CA: North Atlantic Books.
Marx, B. P., Forsyth, J. P., Gallup, G. G., & Fusé, T. (2008). Tonic immobility as an evolved predator defense: Implications for sexual survivors. *Clini. Psychol. Sci. Prac., 15*(1), 74–90. doi:10.1111/j.1468-2850.2008.00112.x
Masi, A. T., & Hannon, J. C. (2008). Human resting muscle tone: Narrative introduction and modern concepts. *Journal Body Work and Movement Therapies, 12*(4), 320–332.
Massion, J. (1992). Movement, posture and equilibrium: Interaction and coordination. *Prog. Neurobiol., 38*(1), 35–56. doi:10.1016/0301-0082(92)90034-C

Matte-Blanco, I. (1998). *Thinking, feeling and being: Clinical reflections on the fundamental antinomy of human beings and worlds*. New York: Routledge.

Mayer, E. A., & Tillisch, K. (2011). The brain-gut axis in abdominal pain syndromes. *Annu. Rev. Med.*, *62*, 381–396.

McCarthy, M. (1998). Skin and touch as intermediates of body experiences with reference to gender, culture and clinical experience. *Journal Bodywork and Movement Therapies*, *2*, 175–182.

McCombe, D., Brown, T., Slavin, J., & Morrison, W. A. (2001). The histochemical structure of the deep fascia and its structural response to surgery. *J. Hand Surg.*, *26*(2), 89–97.

McDougall, J. (1989). *Theaters of the body: A psychoanalytic approach to psychosomatic illness*. London and New York: W.W. Norton.

McGlone, F., Wessberg, J., & Olausson, H. (2014). Discriminative and affective touch: Sensing and feeling. *Neuron*, *82*(4), 737–755.

Meganck, R., Vanheule, S., & Desmet, M. (2013). Affective processing and affect regulation: A clinical interview study. *J. Am. Psychoanal Assoc. Dec.*, *61*(6), NP12–16.

Mehling, W. E., DiBlasi, Z., & Hecht, F. (2005). Bias control in trials of bodywork: A review of methodological issues. *Journal of Alternative and Complementary Medicine*, *11*(2), 333–342.

Mehling, W. E., Gopisetty, V., Daubenmier, J., Price, C. J., Hecht, F. M., & Stewart, A. (2009). Body awareness: Construct and self-report measures. *PLoS One*, *4*(5).

Mehling, W. E., Wrubel, J., Daubenmier, J. J., Price, C. J., Kerr, C. E., & Silow, T. (2011). Body awareness: A phenomenological inquiry into the common ground of mind-body therapies. *Philosophy, Ethics, and Humanities in Medicine*, *6*, 6. doi:10.1186/1747-5341-6-6

Merleau-Ponty, M. (2009). *Fenomenologie van de waarneming*. Amsterdam: Boom.

Mesman, J., van IJzendoorn, M. H., & Bakermans-Kranenburg, M. J. (2009). The many faces of the still face paradigm: A review and meta-analysis. *Developmental Review*, *29*, 120–162.

Meurs, P. (2004). *Gevoelsambivalentie: Het wonderlijke samenspel van liefde en agressie*. Leuven: Lannoo Campus.

Meurs, P., & Cluckers, G. (1996). Lichamelijkheid en affect bij psychosomatiek. *Tijdschrift voor psychoanalyse*, *2*(2), 68–82.

Meyer, K., & Damasio, A. (2009). Convergence and divergence in a neural architecture for recognition and memory. *Trends Neurosci.*, *32*(7), 376–382. doi:10.1016/j.tins.2009.04.002

Meyers, T. W. (2014). *Anatomy trains: Myofascial meridians for manual and movement therapists*. London: Churchill Livingstone Elsevier.

Minelli, A., & Vaona, A. (2012). Effectiveness of cognitive behavioral therapy in the treatment of fibromyalgia syndrome: A meta-analytic literature review. *Reumatismo*, *64*(3), 151–157. doi:10.4081/reumatismo.2012.151

Mitchell, J. (1986). *The selected Melanie Klein*. New York: Free Press.

Mitchell, S. A., & Black, M. J. (1995). *Freud and beyond: A history of modern psychoanalytic thought*. New York: Basic Books.

Mohr, W. K., & Fantuzzo, J. W. (2000). The neglected variable of physiology in domestic violence. *Journal of Aggression, Maltreatment & Trauma*, *3*(1), 69–84. doi:10.1300/J146v03n01_06

Monticone, M., Ambrosini, E., Cedraschi, C., Rocca, B., Fiorentini, R., Restelli, M., . . . Moja, L. (2015). Cognitive-behavioral treatment for subacute and chronic neck pain: A Cochrane review. *Spine (Phila Pa 1976)*, *40*(19), 1495–1504. doi:10.1097/BRS.0000000000001052

Mooij, A. (2002). *Psychoanalytisch gedachtegoed*. Amsterdam: Boom.
Mooij, A. (2006). *De psychische realiteit: Psychiatrie als geesteswetenschap*. Amsterdam: Boom.
Morhenn, V., Beavin, L. E., & Zak, P. J. (2012). Massage increases oxytocin and reduces adrenocorticotropin hormone in humans. *Altern. Ther. Health Med.*, *18*(6), 11–18.
Moyaert, P. (2014). *Opboksen tegen het inerte: De doodsdrift bij Freud*. Nijmegen: Vantilt.
Muschalla, B., Bengel, J., Morfeld, M., & Worringen, U. (2017). Towards a rehabilitation- and participation-oriented psychotherapy. *Rehabilitation (Stuttg.)*. doi:10.1055/s-0043-102553
Nakao, M. (2010). Work-related stress and psychosomatic medicine. *Biopsychosoc. Med.*, *4*(1), 4. doi:10.1186/1751-0759-4-4
Nicolai, N. J. (2010). Moederen: neurobiologisch gezien. In M. Kinet, & A. Bazan (Eds.), *Psychoanalyse en Neurowetenschap: De geest in de machine*. Antwerp and Apeldoorn: Garant.
Nicolai, N. J. (2016). *Emotieregulatie als basis van het menselijk bestaan: De kunst van het evenwicht*. Leusden: Diagnosis.
Nimnuan, C., Hotopf, M., & Wessely, S. (2001). Medically unexplained symptoms: An epidemiological study in seven specialities. *Journal Psychosomatic Research*, *51*, 361–367.
NIP (Nederlands Instituut van Psychologen). (2011). *Beroepsprofiel Lichaamsgericht Werkend Psycholoog*. Utrecht.
Norman, G. J., Berntson, G. G., & Cacioppo, J. T. (2014). Emotion, somatovisceral afference, and autonomic regulation. *Emot. Rev.*, *6*(2), 113–123. doi:10.1177/1754073913512006
Ogden, P., Minton, K., & Pain, C. (2006). *Trauma and the body: A sensorimotor approach to psychotherapy*. New York: W.W. Norton.
Olausson, H., Cole, J., & Valbo, A. (2008). Unmyelinated tactile afferents have opposite affects on insular and somatosensory cortical processing. *Neurosci. Lett.*, *436*, 128–132.
Olausson, H., Lamarre, Y., Backlund, H., Morin, C., Wallin, B. G., Starck, G., Ekholm, S., Strigo, I., Worsley, K., Vallbo, A. B., & Bushnell, M. C. (2002). Unmyelinated tactile afferents signal touch and project to insular cortex. *Nat. Neurosci.*, *5*, 900–904.
Olausson, H., Wessberg, J., & Morisson, I. (2010). The neurophysiology of unmyelinated tactile afferents. *Neuroscience Biobeh. Rev.*, *34*, 185–191.
Orbach, S. (2006). The body in clinical practice. In K. White (Ed.), *Touch: Attachment and the body*. London: Karnac Books.
Ordine, N. (2017). *Het nut van het nutteloze: Een manifest*. Utrecht: Bijleveld.
Ornitz, E. M., & Pynoos, R. S. (1996). Startle modulation in children with posttraumatic stress disorder. *The American Journal of Psychiatry*, *146*(7), 866–870. Accessed via http://ajp.psychiatryonline.org
Osborn, M., & Smith, J. A. (2006). Living with a body separate from the self. The experience of the body in chronic benign low back pain: An interpretative phenomenological analysis. *Scandinavian Journal of Caring Sciences*, *20*, 216–222.
Oschman, J. L. (2012). Fascia as a body-wide communication system. In R. Schleip, T. W. Findley, L. Chaitow, & P. Huijing (Eds.), *Fascia: The tensional network of the human body* (pp. 103–110). London: Churchill Livingstone Elsevier.
Paesen, L. (2005). Denken op grote hoogte: Een verkenning van het mentalisatieproces van patiënten binnen een forensische polikliniek. In M. Kinet, & R. Vermote (Eds.), *Mentalisatie*. Antwerp: Garant.
Painter, J. W. (1986). *Deep bodywork and personal development: Harmonizing our bodies, emotions and thoughts*. Mill Valley: Body Mind Books.

Painter, J. W. (1987). *The technical manual of deep wholistic bodywork: Postural integration*. Mill Valley: Body Mind Books.

Panksepp, J. (2005). Affective consciousness: Core emotional feelings in animals and humans. *Conscious. Cogn.*, *14*(1), 30–80. doi:10.1016/j.concog.2004.10.004

Paton, J. F., Nalivaiko, E., Boscan, P., & Pickering, A. E. (2006). Reflexly evoked coactivation of cardiac vagal and sympathetic motor outflows: Observations and functional implications. *Clin. Exp. Pharmacol. Physiol.*, *33*(12), 1245–1250. doi:10.1111/j.1440-1681.2006.04518.x

Pavan, P. G., Stecco, A., Stern, R., & Stecco, C. (2014). Painful connections: Densifications versus fibrosis of fascia. *Curr. Pain Headache Rep.*, *18*(8), 441.

Payne, H. (2009). The BodyMind Approach (BMA) to psychotherapeutic groupwork with patients with medically unexplained symptoms (MUS): A review of the literature, description of approach and methodology selected for a pilot study. *European Journal for Counselling and Psychotherapy*, *11*, 287–310. doi:10.1080/13642530903230392

Payne, P., & Crane-Godreau, M. A. (2015). The preparatory set: A novel approach to understanding stress, trauma, and the bodymind therapies. *Front. Hum. Neurosci.*, *9*, 178. doi:10.3389/fnhum.2015.00178

Payne, P., Levine, P. A., & Crane-Godreau, M. A. (2015). Somatic experiencing: Using interoception and proprioception as core elements of trauma therapy. *Front. Psychol.*, *6*, 93. doi:10.3389/fpsyg.2015.00093

Perry, B. D. (1997). Incubated in terror: Neurodevelopmental factors in the "cycle of violence". In J. D. Osofsky (Ed.), *Children in a violent society* (pp. 124–149). New York: Guilford. Accessed via https://books.google.be

Piehl-Aulin, K., Laurent, C., & Engström-Laurent, A. (1991). Hyaluronan in human skeletal muscle of lower extremity: Concentration, distribution, and effect of exercise. *J. Appl. Physiol.*, *71*(6), 2493–2498.

Pinkola Estes, C. (1996). *De ontembare vrouw als archetype in mythe en verhalen*. Haarlem: Becht.

Plasmans, K., & Van Asten, G. (2016). *De intuïtie van de psychiater: Een pleidooi voor stille signalen in therapie*. Leuven: Lannoo Campus.

Plotsky, P. M., & Meaney, M. J. (1993). Early, postnatal experience alters hypothalamic corticotropin-releasing factor (CRF) mRNA, median eminence CRF content and stress-induced release in adult rats. *Brain Res. Mol. Brain Res.*, *18*(3), 195–200. doi:10.1016/0169-328X(93)90189-V

Pluess, M., Conrad, A., & Wilhelm, F. H. (2009). Muscle tension in generalized anxiety disorder: A critical review of the literature. *J. Anxiety Disord.*, *23*(1), 1–11. doi:10.1016/j.janxdis.2008.03.016

Pollatos, O., Kirsch, W., & Schandry, R. (2005). Brain structures involved in interoceptive awareness and cardioafferent signal processing: A dipole source localization study. *Hum. Brain Mapp.*, *26*, 54–64.

Pollatos, O., Schandry, R., Auer, D. P., & Kaufmann, C. (2007). Brain structures mediating cardiovascular arousal and interoceptive awareness. *Brain Res.*, *1141*, 178–187.

Porges, S. W. (2009). The polyvagal theory: New insights into adaptive reactions of the autonomic nervous system. *Cleveland Clinic Journal of Medicine*, *76*(2).

Price, M. J. (1993). Exploration of body listening: Health and physical self-awareness in chronic illness. *Advanced Nurse Science*, *15*(4), 37–52.

Prins, A. (2008). *Uit verveling*. Kampen: Klement.

Quinodoz, D. (2003). *Words that touch*. London: Karnac Books.

Raknes, O. (2004). *Wilhelm Reich and orgonomy*. Princeton, NJ: American College of Orgonomy Press.
Reich, W. (1972). *Character analysis*. New York: Touchstone.
Reich, W. (1973). *The function of the orgasm: Sex-economic problems of biological energy*. New York: Farrar, Straus & Giroux.
Reich, W. (1994). *Beyond psychology: Letters and journals 1934–1939*. New York: Farrar, Straus & Giroux.
Reid, H., & Croucher, M. (1986). *De oosterse krijgskunst: De paradox van de martial arts. Techniek Filosofie Rituelen*. Haarlem: Rostrum.
Resnick, H. S., Yehuda, R., Pitman, R. K., & Foy, D. W. (1995). Effect of previous trauma on acute plasma cortisol level following rape. *American Journal of Psychiatry*, *152*, 1675–1677. Accessed via http://ajp.psychiatryonline.org/
Resulaj, A., Kiani, R., Wolpert, D. M., & Shadlen, M. N. (2009). Changes of mind in decision-making. *Nature*, *461*, 263–266. doi:10.1038/nature08275
Rexwinkel, M., Schmeets, M., Pannevis, C., & Derkx, B. (2011). *Handboek Infant Mental Health. Inleiding in de ouder-kindbehandeling*. Assen: Van Gorcum.
Rief, W., & Broadbent, E. (2007). Explaining medically unexplained symptoms-models and mechanisms. *Clinical Psychology Review*, *27*, 821–841.
Ritz, T., Meuret, A. E., Bhaskara, L., & Petersen, S. (2013). Respiratory muscle tension as symptom generator in individuals with high anxiety sensitivity. *Psychosomatic Medicine*, *75*, 187–195. doi:10.1097/PSY.0b013e31827d1072
Roelofs, K., & Spinhoven, P. (2007). Trauma and medically unexplained symptoms towards an integration of cognitive and neuro-biological accounts. *Clin. Psychol. Rev.*, *27*(7), 798–820. doi:10.1016/j.cpr.2007.07.004
Rogosch, F. A., Dackis, M. N., & Cicchetti, D. (2011). Child maltreatment and allostatic load: Consequences for physical and mental health in children from low-income families. *Dev. Psychopathol.*, *23*(4), 1107–1124. doi:10.1017/s0954579411000587
Röhricht, F. (2009). Body oriented psychotherapy: The state of the art in empirical research and, evidence-based practice: A clinical perspective. *Body, Movement and Dance in Psychotherapy*, *4*(2), 135–156.
Röhricht, F. (2015a). Body psychotherapy for severe mental disorders. In G. Marlock, & H. Weiss (Eds.), *The handbook of body psychotherapy & somatic psychology*. Berkeley, CA: North Atlantic Books.
Röhricht, F. (2015b). "Body schema", "body image", and bodily experience: Concept formation, definitions, and clinical relevance in diagnostics and therapy. In G. Marlock, & H. Weiss (Eds.), *The handbook of body psychotherapy & somatic psychology*. Berkeley, CA: North Atlantic Books.
Rome, H. P., & Rome, J. D. (2000). Limbically augmented pain syndrome (LAPS): Kindling, corticolimbic sensitization, and the convergence of affective and sensory symptoms in chronic pain disorders. *Pain Medicine*, *1*(1), 7–23.
Rosen, M., and Brenner, S. (2003). *Rosen Method Bodywork: Accessing the Unconscious through Touch*. Berkeley, California: North Atlantic Books.
Roxendal, G. (1985). *Body awareness therapy and the body awareness scale: Treatment and evaluation in psychiatric physiotherapy*. Sweden. Accessed via www.ibk.nu/abstracts/avhandling_roxendal.pdf
Ruden, R. A. (2005). Neurobiological basis for the observed peripheral sensory modulation of emotional responses. *Traumatology*, *11*(3), 145–158. Accessed via www.energypsych.org/
Russell, W. A., Wickson, F., & Carew, A. L. (2008). Transdisciplinarity: Context, contradictions and capacity. *Futures*, *40*, 460–472.

Sabbe, B. (2010). All are equal but some are more equal than others: Het biopsychosociale model voorbij. In B. Van Houdenhove, P. Luyten, & J. Vandenberghe (Eds.), *Luisteren naar het lichaam: Het dualisme voorbij* (hoofdstuk 1). Leuven: Lannoo Campus.

Sainsbury, P., & Gibson, J. G. (1954). Symptoms of anxiety and tension and the accompanying physiological changes in the muscular system. *J. Neurol. Neurosurg. Psychiatry, 17*(3), 216–224.

Saltzman, K. M., Holden, G. W., & Holahan, C. J. (2005). The psychobiology of children exposed to marital violence. *Journal of Clinical Child & Adolescent Psychology, 34*(1), 129–139. doi:10.1207/s15374424jccp3401_12

Saper, C. B. (2000). Pain as a visceral sensation. In E. A. Mayer, & C. D. Saper (Eds.), *The biological basis for mind body interactions* (pp. 237–243). Amsterdam: Elsevier Science. Accessed via https://books.google.be

Satterfield, J. M., Spring, B., Brownson, R. C., Mullen, R. J., Newhouse, R. P., Walker, B. B., & Withlock, E. P. (2009). Toward a transdisciplinary model of evidence-based practice. *The Milbank Quarterly, 87*(2), 368–390.

Sayar, K., Gulec, H., & Topbas, M. (2004). Alexithymia and anger in patients with fibromyalgia. *Clin. Rheumathology, 23*, 441–448.

Scaer, R. C. (2001). The neurophysiology of dissociation and chronic disease. *Applied Psychophysiology and Biofeedback, 26*(1), 73–91. Accessed via http://media.proquest.com.bib-proxy.uhasselt.be/

Schleip, R. (2003a, January). Fascial plasticity: A new neurobiological explanation. Part 1. *Journal of Bodywork and Movement Therapies*, 11–19.

Schleip, R. (2003b, April). Fascial plasticity: A new neurobiological explanation. Part 2. *Journal of Bodywork and Movement Therapies*, 104–116.

Schleip, R. (2011). Fascia as a sensory organ a target of myofascial manipulation. *Retrieved from: http://axissyllabus.org/assets/pdf/Schleip_Fascia_as_a_sensory_organ.pdf*

Schleip, R., Findley, T., Chaitow, L., & Huijing, P. (2012). *Fascia: The tensional network of the human body*. New York: Elsevier.

Schleip, R., Gabianni G., Wilke, J., Naylor, I., Hinz, B., Zorn, A., Jäger, H., Breul, R., Schreiner, S. & Klingler, W. (2019). Fascia is able to actively contract and may thereby influence musculoskeletal dynamics: A histochemical and mechanographic investigation. *Frontiers Physiology.* doi.org/10.3389/fphys.2019.00336

Schleip, R., & Jäger, H. (2012). Interoception: A new correlate for intricate connections between fascial receptors, emotion and self-recognition. In R. Schleip, T. Findley, L. Chaitow, & P. Huijing (Eds.), *Fascia: The tensional network of the human body* (pp. 89–94). New York: Elsevier.

Schleip, R., Jäger, H., & Klingler, W. (2012). What is 'fascia'? A review of different nomenclatures. *J. Bodyw Mov. Ther., 16*(4), 496–502. doi:10.1016/j.jbmt.2012.08.001

Schleip, R., Klingler, W., & Lehmann-Horn, F. (2005). Active fascial contractility: Fascia may be able to contract in a smooth muscle-like manner and thereby influence musculoskeletal dynamics. *Medical Hypotheses, 65*, 273–277.

Schleip, R., Naylor, I. L., Ursu, D., Melzer, W., Zorn, A., Wilke, H., Lehmann-Horn, F., & Klingler, W. (2006). Passive muscle stiffness may be influenced by active contractility of intramuscular connective tissue. *Medical Hypotheses, 66*, 66–71.

Schore, A. (2001). Neurobiology, developmental psychology and psychoanalysis: Convergent findings on the subject of projective identification. In J. Edwards (Ed.), *Being alive: Building on the work of Anne Alvarez* (pp. 57–74). Sussex: Routledge.

Schore, A. (2003). *Affect regulation and the repair of the self*. New York: W.W. Norton.

Sercu, P., & Bourggeois, D. (2016). *Bewegingsperceptie ontrafeld: Fasciatherapie: een vernieuwende visie*. Temse: uitgegeven in eigen beheer.
Seth, A. K. (2013). Interoceptive inference, emotion, and the embodied self. *Trends Cogn. Sci., 17*, 565–573.
Shedler, J. (2010). The efficacy of psychodynamic psychotherapy. *American Psychologist, 65*(2), 98–109.
Siegel, D. J. (1999). *The developing mind*. New York: Guilford Press.
Siegel, D. J. (2009). Mindful awareness, mindsight and neural integration. *The Humanistic Psychologist, 37*(2), 137–158.
Siegel, D. J. (2010). *Mindsight: De psychologie van het nieuwe bewustzijn*. Antwerp: Spectrum.
Siegel, D. J. (2017). *Mind: Een reis naar de essentie van ons mens-zijn*. Eeserveen: Mens!
Sifneos, P. E. (1973). The prevalence of 'alexithymic' characteristics in psychosomatic patients. *Psychotherapy and Psychosomatics, 22*, 255–262.
Simmons, W. K., Avery, J. A., Bodurka, J., Drevets, W. C., & Bellgowan, P. (2013). Keeping the body in mind: Insula functional organization and functional connectivity integrate interoceptive, exteroceptive, and emotional awareness. *Hum. Brain Mapp., 34*, 2944–2958.
Simons, D. G., & Mense, S. (1998). Understanding and measurement of muscle tone as related to clinical muscle pain. *Pain, 75*(1), 1–17.
Simons, L. E., & Basch, M. C. (2016). State of the art in biobehavioral approaches to the management of chronic pain in childhood. *Pain Manag., 6*(1), 49–61. doi:10.2217/pmt.15.59
Slatman, J. (2008). *Vreemd lichaam: Over medisch ingrijpen en persoonlijke ideniteit*. Amsterdam: Ambo.
Smith, A. M., & Flannery-Schroeder, E. C. (2013). Childhood emotional maltreatment and somatic complaints: The mediating role of alexithymia. *Journal of Child & Adolescent Trauma, 6*(3), 157–172. doi:10.1080/19361521.2013.811456
Smith, A. M., Russell, A., & Hodges, P. (2006). Disorders of breathing and continence have a stronger association with back pain than obesity and physical activity. *Australian Journal of Physiotherapy, 52*, 11–16.
Smith, R. C., Gardiner, J. C., Lyles, J. S., Sirbu, C., Dwamena, F., Hodges, A., . . . Goddeeris, J. (2005). Exploration of DSM-IV criteria in primary care patients with medically unexplained symptoms. *Psychosomatic Medicine, 67*, 123–129.
Soenen, S., & Van Balen, R. (2004). De genezende werking van het gesprek in psychotherapie: Een dialoog met E.T. Gendlin en J. Lacan. In G. Lietaer, & M. Van Kalmthout (Eds.), *Praktijkboek gesprekstherapie: Psychopathologie en experiëntiële procesbevordering*. Utrecht: De Tijdstroom.
Soth, M. (2005). Embodied countertransference. In N. Totton (Ed.), *New dimensions in body psychotherapy* (pp. 40–55). Maidenhead: Open University Press.
Soth, M. (2015). Transference, counter-transference and supervision in the body psychotherapeutic tradition. In G. Marlock, & H. Weiss (Eds.), *The handbook of body psychotherapy and somatic psychology*. Berkeley, CA: North Atlantic Books.
Southwick, S. M., Krystal, J. H., Morgan, C. A., Johnson, D., Nagy, L. M., Nicolaou, A., . . . Charney, D. S. (1993). Abnormal noradrenergic function in posttraumatic stress disorder. *Archives of General Psychiatry, 50*(4), 266–274. Accessed via http://archpsyc.jamanetwork.com
Spaans, J. A., Veselka, L., Luyten, P., & Bühring, M. E. F. (2009). Lichamelijke aspecten van mentalisatie: therapeutische focus bij ernstige onverklaarde lichamelijke klachten. *Tijdschrift Voor Psychiatrie, 51*, 239–248.

Stanghellini, G. (2009, February). Embodiment and schizophrenia. *World Psychiatry: Official Journal of the World Psychiatric Association (WPA)*, *8*, 56–59.

Stecco, C. (2015). *Functional atlas of the human fascial system*. London: Churchill Livingstone Elsevier.

Stecco, C., Cagey, O., Belloni, A., Pozzuoli, A., Porzionato, A., Macchi, V., Aldegheri, R., De Caro, R., & Delmas, V. (2007). Anatomy of the deep fascia of the upper limb. Second part: Study of innervation. *Morphology*, *91*, 38–43.

Stecco, C., Stern, R., Porzionato, R., Macchi, V., Masiero, S., Stecco, A., & De Caro, R. (2011). Hyaluron within fascia in the etiology of myofascial pain. *Surg. Radiol. Anat.*, *33*(10), 891–896.

Steinbrecher, N., Koerber, S., Friesser, D., & Hiller, W. (2011). The presence of medically unexplained symptoms in primary health care. *Psychosomatics*, *52*, 263–271.

Stern, D. (1985). *The interpersonal world of the infant: A view from psychoanalysis and development psychology*. London: Karnac Books.

Störig, H. J. (1998). *De geschiedenis van de filosofie 2*. Utrecht: Spectrum.

Stroeken, H. P. J. (2008). *Psychoanalytisch woordenboek: Begrippen, termen, personen, literatuur* (Vol. 3 de editie). Amsterdam: Boom.

Stucki, G., Prodinger, B., & Bickenbach, J. (2017). Four steps to follow when documenting functioning with the international classification of functioning, disability and health. *Eur. J. Phys. Rehabil. Med.*, *53*(1), 144–149. doi:10.23736/S1973-9087.17.04569-5

Suetterlin, K. J., & Sayer, A. A. (2013). Proprioception: Where are we now? A complementary on clinical assessment, changes across the life course, functional implications and future interventions. *Age Ageing*, *43*, 313–318. doi:10.1093/ageing/aft174

Tang, N. K. (2017). Cognitive behavioural therapy in pain and psychological disorders: Towards a hybrid future. *Prog. Neuropsychopharmacol Biol. Psychiatry*. doi:10.1016/j.pnpbp.2017.02.023

Taylor, C. (2008). *Merleau-Ponty*. London and New York: Routledge Philosophers.

Taylor, S. E., Klein, L. C., Lewis, B. P., Gruenewald, T. L., Gurung, R., & Updegraff, J. (2000). Biobehavioral responses to stress in females: Tend-and-befriend, not fight-or-flight. *Psychological Review*, *107*(3), 411–429.

Tesarz, J., Eich, W., Treede, R. D., & Gerhardt, A. (2016). Altered pressure pain thresholds and increased wind-up in adult patients with chronic back pain with a history of childhood maltreatment: A quantitative sensory testing study. *Pain*, *157*(8), 1799–809. doi:10.1097/j.pain.0000000000000586

Tesarz, J., Gerhardt, A., Leisner, S., Janke, S., Treede, R. D., & Eich, W. (2015). Distinct quantitative sensory testing profiles in nonspecific chronic back pain subjects with and without psychological trauma. *Pain*, *156*(4), 577–586. doi:10.1097/01.j.pain.0000460350.30707.8d

Thayer, J. F., & Brosschot, J. F. (2005). Psychosomatics and psychopathology: Looking up and down from the brain. *Psychoneuroendocrinology*, *30*, 1050–1058.

Thoma, N., Pilecki, B., & McKay, D. (2015). Contemporary cognitive behavior therapy: A review of theory, history, and evidence. *Psychodyn. Psychiatry*, *43*(3), 423–461. doi:10.1521/pdps.2015.43.3.423

Tietjen, G. E., Brandes, J. L., Peterlin, B. L., Eloff, A., Dafer, R. M., Stein, M. R., Drexler, E., Martin, V. T., Hutchinson, S., Aurora, S. K., Recober, A., Herial, N. A., Utley, C., White, L., & Khuder, S. A. (2010). Childhood maltreatment and migraine (part II). Emotional abuse as a risk factor for headache chronification. *Headache*, *50*(1), 32–41. doi:10.1111/j.1526-4610.2009.01557

Totton, N. (1998). *The water in the glass: Body and mind in psychoanalysis*. London: Rebus Press.

Totton, N. (2005). *New dimensions in body psychotherapy* (T. Nick, Ed.). Maidenhead: Open University Press.

Totton, N., & Edmondson, E. (2013). *Reichian Growth work. Melting the blocks of life and love.* Ross-on-Wye: PCCS Books.

Tozzi, P. (2014). Does fascia hold memories? *Journal of Bodywork and Movement Therapies, 18,* 259–265.

Tracey, I., & Bushnell, M. C. (2009). How neuroimaging studies have challenged us to rethink: Is chronic pain a disease? *J. Pain, 10*(11), 1113–1120. doi:10.1016/j.jpain.2009.09.001

Tsakiris, M. (2010). My body in the brain: A neurocognitive model of body-ownership. *Neuropsychologia, 48,* 703–712.

Tsakiris, M., Hesse, M. D., Boy, C., Haggard, P., & Fink, G. R. (2007). Neural signatures of body ownership: A sensory network for bodily self-consciousness. *Cerebral Cortex, 17,* 2235–2244.

Tune, D. (2005). Dilemmas concerning the ethical use of touch in psychotherapy. In N. Totton (Ed.), *New dimensions in body psychotherapy.* Berkshire: Open University Press.

Turvey, M. T., & Fonseca, S. T. (2014). The medium of haptic perception: A tensegrity hypothesis. *Journal of Motor Behavior, 46,* 143–187.

Twisk, F. N., & Maes, M. (2009). A review on cognitive behavorial therapy (CBT) and graded exercise therapy (GET) in myalgic encephalomyelitis (ME)/chronic fatigue syndrome (CFS): CBT/GET is not only ineffective and not evidence-based, but also potentially harmful for many patients with ME/CFS. *Neuro Endocrinol Lett, 30*(3), 284–299.

Vaitl, D. (1996). Interoception. *Biol. Psychol., 42,* 1–27.

Van Baak, J., Bartels, J., Van Heusden, B., & Wildevuur, C. (Eds.). (2007). *Lichaam en geest: Het lichaam/geest-probleem vanuit verschillende invalshoeken benaderd.* Budel: Damon.

Van Camp, I. (2012). Heterogeniteit van het 'snijden in eigen vlees' . . . en haar therapeutische implicaties. In M. Kinet (Ed.), *Zelfverwonding: Psychodynamiek en psychotherapie.* Antwerp and Apeldoorn: Garant.

Vancampfort, D., Correll, C. U., Scheewe, T. W., Probst, M., De Herdt, A., Knapen, J., & De Hert, M. (2013). Progressive muscle relaxation in persons with schizophrenia: A systematic review of randomized controlled trials. *Clin. Rehabil., 27*(4), 291–298. doi:10.1177/0269215512455531

Vancampfort, D., Firth, J., Schuch, F., Rosenbaum, S., De Hert, M., Mugisha, J., . . . Stubbs, B. (2016). Physical activity and sedentary behavior in people with bipolar disorder: A systematic review and meta-analysis. *J. Affect Disord., 201,* 145–152. doi:10.1016/j.jad.2016.05.020

Vancampfort, D., Probst, M., Helvik Skjaerven, L., Catalan-Matamoros, D., Lundvik-Gyllensten, A., Gomez-Conesa, A., . . . De Hert, M. (2012). Systematic review of the benefits of physical therapy within a multidisciplinary care approach for people with schizophrenia. *Phys. Ther., 92*(1), 11–23. doi:10.2522/ptj.20110218

Vancampfort, D., Vanderlinden, J., De Hert, M., Soundy, A., Adamkova, M., Skjaerven, L. H., . . . Probst, M. (2014). A systematic review of physical therapy interventions for patients with anorexia and bulimia nervosa. *Disabil. Rehabil., 36*(8), 628–634. doi:10.3109/09638288.2013.808271

Van den Bergh, B. (2007). De prenatale oorsprong van welvaartsziekten en gedragsproblemen. In B. Van Houdenhove (Ed.), *Stress, het lijf, en het brein: Ziekten op de grens tussen psyche en soma* (hoofdstuk 5). Leuven: Lannoo Campus.

Vandenberghe, J. (2010). Grenzen aan evidence b(i)ased psychiatrie? In R. Abma, A. Verbrugge, A. Van Heijst, M. Gerritsen, J. Vandenberghe, P. Verhaeghe, N. Stinckens, &

G. Glas (Eds.), *Evidentie en Existentie: Evidence-based handelen en verder . . .* Tilburg: KSGV.

Vandenberghe, J., & Luyten, P. (2010). Inleiding bij een Festschrift. In B. Van Houdenhove, P. Luyten, & J. Vandenberghe (Eds.), *Luisteren naar het lichaam: Het dualisme voorbij* (pp. 9–16). Tielt: Lannoo Campus.

Van den Bossche, M. (2008). Lijfelijke spiritualiteit en horizontale transcendentie. In G. Coene (Ed.), *De kunst buiten het zelf te treden: Naar een spiritueel atheïsme.* Brussels: VUB Press.

Van der Kolk, B. A. (1994). The body keeps the score: Memory and the emerging psychobiology of post traumatic stress. *Harvard Review of Psychiatry, 1*, 253–265. Retrieved from www.ncbi.nlm.nih.gov/pubmed/9384857

Van der Kolk, B. A. (2005). Developmental trauma disorder. *Psychiatric Annals, 35*, 401–409.

Van der Kolk, B. A. (2009). Developmental trauma disorder: Towards a rational diagnosis for chronically traumatized children. *Praxis Der Kinderpsychologie Und Kinderpsychiatrie, 58*, 572–586.

Van der Kolk, B. A. (2014). *The body keeps the score: Mind, brain and body in the transformation of trauma.* London: Penguin Books.

Van der Moolen, C., & Eisinga, R. (2004). Procesbevordering bij cliënten met onbegrepen lichamelijke klachten. In G. Lietaer, & M. Van Kalmthout (Eds.), *Praktijkboek gesprekstherapie: Psychopathologie en experiëntiële procesbevordering.* Utrecht: De Tijdstroom.

Vandessel, N., Leone, S. S., Vanderwouden, J. C., Dekker, J., & Vanderhorst, H. E. (2014). The prospect studies: Design of a prospect cohort study on prognosis and perpetuating factors of MUPS. *J. Psychosomatic. Res., 76*(3), 200–206.

Van Dongen, H. (2014). *Bergson.* Amsterdam: Boom.

Van Gael, M. (2012). Betekenaars van vlees en bloed: Psychodynamische perspectieven op begrijpen en behandelen van zelfverwondend gedrag. In M. Kinet (Ed.), *Zelfverwonding. Psychodynamiek en psychotherapie* (pp. 33–55). Antwerp and Apeldoorn: Garant.

Vanheule, S. (2005). Lacan's constructie en deconstructie van de dubbele spiegelopstelling. *sKRIPTa, Bulletin van de kring voor psychoanalyse van de New Lacanian School, 1*, 27–39.

Vanheule, S. (2013). *Psychose Anders bekeken: Over het werk Van Jacques Lacan.* Leuven: Lannoo Campus.

Vanheule, S. (2014). *Diagnosis and the DSM: A critical review.* London and New York: Palgrave Macmillan.

Vanheule, S., Desmet, M., Meganck, R., Inslegers, R., De Schryver, M., & Devisch, I. (2014). Reliability in psychiatric diagnosis with the DSM: Old wine in New Barrels. *Psychother Psychosom, 83*, 313–314.

Vanheule, S., Meganck, R., & Desmet, M. (2011a). Alexithymia, social detachment and cognitive processing. *Psychiatry Research, 190*, 49–51.

Vanheule, S., Verhaeghe, P., & Desmet, M. (2011b). In search of a framework for the treatment of alexithymia. *Psychology and Psychotherapy, 84*, 84–97; discussion 98–110.

Van Houdenhove, B. (Ed.). (2007a). *Stress, het lijf, en het brein: Ziekte op de grens tussen psyche en soma.* Leuven: Lannoo Campus.

Van Houdenhove, B. (2007b). Chronisch vermoeid, overal pijn: een heel verhaal. In P. Luyten, P. Van Haute, & A. De Block (Eds.), *Psychoanalyse, cognitieve psychologie en evidence-based medicine.* Leuven: Lannoo Campus.

Van Houdenhove, B. (2007c). Slechte start in het leven: kwetsbaarder voor stressgebonden ziekten? In B. Van Houdenhove (Ed.), *Stress, het lijf, en het brein. Ziekten op de grens tussen psyche en soma* (hoofdstuk 4). Leuven: Lannoo Campus.

Van Houdenhove, B. (2010). Luisteren naar het lichaam: Waarom het 'verhaal' van de CVS-patient belangrijk is. In B. Van Houdenhove, P. Luyten, & J. Vandenberghe (Eds.), *Luisteren naar het lichaam: Het dualisme voorbij* (hoofdstuk 13). Leuven: Lannoo Campus.

Van Houdenhove, B., Luyten, P., & Vandenberghe, J. (Eds.). (2010). *Luisteren naar het lichaam: Het dualisme voorbij*. Leuven: Lannoo Campus.

Van Os, J. (2014). *De DSM-5 voorbij! Persoonlijke diagnostiek in een nieuw GGZ*. Leusden: Diagnosis.

Van Oudenhove, L. (2007a). Het brein en de buik: stress, emoties en maagdarmklachten. In B. Van Houdenhove (Ed.), *Stress, het lijf, en het brein: Ziekten op de grens tussen psyche en soma* (hoofdstuk 6). Leuven: Lannoo Campus.

Van Oudenhove, L. (2007b). Stress, emoties en pijn: een vicieus samenspel. In B. Van Houdenhove (Ed.), *Stress, het lijf, en het brein: Ziekten op de grens tussen psyche en soma* (hoofdstuk 3). Leuven: Lannoo Campus.

Van Oudenhove, L. (2010). Vroegtijdige negatieve levensgebeurtenissen en functionele gastro-intestinale aandoeningen: Van epidemiologie naar pathofysiologie. In B. Van Houdenhove, P. Luyten, & J. Vandenberghe (Eds.), *Luisteren naar het lichaam: Het dualisme voorbij* (hoofdstuk 10). Leuven: Lannoo Campus.

Van Praag, D. (1998). *Gestalttherapie: Veld en existentie*. Leusden: De Tijdstroom.

Van Sluis, J. (1998). *Leeswijzer bij Zijn en Tijd van Martin Heidegger*. Best: Damon.

Van Winkle, E. (2000). The toxic mind: The biology of mental illness and violence. *Med. Hypotheses, 55*(4), 356–368. doi:10.1054/mehy.2000.1146

Verhaeghe, P. (2003). *Over normaliteit en andere afwijkingen: Handboek klinische psychodiagnostiek*. Leuven: ACCO.

Verhaeghe, P. (2006). *Tussen hysterie en vrouw: Van Freud tot Lacan: een weg door honderd jaar psychoanalyse*. Leuven: ACCO.

Verhaeghe, P. (2009). *Het einde van de psychotherapie*. Amsterdam: De Bezige Bij.

Verhaeghe, P. (2010). Psychotherapie vanuit de psychotherapeut. *Tijdschrift Cliëntgerichte Psychotherapie: Procesgericht Experiëntieel Interactioneel Integratief, 48*(2), 164–174.

Verhaeghe, P. (2015). Angst en object vanuit Lacan. *Tijdschrift voor psychoanalyse, 21*(2), 118–128.

Verhaeghe, P., & Vanheule, S. (2005). Actual neurosis and PTSD: The impact of the other. *Psychoanalytic Psychology, 22*(4), 493–507.

Vermote, R. (2005). Mentaliseren en psychopathologie: Een klinische benadering van het werk van Bion. In M. Kinet, & R. Vermote (Eds.), *Mentalisatie*. Antwerp and Apeldoorn: Garant.

Vermote, R. (2010). De irrationale dimensie van de psychoanalyse. *Tijdschrift voor Psychoanalyse, 16*, 239–247.

Vermote, R. (2011). Het onbewuste. In J. Dirkx, M. Hebbrecht, A. W. M. Mooij, & R. Vermote (Eds.), *Handboek psychodynamiek*. Utrecht: De Tijdstroom.

Vermote, R. (2015). Een geïntegreerd psychoanalytisch model in het licht van neurowetenschappelijke bevindingen. *Tijdschrift voor Psychoanalyse, 21*, 3–12.

Victoria, H. K., & Caldwell, C. (2013). Breathwork in body psychotherapy: Clinical applications. *Body, Movement and Dance in Psychotherapy, 8*, 216–228.

Waller, E., & Scheidt, C. E. (2006). Somatoform disorders as disorders of affect regulation: A development perspective. *International Review of Psychiatry, 18*, 13–24.

Walsh, R. (1999). Asian contemplative disciplines: Common practices, clinical applications, and research findings. *The Journal of Transpersonal Psychology, 31*(2).

Walusinski, O. (2006). Yawning: Unsuspected avenue for a better understanding of arousal and interoception. *Med Hypotheses*, *67*, 6–14.
Wand, B. M., Parkitny, L., O'Connell, N. E., Luomajoki, H., McAuley, J. H., Thacker, M., & Moseley, G. L. (2010). Cortical changes in chronic low back pain: Current state of the art and implications for clinical practice. *Manual Therapy*. doi:10.1016/j.math.2010.06.008
Wearden, A. J., Lamberton, N., Crook, N., & Walsh, V. (2005). Adult attachment, alexithymia, and symptom reporting: An extension to the four category model of attachment. *Journal of Psychosomatic Research*, *58*, 279–288.
Weaver, J. O. (2015). The influence of Elsa Gindler. In G. Marlock, & H. Weiss (Eds.), *The handbook of body psychotherapy and somatic psychology*. Berkeley, CA: North Atlantic Books.
Weinberg, M. K., Beeghly, M., Olson, K. L., & Tronick, E. (2008). A still-face paradigm for young children: 2(1/2) year-olds' Reactions to maternal unavailability during the still-face. *J. Dev. Process*, *3*(1), 4–22.
Weinberg, M. K., & Tronick, E. Z. (1994). Beyond the face: An empirical study of infant affective configurations of facial, vocal, gestural, and regulatory behaviors. *Child Dev.*, *65*(5), 1503–1515.
Weisfeld, G. E., & Beresford, J. M. (1982). Erectness of posture as an indicator of dominance or success in humans. *Motiv. Emot.*, *6*(2), 113–131. doi:10.1007/BF00992459
Weston, C. S. (2014). Posttraumatic stress disorder: A theoretical model of the hyperarousal subtype. *Front Psychiatry*, *5*, 37. doi:10.3389/fpsyt.2014.00037
White, K. (Ed.). (2006). *Touch: Attachment and the body*. London: Karnac Books.
Wiebking, C., Duncan, N. W., Tiret, B., Hayes, D. J., Marjanska, M., Doyon, J., Bajbouj, M., & Northoff, G. (2014). GABA in the insula – a predictor of the neural response to interoceptive awareness. *Neuroimage*, *86*, 10–18.
Wilber, K. (1984a). The developmental spectrum and psychopathology: Part 1, stages and types of pathology. *The Journal of Transpersonal Psychology*, *16*(1).
Wilber, K. (1984b). The developmental spectrum and psychopathology: Part 2, treatment modalities. *The Journal of Transpersonal Psychology*, *16*(2).
Wilber, K. (1985). *Oog in Oog: Veranderende denkbeelden voor deze tijd*. Rotterdam: Lemniscaat.
Wilber, K. (1992). *Het atman project: Een transpersoonlijke visie op menselijke ontwikkeling*. Utrecht: Servire.
Wilber, K. (1996). *Up from Eden: A transpersonal view of human evolution*. Wheaton: Quest Books.
Wilber, K. (1998a). *The eye of spirit: An integral vision for a world gone slightly mad*. Boston and London: Shambala Publications.
Wilber, K. (1998b). *De integratie van wetenschap en religie*. Utrecht: Servire.
Wilber, K. (1999). *The collected works of Ken Wilbur, Vol. 4: Integral psychology, transformations of consciousness, selected essays*. Boston and London: Shambala Publications.
Wilber, K. (2000). *Sex, ecology, spirituality: The spirit of evolution*. Boston: Shambhala Publications.
Wilber, K. (2001a). *Integrale psychologie*. Deventer: Ankh-Hermes.
Wilber, K. (2001b). *Eye to eye: The quest for the new paradigm*. Boston and London: Shambala Publications.
Wilber, K. (2001c). *Zonder grenzen*. Amsterdam: Karnac Books.
Wilber, K. (2006). *Integral spirituality: A startling new role for religion in the modern and postmodern world*. Boston and London: Integral books.

Wilber, K. (2017). *The religion of tomorrow: A vision for the future of the great traditions.* Boulder: Shambala Publications.

Wilde, M. H. (1999). Why embodiment now? *Advances in Nursing Science, 22*(2), 25–28.

Wilde, M. H. (2003). Embodied knowledge in chronic illness and injury. *Nursing Inquiry, 10*(3), 170–176.

World Health Organization. (2002). *Towards a common language for functioning, disability and health: ICF the international classification of functioning, disability and health.* Retrieved from www.who.int/icidh

Yalom, I. D. (1980). *Existential psychotherapy.* New York: Basic Books.

Younger, J. W., Shen, Y. F., Goddard, G., & Mackey, S. C. (2010). Chronic myofascial temporomandibular pain is associated with neural abnormalities in the trigeminal and limbic systems. *Pain, 149*(2), 222–228. doi:10.1016/j.pain.2010.01.006

Zeiler, K. (2010). A phenomenological analysis of bodily self-awareness in the experience of pain and pleasure: On dys-appearance and eu-appearance. *Medicine, Health Care and Philosophy, 13*, 333–342.

Ziegelaar, A. (2016). *Oorspronkelijk bewustzijn.* Leusden: ISVW Uitgevers.

Index

anamnesis 19, 21, 29, 37–38, 43–44, 53, 127–133, 136–137, 149, 163n2
anxiety 19, 32, 34n6, 47, 58–59, 73–77, 93, 103, 117–122, 123n7, 123n12, *141–142*, 146–147, 161

body psychotherapy 12n2, 72, 116, 118, 133, 153, 157, 158, 161, 165–166
body reading 74–75, 134, 163n3
bodywork 8–9, *10*, 11, 24, 30, 32, 48–51, 65, 72–73, 76, 80, 85, 89, 93–94, 99, 118, 127, 132–135, *133*, 137–138, *139*, 140, *141*, 144, 151–153, 157–158, 161, 163, 164n11, 165–166
breathing 6–10, 30–31, 41–42, 64, 73–76, 79–85, 89, 117–119, 136, 139, 144–145, 154–162

conceptual self-awareness 45–46, 50, 92
(counter)-transference 72, 131, 157–158, 164n9, 164n10

developmental dynamics 24, 116, 130
developmental dynamic treatment template 9, 26, 111, 116, 140, *141–142*, 143
dyadic 103, 111–114, 119–123, 124n6, 139–140

embodied self-awareness 45–46, 50–51, 64, 92, 119, 137, 153
embodiment 45–52, 53n6, 58, 67, 79, 92, 152, 161–162

four quadrant model 16, *17–18*, 33, 84, 129
fulcrum 1 *24*, 27, *28*, 101–105, 114, *141*, 143, 146–147

fulcrum 2 *24*, 26, *28*, 103–105, 114, 119–120, 124n5, *141*, 146–147, 150, 159, 161
fulcrum 3 *24*, 26, *28*, 116, 124n5, *141*, 146–147, 150
fusion/identification/differentiation/integration (FIDI) 25–28, *27*, *28*, 33, 100, 114, 119–120

interoception 51, 86, 89–90, *89*, 92

light sensual touch 89
listening touch 64–65, 74–75, 94, 132, 134, 137–138, 140, 143, 149–151, 163n3

muscle tension 5, 46, 54n6, 73, 77, 79, 89–90, 116, 118
muscular armour 6, 30, 45, 65, 71–76, 79–89, 92, 95, 95n3, 99, 117–118, 132–139, 145, 152, 158
myofascial middle layer (MML) 80–88, *81–83*, 99, 118, 123, 135, 151–152, 156

narrative 32–33, 37–48, 52, 60, 64, 73, 79, 128–132, 136

objectal foundation 40–44, 52, 79, 128, 131, 159

pleromatic *24*, *28*, 100–105, *105*, 114, 117, 122–123, *141*, 160

Reich, W. 5–6, 10, 72–74, 76, 95, 95n1, 95n2, 95n3, 116–117, 137, 157
request for help 20–23, 34n7, 37–41, 44, 61, 93, 106, 16, 121, 128–132, 146, 161
reverie 50–51, 111–114, 124n11, 128

self-other-world 29–30, 39, 42, 100
slow melting pressure 87, 151–152
subject development 24, 28, 84, 95, 99–103, 106, 111, 113, 121–123, 123n1, 146, 160

unconscious 5, 15–16, 41–48, 51, 53, 58, 63, 73, 77–79, 90–93, 99–106, 107n6, 111–116, 120, 123, 136–137, 146, 157–158, 166

uroboric-pranic body 83–84, 95, 99, 105–106, 115, 123, 151–152
uroboros 101–105, *102*, 107n10, 117–118, 122, 131, 160

Wilber, K. 16–18, *17*, *18*, 22–28, *24*, *27*, *28*, 33n3, 33n4, 34n8, 34n10, 34n11, 34n12, 58, 100–106, *105*, 107n10, 107n12, 114–119, 121, 124n5, 124n9, *129*, *141*, 163, 163n6